Business and the Language Barrier

BUSINESS
AND THE
LANGUAGE
BARRIER

by Richard Simpkin and Rosemarie Jones

BUSINESS BOOKS LIMITED
London

First published 1976

ISBN 0 220 66297 5

This book has been photoset 11 on 12 point Baskerville by Jetset Typesetters Ltd. Brighton, Sussex prepared for press by The Ivory Head Press, 170 Murray Road, London W5, and printed in England photo-litho reprint by W & J Mackay Limited, Chatham from earlier impression for the publishers, Business Books Limited, 24 Highbury Crescent, London N5.

Contents

Preface

The idea for this book sprang naturally enough from Britain's entry into the European Economic Community.

In the months before entry there was indeed a significant increase in the volume of EEC-oriented language work as firms which had not already established themselves in Europe explored the market, and in some cases decided to move into it. But in our experience at least, this bulge has not been maintained except perhaps in the case of France; indeed the availability in English of many official and semi-official documents which previously had to be translated has probably diminished the load of language work overall. In fact, many would-be exporters to Europe quickly discovered what some had suspected all along—that the idea of the Six as a wide-open 'export' market was an illusion, dare one say an illusion carefully fostered in certain quarters.

While our membership is still in its preliminary phases and the state of our economy continues to make our products less than competitive and our country a less than attractive investment prospect, the principal effect of entry—for manufacturing industry at least—seems rather to be a broadening of the economic base. Those companies that had already established themselves within the Six or already did business with them have continued to do so, and indeed to strengthen their links and expand xiv their business; but market penetration as such seems so far to be the exception rather than the rule.

The undoubted growth in the volume and importance of commercial language work that has taken place over the past few years appears to be due to quite different geopolitical and economic factors which are at best no more than indirectly connected with our approach to and entry into the EEC. The decline of the Commonwealth as a guaranteed market in our case, and the weakening or loss of sectors of politico-economic influence in that of the States have combined with emerging economic dominance of third-world primary producers, notably OPEC, to force our two countries into third-world markets that had previously been associated, colonially or otherwise, with European countries of another language. In these markets the number of English-speakers is negligible, the willingness to work in English is slight and we are facing competition well backed with language resources and only too happy to work in whatever language may be called for. Basic English uttered in a loud voice is not enough, and it may be that such conventions as letters being sent in the originator's language and translated at the other end have to go by the board because there is no-one at the other end capable of translating them. And with this growth in quantity of language work has come a requirement for high quality because of the need to avoid breakdown of communication and misunderstandings in dealing with people who are at once resolute bureaucrats and unpractised in negotiating the bureaucratic maze.

English having been the language of two successive top nations, less emphasis has been given to education in languages, to the development of the language profession or to the interface of that profession with commerce and industry in Britain and the States than in other countries. It is thus perhaps surprising that while other European countries put much more intensive and successful effort into the teaching of foreign languages and thus have greater language resources, neither the organisation of these resources nor their interface with those who use them is in a very much better state. At present the speedy and cost-effective execution of language work is inhibited by two wide gaps of understanding. One is between the real language and language-related needs of commerce and industry and management's understanding of these needs. The other is between these real needs and the services the language profession is geared to provide. This book sets out to bridge these gaps. It suggests ways in which a realistic and effective interface between the needs of commerce and industry on the one hand and the available language resources on the other might be developed.

The first part of the book explains to management the strengths, limitations and problems of the techniques available to meet their language needs and the nature of the resources on which they are likely to have call. This Part is deliberately presented in rather general terms at one remove from actual management situations. Part 2 applies Part 1 to the general field of foreign working and to particular types of management situation associated with it. To save managerial time an effort has been made to make each Part and to some extent each chapter self-contained. This approach has inevitably led to a fair amount of repetition, both between chapters and between Parts 1 and 2; but we feel that this repetition will help to throw light on some of the more difficult problems by tackling them from several different angles. To make this book into a practical management tool, some chapters of Part 2 have been summed up in comprehensive checklists and programmed instructions.

The book is primarily intended as a reference guide to management, principally perhaps in medium and small firms and organisations, when they have to embark on foreign-language working. However, the content and layout have also been devised to make the book suitable for the support of teaching in polytechnics and colleges of further education, as well as in other institutions concerned with business and management training — and with the teaching of applied languages.

While realising that some of the comments and suggestions made are controversial and unlikely to find favour with the more conventionally minded members of the language profession, these remarks and proposals are based on successful experience. We hope that discussion of them may have some influence in shaping the language profession more closely to the needs of what has now become and is likely to remain its principal user, and of improving the chances of a satisfying and rewarding career for the many starry-eyed young linguists who embark on this seemingly glamorous profession.

Part 1
THE LANGUAGE PROBLEM

1
Languages and market coverage

The power of speech has traditionally been held to be the feature that distinguishes man from the rest of the animal kingdom and has enabled him to become the master rather than the slave of his environment. And, despite recent discoveries on communication among primates and marine mammals, we all regard language as a gift unique to the human race. Language is the foundation on which much of our culture and social structure is built and organised; it is so much a part of our life that we cannot take an objective and detached view of it. We thus become frustrated and resentful when it fails us as our principal means of communication.

It is this emotional attitude rather than the practical problems involved that causes on the one hand the language barrier to loom so large and rugged in the eyes of those wishing to cross it and on the other the language profession to be so lowly regarded. Management cannot afford the luxury of emotions in this field—whether they be an undue respect for language deriving from its cultural associations or, in effect, xenophobia. Like most environmental hazards the language barrier is of itself generally speaking neutral; those who understand how to relate it with their aims and make it work for them can gain advantage from it; for others it may remain an insurmountable obstacle.

Once stripped of all its emotional associations, the need to work across two or more languages will appear to the exporter as a factor in the planning of his export programme, something in fact falling within the communications factor as a whole which will include telephone facilities, postal turnround time, travel costs, surface and air freight rates and so on. His response to the language barrier, just as to these other elements, then becomes twofold. On the one hand he must find out as much as he can about it and come to terms with its in his timing and costing; he must then go further and explore how he can shape from it tools that will support his programme and give him an edge on his competitors.

1.2   Language distribution

The first concept in this rational approach is the grading of languages by the value of the market they cover rather than by some subjective criterion of cultural or social acceptability. The effect of this differential 'market value' of languages is compounded by the fact that it is possible to work faster, to a higher standard and more cheaply in the European languages with the largest coverage. Here one might use the simple engineering analogy of mains electricity. Suppose that one's home market and, a substantial sector of the potential export market works on 240 V, 50 Hz AC as its single-phase basis, and a further large market (in fact, the American one) is on 220 V, 60 Hz AC, then it is clearly logical to design equipment to accept alternating current at voltages between 200 and 250 and to provide easy conversion or alternative models for the two frequencies – the more so as suitability for an AC supply greatly broadens the scope open to the designer even of relatively simple equipment. But it would be quite irrational and anything but cost-effective to produce equipment compatible with the 110 V direct current supply still to be found in a few small countries, even if one's family happened to trace its origins back to one of these countries.

Taking this analogy one stage further only certain highly developed languages, equivalent to AC supplies, will be able to cope with the full span of requirements of modern science and technology; in others it will be necessary to adopt the clumsy and inefficient expedient of word-borrowing, just as the DC supply will have to be put through rotary converters. On the other hand for certain specialised purposes – particularly at political level – the use of a minor language will offer unique advantages, just as a DC supply does for the speed control of motors.

Table 1.1. below puts languages into order of importance in terms of numbers and gross product. (language coverage by population and gross product is tabulated fully in Appendix 1). At the risk of offending many readers it deliberately ignores their cultural value and any traditional affiliation or enmity between those who speak them. It is necessary to draw a distinction between primary coverage, i.e. the countries or areas in which

TABLE 1.1*

A Languages in order of importance by population		B Languages in order of importance by gross product, i.e. total of GNPs	
Language	Population,'000s	Language	Gross product, US $m
English	1,347,169	English	1,600,630
Chinese	805,647	Russian	520,530
Russian	355,458	German	414,430
French	250,880	French	280,300
Spanish	221,416	Japanese	247,890
German	196,436	Spanish	177,500
Arabic	129,568	Chinese	145,100
Portuguese	122,450	Italian	114,900
Japanese	106,960	Portuguese	64,400
Italian	56,410	Dutch	53,510
Polish	33,068	Polish	49,640
Roumanian	20,700	Swedish	49,350
Dutch	18,185	Arabic	46,330
Swedish	12,750	Roumanian	16,770

*See also Appendix 1 for further details.

the language is the mother-tongue of the inhabitants, and secondary coverage, i.e. areas in which for ethnic, cultural, political or economic reasons it has become the *lingua franca*. Some of the figures in this table are undoubtedly open to question in detail, but they are the best available and are accurate enough for the purpose in hand; and a few arbitrary decisions have had to be made in compiling it. As readers may observe, the table and subsequent discussion contain the hidden assumption that the bulk of manufactured exports to developing countries will be of a medium to high technology nature.

1.3 'Main languages' and 'technological languages'

The special problems presented by Arabic and Chinese will be discussed below, but considering for the moment the European or Europe-based languages, we come out with three — English, French and Russian — which gain top rating on both counts. Then comes German, which despite its excellence for scientific and technological purposes only makes the big league through its use in scientific, technological and commercial circles in much of Eastern Europe — rather surprisingly, it would seem, in preference to Russian. As well as being, for political reasons that have never been entirely clear to us, a United Nations language, Spanish gains its importance from the Central and South American markets, and these factors are generally considered sufficient to gain it a place among the 'main languages' despite limitations in its scientific and technological vocabulary.

Although it is the largest single market in Latin America, Brazil alone would not justify inclusion of Portugese among the main languages, on the one hand because most Brazilian businessmen and engineers are reasonably well versed in either Spanish, English or German and on the other because the language's powers of technological expression rate considerably below those of Spanish; but the enormously interesting market presented by the former Portuguese African colonies may justify the treatment of Portuguese as a major language in some cases if in fact these countries decide to adopt it for international and technological purposes.

Hurtful as it may be and despite their fine cultural traditions, the other European languages are not in the running. The combination of political and economic pressures makes it likely that they may over a generation or two slide towards the status of the Celtic languages, kept alive perhaps by nationalist political and cultural groups. Looking rather further ahead one can see German joining them unless Germany's post-war sterility in culture and science gives way to a resurgence of her former splendid creativity in every field.

At the same time efforts now being made suggest that the structures of the major oriental languages are likely to be evolving in a direction that will enable them to carry scientific and technological terminology and thus eventually eliminate European languages from those countries.

English is perhaps the most widespread and certainly the most widely and generously abused of languages. One of us recalls, when sailing in Hong Kong harbour some 15 years ago — well after the establishment of the Communist régime — an exchange of courtesies conducted in pidgin English between the crews of a local sampan and a junk from Shanghai, of which he could understand not a single word. (On a similar occasion, however, when being crewed by a shy young girl, he was unable to escape the appalling intelligibility of the pre-liberty briefing given over the ship's broadcast of a US Navy carrier that had just dropped anchor.) But all major languages are used, both as mother-tongues and by adoption, over a sufficiently large area for marked variations to be inevitable. Sometimes these may lead to a genuine risk of misunderstanding, but the more usual problem arises in the preparation of advertising copy or promotional literature designed to appeal right across the language market.

1.4.1   English

As Mark Twain wrote in *Puddn'head Wilson's Journal:* 'The King's English is not the King's; it's a joint stock company and Americans own most of the shares'. Certainly from the commercial viewpoint and probably from others as well, American English is now the more widespread and generally acceptable branch of the language. Being the younger it is also the livelier and the richer in innovation, although the transatlantic trade in neologisms is better balanced than most.

At the colloquial level, and more particularly where dialects or dialect-influenced speech is concerned, there is sufficient risk of misunderstanding for books like Norman Moss's *What's the difference?*(Hutchinsons, 1973) to have a wide sale in many market sectors. But despite certain pitfalls of terminology and orthography which must be known and avoided, Anglo-American 'mandarin' represents in itself one of those rare instances of a marriage bringing out the best in both partners and provides a lucid and acceptable means of communication between speakers of the two branches of the language.

As for the secondary coverage of these branches, British English and its derivatives prevail throughout the Commonwealth. The pidgin English of Africa and the Far East also springs from this root. But American English has spread not only north and south in the American Continent but also in a girdle round the earth across the latitudes of Europe and the USSR.

Finally it is worth noting that most other advanced countries are now teaching British and American English as separate subjects at university, and in the USSR at least at sixth-form level too. This increases the likelihood of an Englishman having difficulties of communication with those who have a foreign mother-tongue but are fluent in American English; their cultural and linguistic background lacks the commonalty enabling the English and the Americans themselves to bridge this gap.

It is often tempting to describe France as a nation of exceptions which prove no rule, but in respect of dialect and other local variations their language is the exception that proves the rule.Until very recently, *patois* apart, the French language has been completely standardised under the autocratic rule of the *Académie Française* backed up by an educational system that, although in some respects antiquated, has managed to combine egalitarianism and élitism in a unique way. The only local variations concern objects or concepts peculiar to France's former dependencies, and even here — as with so many neologisms and pieces of *franglais* — the *Académie Française* will generally be found to have pronounced. The ex-colonies, even those which are trying to develop say Arabic as their primary language in the long term, take even greater pride than the French themselves in the purity of their French and must be a major factor in conserving the classical form of the language.

Inextricably bound up with the French language, and considerably more difficult than the language itself for a foreigner to come to terms with, is the *dialectique* of thesis, synthesis and antithesis, which pervades the French educational system and tends to be the basis of their thought and argument. The French are perhaps the only people who would claim to arrive at political, economic, military and commercial decisions by logical arguments — it is even possible that they occasionally do so.

Against this current of pure water there flows from Belgium — mainly from the EEC headquarters but increasingly perhaps from the international community as a whole and from the Walloons themselves — a tide of 'Euro-French'. The differences between this and French French are as yet neither pronounced nor easy to define, although one can usually spot the origin of a text by such minor differences as the prevalence of *'qui suit/qui suivent'* or *'comme suit'* over *'le(s) suivant(e)(s)'*. It is so far on precision and lucidity that the influence of Anglo-Saxon and Germanic thought and language has mainly left its mark; in other words these documents are very much more difficult to understand than something written by a Frenchman.

1.4.3 Russian

Just as it is difficult to comprehend the geographical, climatic and ethnic scope of the USSR, it is easy to forget that this vast political entity embraces numerous and diverse cultures and mother-tongues. Russian as we now know it, including the Cyrillic alphabet, is in any event largely an imposed language of comparatively recent origin — say the late 18th century — which has borrowed almost the whole of its specialised terminology, either direct or at one complicating remove, from the French, German and to a lesser extent English that its upper and professional classes habitually spoke.

The impact of Marxism on what was then still a comparatively young and rapidly developing language and culture was very far-reaching, so that one might say that Russian is a young language being at once developed and constrained by a ponderous educational system working within the constraints of the strongest, thickest and most frequent red tape in the world.

For all these reasons it is possible to get away with a much lower standard of both spoken and written Russian than would be acceptable in the case of French or German.

On the other hand in Western Europe, though perhaps not to the same extent in the United States, Russian is largely taught by White Russians and their descendandts. This is a beautiful language, having much in common with Edwardian English, but nostalgia has helped to crystallise it and to separate it out from the language now spoken in the Soviet Union. Russian is thus one of the few instances in which it may, for commercial, scientific and technological purposes, be better to use an English native-speaker with excellent knowledge of Soviet Russian than a non-Soviet native-speaker.

1.4.4 Spanish

It is the varieties of Spanish that perhaps present the most severe problem of all. It is widely known that there is an appreciable difference in pronunciation, terminology and syntax between Spain and Latin America, broadly comparable perhaps in terms of its effect on communication to the difference between British and American English. But it may not be generally appreciated that on the one hand the language spoken and written in many parts of Spain diverges significantly from pure Castilian, or that within Latin America usage differs between countries and regions to the point where the same word may have completely opposite meanings.

In writing or translating into Spanish, it is thus necessary to know the readership very specifically if the appeal of a native-speaking standard is sought; and it may also be very difficult to find anyone capable of writing the precise variety of language called for. However — and again the analogy with British and American holds — there is a 'mandarin' which is generally acceptable in most professional fields and in commerce outside the everyday expressions of routine correspondence and basic procedures such as invoicing. The trouble is that like Anglo-Saxon 'mandarin', Spanish 'mandarin' is easily recognisable and comparatively easy for someone of the right background to write; but it is extremely difficult to define in general terms.

1.4.5 German

Modern German is of comparatively recent development. On a general impression based on orthography and intelligibility, the difference between the language of Göethe and modern German is at least as great as that between the language of Shakespeare, born almost two centuries earlier, and modern English. Further, the unifying political influences on the language began to make themselves felt only in the early to mid-19th century. The political events of the 20th, with the *Verdeutschung* of the '30s being followed by a frantic chase to escape from German roots and adopt foreign ones in the post-war period, have given *Hochdeutsch,* despite its officially acknowledged existence, little chance to settle down and develop. Unless the political climate changes and nationalism sets in, the masochism — one might perhaps almost say the guilt complex — of the West Germans seems likely to be cast out once and for all into their language and to send it charging down the Gadarene slope on the brink of which it is now poised.

The East Germans by contrast, with all the chauvinism that is the hallmark of international Marxism, and also inspired perhaps by the determination to 'dew different' (as we say in Norfolk) from the West, have tended to follow a policy of purification and *Verdeutschung* that the Nazis themselves might well have envied. Here, in contrast to dichotomies that have arisen more naturally and more gradually, the most pronounced differences lie in the formal and official language and, allowing for local hazards, the greatest commonalty in the idiom of everyday speech. The differences in terminology are sufficient to make accurate translation of, say, contracts, a considerable problem for anyone in the West, of German mother-tongue or otherwise.

This modern, artificial and hopefully temporary distinction is superimposed on a wealth of dialect variety greater perhaps than that of any other Western language and ranging from Schleswig-Holstein and Friesland to Silesia, Austria and Switzerland. This combined pattern of dialect and political separation calls for particularly careful treatment. Within any one of the four nation-states concerned, the formal language will clearly be the same while the differences in dialect — for instance between *Plattdeutsch* and *Bayrisch* — are far greater than those on one side or the other of any of the frontiers. On the other hand East and West Germany, Austria and Switzerland all have radically different official and legal terminologies, and there is no 'mandarin' that would be acceptable in, say, a court of law of any of the four countries.

If détente continues and relationships between the two Germanies increase greatly in scope and intensity, one will probably see the re-establishment of a *Hochdeutsch* accepted in both those countries, and then the Austrians and the German-speaking Swiss will have to make the best of it as in the past. But we are clearly a very long way from this situation, and this diversity scarcely strengthens the position of the German language at international level. So it is very possible that fractionation· will accelerate the decline in status of a language that cultural attainment and scientific achievement had combined to make one of the greatest in the world.

Two things will by now be clear to the reader. First, if it is purely a question of imparting information to professional men and others of equivalent education, there is no need whatever to go outside the main or major languages, and in any hard science or engineering field the level of communication may fall if one does so. Secondly, the cost-effectiveness of translation or other use of the language falls off almost exponentially (reducing market, increasing cost, loss of quality) as we move down the league table.

The justification for venturing into a minor language will therefore be either political or promotional, and two solutions which avoid many of the drawbacks of a direct full-scale venture into the minor language thus present themselves. One is to dress the presentation up in the minor language rather as a non-linguist host may learn by heart a sentence or two of his guests' language for his speech of welcome, and offering the bulk of the documentation in any one of a choice of major languages. For example in that most important of all future markets, Iran, the European language used as a *lingua franca* within a particular profession, industry or large firm may be English, French, German or Russian depending on where the bulk of the managers and technologists of that particular organisation have been trained. It thus becomes necessary to agree a working language at a preliminary meeting. It is perfectly feasible and relatively quick and cheap to produce, in this case in Farsi, something between a glorified compliments slip and a short glossy couched in general terms and aimed at political level readership and submit the rest of the documentation in the agreed major European language under cover of, or in association with this.

The second possibility, which applies perhaps especially to the East European market, is an indirect approach. It may for example be very difficult to get complex technical documentation well translated from English into, say, Czech. But once the documentation is established in German and the sponsor is set up in—in this case—either of the Germanies, it will be far simpler to move from German to Czech. The price here, of course, will be delay in penetration of one of the target markets.

The decision on how to tackle minor language markets, further dicussed in Part 2 of this book, is in fact a relatively straightfoward management decision provided the person taking it is aware of all the factors. When full consideration is given to them all, there may well sometimes be a case for letting the tail wag the dog a little — letting optimisation of language costs and procedures influence the marketing plan itself.

1.6   Problems of non-European languages

At the practical level to which we and, hopefully, the reader are trying to confine ourselves, there are perhaps four reasons for learning or working in a country's language. Either you want to export to it, or you want to borrow money from it, or you expect to go to war with it and/or to be conquered by it. With this checklist it is easy to see that there is little reason for concerning ourselves further with Japanese, Japan being at once a politico-military dwarf and an economic giant which is increasingly short of money and where enthusiasm for exports is equalled only by an opposition to imports backed up by the sharpest of statutory teeth.

The problem with the great Oriental languages is that they are structured round a culture and mode of thought so different to our own as to be incomprehensible to us. They lack the roots and syntax on which to build a vocabulary for a body of science and technology which—to a greater extent than many scientists or engineers might care to admit, and particularly in the earlier descriptive stages—has in some measure been shaped by classical and modern European languages and the concepts and roots available in these. (In a later chapter we shall be considering the nomenclature of botany and organic chemistry as examples of linguistic codes rather than parts of a true language.) At the moment the resulting gap is so wide that it is easier for the speakers of the Oriental language to work in a European language than for anyone to attempt to bridge it.

On the other hand the racial and ideological pressures at work in many parts of the third world are so powerful that it is unlikely that third world countries will accept the use of a European language indefinitely. There have already been a number of serious attempts, notably in the development of the Malaysian National Language from Malay, to impose an economic and technological vocabulary on an Oriental language, but so far as the authors know these have had very limited success. Since however it takes at least two generations for a country's educational system to develop a useful level of resources in teaching a language and produce speakers of it, one may perhaps be permitted a little rather wild speculation here.

In identifying a language as suitable for development to fulfil the complete needs of an advanced society, to the exclusion of any language borrowed from another society, one should perhaps look for three criteria: a primary and secondary population coverage of the same order as that of the major European languages; a society within the primary coverage that possesses, or has in the past possessed, a very advanced culture, being for example the mother-tongue of one of the great religions of the world; and more broadly a society which has in the past developed or acted as a vehicle for the science and technology of the era. Taking this subjective speculation one stage further, the languages that leap out as satisfying these criteria are Arabic and Chinese.

Without developing this topic in full, one could perhaps fairly say that 'five major languages is about right.' On the one hand it provides for sufficient diversity to represent the full span of advanced cultures without distortion or the superimposition of foreign concepts. On the other it is about as many as any educational system can carry or as any international organisation can reasonably handle in the long term. Thus one might ultimately see Arabic replace Spanish (or possibly French in view of the many French-speaking Arab countries) at United Nations level, while in

the scientific and technological fields Chinese and Arabic might join
English, French and Russian, displacing German and, to the extent that it applies, Spanish. But since the development of both those languages is coupled with an education problem of shattering dimensions in the societies whose mother-tongues they are, it could well be that, by the time they are ripe to replace European languages, the political pressures that motivated their development will have disappeared and been replaced by a pride in the conservation of two parallel cultures, one indigenous and one received.

1.7 The development of a language policy

While some of the discussion in this chapter is deliberately specious in nature and intended to provoke interest and thought, the basic information presented in it is factual. And this makes it clear that every organisation which works or intends to work across a language barrier, from the United Nations organisation to the smallest exporter, needs to work out and implement a language policy. It seems reasonable to expect that the trend in commerce and technology will be more and more towards working in the major languages, as has long been the custom in scientific fields. But if languages are to cease to be a barrier to international working and become a tool that can help fashion and launch an export programme, the language factors must be studied in the same depth as other marketing factors and given due weight in framing the marketing plan.

It will also seem that educational organisations other than those concerned with the needs of the Armed Forces and the Diplomatic Service should be beginning to consider the implications of introducing the teaching of Oriental languages, say Arabic and Chinese, into secondary and further education.

2

The nature of translation

One of the major impediments to effective communication across a language barrier is probably the total incomprehension of the non-linguist (one uses this extreme term literally and with no suggestion of deprecation) of what the act of translation involves. This is scarcely surprising, since it is only recently — probably since the end of World War 2 — that the language profession itself or the relatively few academic institutions which have interested themselves in the more practical aspects of the use of languages attempted any deliberate study or analysis of the procedures and skills involved in written or oral translation.

Since then, with the development of the great Continental schools and faculties of translation and interpreting, and with the emergence of linguistics as a discipline in its own right, a number of attempts have been made to describe, organise and teach theories of translation. These attempts, together with practical experience of 'applied language' teaching at various levels, are gradually providing a framework that will one day doubtless improve methods of selecting translators and the standard to which they can be trained. These attempts will also establish procedures to solve specific translation problems.

Meanwhile these hypotheses, couched in language barely intelligible even to the practising linguist, are of little help to him and of no value

whatever to the businessman who employs him. This chapter attempts to
set out in simple terms some of the aspects of translation which managers
need to know if they are to tackle their language problems and handle their
linguists sensibly.

2.1 Translation—a four-step process

When you read or hear a word or phrase, you either 'know' it or you accept
it as a word without in fact understanding what it represents. In the latter
case you retain it as a word until you learn its meaning from the context,
from enquiry or from research. In the former and more usual case the word
calls up in your consciousness a certain concept; once this has happened
the received word is of no further importance; it can be and is forgotten.
Very often a single word will not suffice to define the concept; a phrase or
even a complete sentence is needed. After hearing or reading a passage,
what you will retain is not the language or indeed the precise message of the
original, but a concept representing the message modified by your own
experience and deductions.

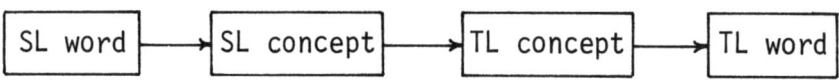

Figure 2.1   SL = language of origin,
             TL = language of translation

Accomplished linguists are often embarrassingly unable to answer
simple questions such as: 'What is the German for "window"?' The word
'window' in isolation simply does not call up *Fenster* or *fenêtre* or whatever.
In the linguist's mind the transition from one language to the other does
not occur between words or phrases but between concepts. (The common
saying: 'You'll never speak a language unless you think in it' would appear
to be relevant here.) It is, of course, far easier to 'work' completely in a
foreign language than to translate or interpret between two languages,
since translation involves the constant transition between one set of
concepts and another.

You will now see why, as Figure 2.1 indicates, translation even at quite
an elementary level is a four-step, not a two-step process; and why the fate
of unintelligibility so often overtakes those who attempt to translate from
dictionaries. After examining some of the broader aspects of verbal and
language-based communication, we shall pursue in more depth the key
parameters of translation.

2.2 Characteristics of verbal communication

Unlike mathematical or scientific symbols, words are imprecise, and much of the content of the message they carry is subjective. When we try to write 'instructions in words of one syllable', i.e. that will be clear to the least intelligent and experienced reader, or to prepare an agreement or other legal document, we attempt to strip words down so that they carry only a basic and objective meaning. But if we took this process to its extreme, defining every term like any Schoolman, explaining every contingency or ambiguity and (literally) leaving nothing to the imagination, the text would contain so much information redundant for the most likely reader that it would be psychologically unacceptable to him — or in the common sense of the term 'unreadable'.

At the other extreme consider communication between members of a close-knit family. This is apt to be completely unintelligible to an outsider. Coined 'family words' are used to convey any one of an absurdly wide span of meanings. Standard words are used in a sense completely foreign to their conventional meaning, and even standard words more or less correctly used carry a vast overload of subjective implications.

The text with which a translator is faced will lie somewhere between these two extremes, very often nearer to the second of them. In normal professional or commercial correspondence, a very high proportion of the message is taken as common knowledge and therefore omitted, and much else is covered by allusions to common experiences or reference bases; and if the correspondents know one another personally, a great deal more will be left to be read between the lines.

A translator receiving a text of this kind through the post and knowing nothing of the background, the circumstances or the personalities stands no chance whatever of conveying to the ultimate reader the full and precise message that the writer intended. But the difficulty does not end there; coming cold to the text the translator will find in it not only ambiguities of factual statement, which can often be cleared on the telephone, but ambiguities of implication or nuance on which he must take a decision for himself. A series of erroneous decisions of this kind, each of them perfectly justifiable in itself, can take the translation far away from both the explicit meaning and the tone of the original. Add to this the fact that, professional and specially trained writers apart, few originators express themselves accurately, clearly or correctly, and that most typists throw in a liberal dollop of spelling and typing errors, and the translator is faced with a mountainous task of comprehension before the problem of transition to the language of translation is even considered. The deliberate misuse or transposition of a word is an attractive and effective trick of style which anyone is entitled to play with his own language in literature or in everyday communication; and since the whole point of this flourish is that the 'error' should be clearly recognisable, the translator or any other reader has only himself to blame if he is puzzled or misled. But the accidental misuse of words is quite a different matter and is a fault so common as to represent a major cause of failure of communication.

The authors, who at this point must confess to working 'the wrong way', usually with the help of a native speaker of the language of translation, find that the problem of understanding fully and correctly texts presented for translation is far more difficult than that of conveying the comprehended message in the language of translation — and this although these texts are received in their own mother tongue and they know most originators personally. This will perhaps serve to make clear to the users of translators that in the conventional procedures of commercial translation a high and sometimes a critical loss of information is inevitable.

2.3   Communication on the aesthetic plane

The term 'aesthetic' is used here to describe communication in which the literal message is reinforced by secondary signals of a consistent pattern.

The power of speech may be the characteristic that singles out man from the rest of the animal kingdom, but language used or misused on the literal or prosaic level is not merely a blunt instrument but a remarkably ineffective means of communication. Wherever a negotiating situation exists or indeed it becomes important for one person to influence another, the successful man of business will, loth as he may be to admit it, quickly resort to the use of language for communication on some higher plane. So we are faced with a progression of combinations of basic and secondary communication ranging from the unadorned statement of fact to communication on the aesthetic level on which most literature depends.

As soon as he becomes airborne in this way the originator is in fact asking the translator not simply to convey a message — difficult enough as we have seen — but to condition the reader to accept or respond in some desired way to the content of the message. Clearly the first prerequisite is for the translator to be able to write in any style required of him; but this appears to be a characteristic, perhaps humiliating, perhaps signifying a noble detachment, which successful translators and interpreters appear to share with members of the performing arts. The next requirement is for the translator to have enough knowledge of the originator to judge exactly where on some arbitrary scale of intensity the language used is intended to lie.

Neither of these problems is insuperable, particularly if a pair of translators, one of each mother tongue, are working together. Here the difficulty lies not in comprehension but in making the appropriate transition to the new language. This requires understanding of and feel for not only the language but also the particular combination of language and field. Most Germans like to conduct commercial and professional communications down to earth and man to man, with the implication of a glazed eyeball always poised for confrontation and a hearty hand never more than an inch or two from the other man's shoulder blades. But stumble on even the most improbable of cultural tripwires and you are at once transported into the groves of Academe, with Goethe or even Kant lurking behind every tree.

The Frenchman insists that communication be served up with the proper dressing of formality and courtesy, but under these he likes to find the matter set out with all the power of *dialectique* in which his language excels. But there are exceptions: to anyone other than a French doctor even the most mundane piece of French medical documentation reads like the product of a kind of space-age Olympus in which every least feature and event receives the full grand opera treatment.

The translator's task is therefore to adopt the particular style and strength of expression that will bring the reader to the precise point on the precise plane that the originator intends. We shall return later to this requirement and the practical difficulties that surround it in the discussion of various aspects of promotional literature.

2.4 Spoken and written communication

Figure 2.2 illustrates spoken, personal written and typewritten communication within a single language. It is at once evident that in spoken communication a welter of information is available, so that some of it is almost certainly redundant. We shall return to this diagram when we consider interpreting, but briefly it can be said that the problem in moving

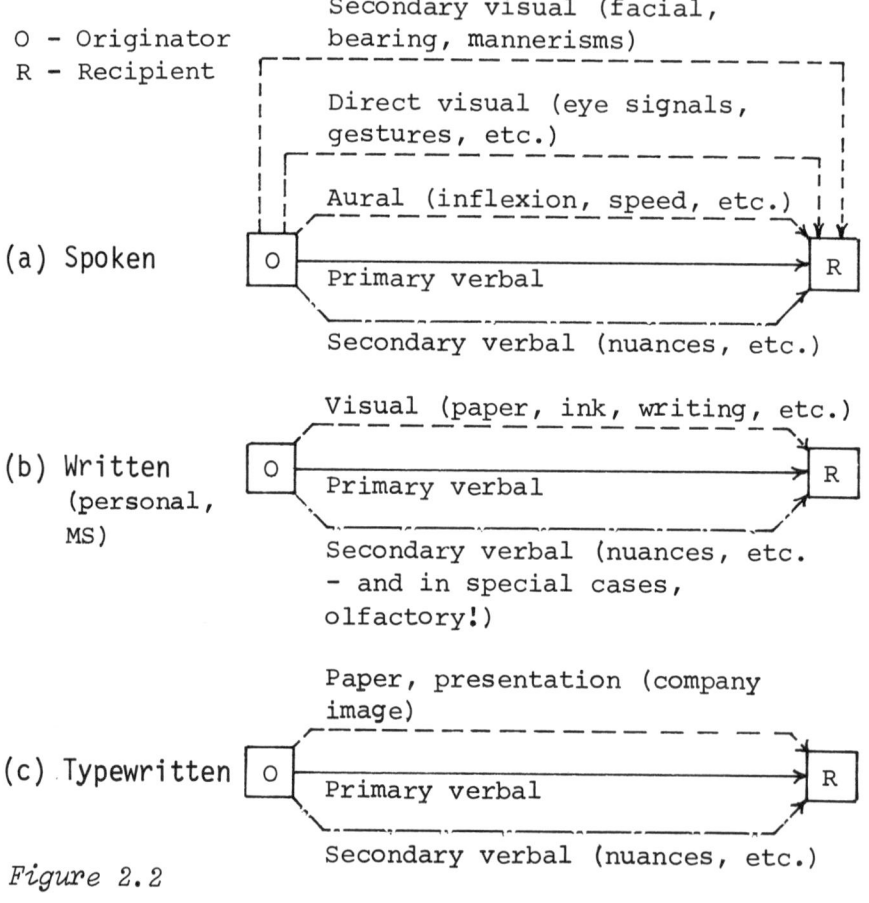

Figure 2.2

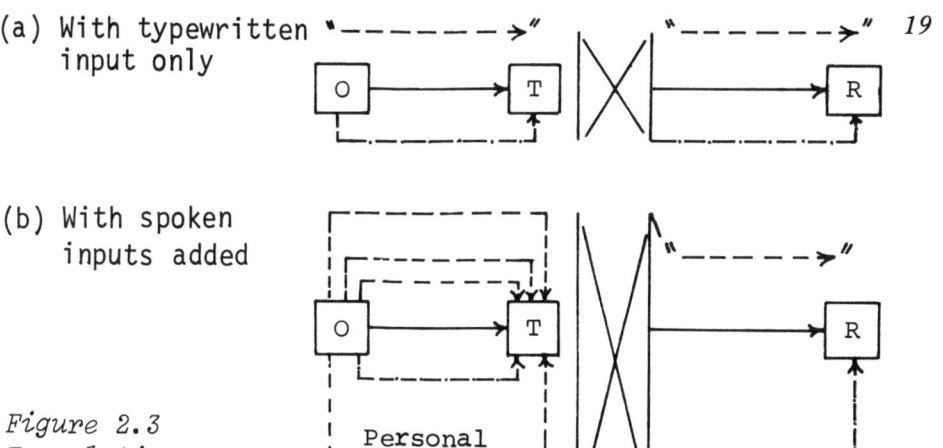

(a) With typewritten input only

(b) With spoken inputs added

Figure 2.3
Translation
inputs and outputs

Personal knowledge

across a language barrier is essentially one of synchronisation of the signals on the various channels. The personal letter, quite apart from the likelihood of the correspondents being known to one another, gives scope for a good deal of visual back-up which can in fact be interwoven with the secondary verbal channel, for example by changing the style or size of writing to give emphasis. When we come down to the typewritten official or commercial communication, we are down to the two verbal channels, and the secondary verbal signal may have lost much of its significance. The visual information imparted by paper and presentation respresents, in fact, not the individual originator but his organisation or company. Near-perfection will be expected, and any falling short of this will greatly reduce the acceptability of the communication. When we consider promotional literature we begin of course to add new factitious channels and so attempt to move towards a situation with a fullness and impact analogous to that of the spoken word.

It is of course in the third 'typewritten' category that the bulk of the professional translator's work lies. He can only attempt to pass on what he receives, or believes he has received.

Suppose that he has received only the 'typewritten' inputs. There will be some degradation of the information in the translation process so that the overall loss of information between originator and recipient is at best considerable. Suppose now (see Figure 2.3) that the originator hands the text to the translator in person and goes over and discusses it with him. The translator has open to him the full range of 'spoken' inputs and over and above this he will — quite quickly if he is experienced — acquire personal knowledge of the originator. He therefore sets about the task of translation with the fullest possible range of information at his disposal. The risk of misunderstandings is virtually eliminated and because he is condensing information and discarding redundant elements there is no reason why he should not convey to the recipient the content and tone of the originator's message virtually intact.

As Figure 2.3 shows it is easy to make meaningful and useful distinctions between channels, although there may be some room for argument as to the channel in which particular elements of the total signal belong. While one can have perfectly clear and varied concepts of 'primary signals' and 'secondary signals', there is in this case a grey zone wide enough to complicate discussion of what proportion of the total signal may be regarded as primary. One may perhaps fairly say that the direct and principal meaning of a word, phrase or sentence belongs squarely in the primary verbal channel, while any overtones or nuances offered to the reader by a sentence or paragraph as a whole can be regarded as secondary verbal signals. Problems arise when a word or phrase is made to carry a special or subjective meaning as well as the direct meaning appropriate to the context.

We can consider this difficult area under three heads. First there may be reference to some experience or verbal exchange specifically shared by the correspondents, so that a proper name or a particular phrase carries some unique and special meaning for them. This arises mainly at the family and personal level, but it is surprising how often allusions of this kind come up in more formal correspondence. The second is allusion to a historical event that will convey a particular set of concepts briefly — 'if Smith represents us, it'll only be another Munich', 'we're getting uncomfortably near *les événements* again'. The third, likely to arise in correspondence between two specialists in the same field, is the use of a word or short phrase as a shorthand description of a complete set of concepts or system. For instance we speak of a 'rigid' meaning 'a non-articulated lorry' or 'a body installation for a non-articulated lorry'; or, using a proper name, of a 'Stephenson valve gear' to describe a particular design of steam-engine valve arrangement.

Even if they lend themselves to literal translation, words and phrases of this kind may easily mislead the translator and thus the recipient. In the case of 'private' meanings, the originator has only himself to blame, for unless he was present on the occasion referred to, it is pure chance whether the translator will choose the particular word that will evoke this special response in the recipient or will prefer some perfectly valid synonym. In the second and third cases it may fairly be argued that a professional translator should have sufficient general and specialised knowledge to appreciate the allusions; but there are limitations in this direction, particularly in the engineering field and particularly when, as is normal, the translator's mother tongue is the language of translation.

Thus a very substantial and critically important part of the signal may be carried within this grey zone between primary and secondary, and in considering this we see that Figure 2.3 does not fully represent the situation. It depicts all the dynamic channels on which information is passed, but it fails to superimpose these on a static matrix of what we may call common memory or common understanding possessed by originator and recipient. The problem lies in the extent to which the translator shares this reference base; in addressing himself, very properly, to the final reader, the originator may easily make unconscious but wholly unwarranted assumptions about the translator's common understanding.

We can now see the full significance of the additional channel marked 'personal knowledge' at the bottom of Figure 2.4. What is really happening is that the briefing session described is building up in the translator this matrix of common understanding, just as reference data are fed into the library or slow-access memory of a computer. We can now redraw Figure 3 to indicate the importance both of briefings and of feedback from the recipient in building up in the translator the requisite matrix of common experience.

The moral is clear enough. Even in the 'typewritten' situation depicted in Figure 2.2, a high proportion of the information is carried on the secondary verbal channel or as an overload on the primary verbal channel. Further the actual content of the signal is often in effect an instruction to the reader to retrieve from the common memory shared by the originator and reader a particular block of information. It is difficult to put a figure on the breakdown of the total message between primary and secondary, but clearly in all but the most routine communications a substantial proportion of the signals may be lost and the whole import of the message may be obscured or misrepresented if the secondary element is lost or distorted. To carry the intended message across a language barrier requires that the translator be fully briefed, that he be allowed to develop his background knowledge and understanding by continuity of work and that, even if he is not required to handle replies coming in from the recipient, he must have access to these.

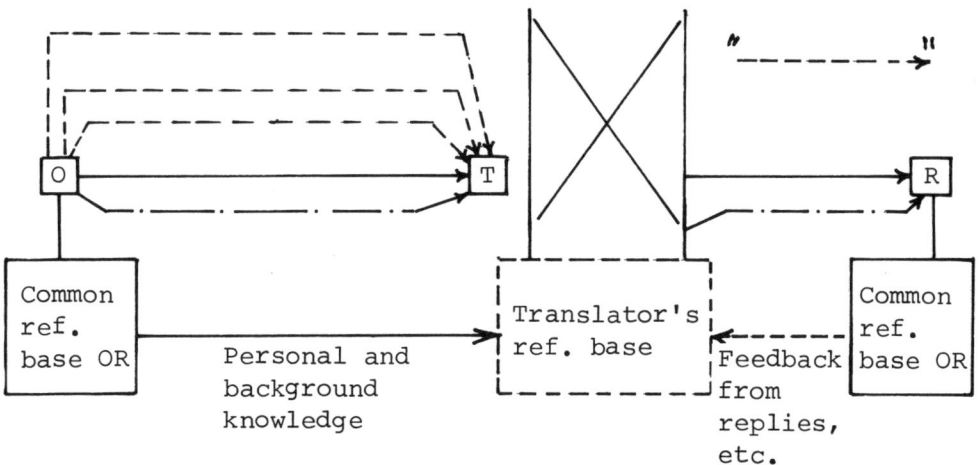

Figure 2.4 Translator's reference base (cf. Figure 2.3b 'with spoken inputs')

The classification of words as concrete or abstract is not particularly helpful, as extreme complexities of meaning can arise in concrete and wholly unevocative words. If for example we take the word 'pin' — — one can't get much simpler than that — and build round it an interlocking pattern of related English, French and German words, we finish up with a jigsaw of twenty or more words any of which could bring us back to 'pin'. It may be more constructive to think of precise terms on the one hand and general words on the other.

Figure 2.5 gives an example of a precise term, and we note that we can expand this to a collective without any loss of precision (although the number of compounds covered by the term 'the alcohols' is legion).

In describing general words the authors find it helpful, with apologies to Eysenck and others, to use the concept of a meaning grid, preferring Cartesian to polar coordinates simply because they are easier to explain and follow. To determine the intersection of the axes we need a concept of primary meaning; here let us avoid linguistic controversy and say simply that 'primary meaning' is the first definition given in a dictionary or the concept evoked in an educated person hearing the word in isolation. We can allow the abscissa to represent the span of meanings covered by the word and the ordinate to represent the span of its connotations (good, neutral, bad). The reader will see that the word may be used to define any point within this grid, and conversely that the word may signify any point within the grid. The person who speaks or writes it must indicate its place within the grid both by context and by such secondary signals as are available within the method of communication being used. Likewise the reader must deduce the word's intended place in its grid, and hence its contribution to the message, from context and secondary signals.

There is, of course, no reason why this grid should be square or symmetrical about its focus. In fact, assuming we use some arbitrary but constant scale, the shape of the grid and any asymmetry of its focus will tell us a great deal about the word.

Within the same language we can construct patterns of overlapping grids, the overlaps themselves representing situations in which two or more words are truly synonymous. Figure 2.5c gives a rather crude indication of this notion, and the reader may find it amusing to construct similar patterns for himself.

When we turn to the translation situation, involving two languages, we get a much more complicated pattern of overlapping grids. Figure 2.5d suggests the development of such an exercise starting with the English word 'true'. If we developed this fully in English and German and then superimposed French on it, showing the grids instead of just the words, we should quickly reach a pattern so complex as to be indecipherable.

Since we know from experience how frequently misunderstandings and failures of communication occur among people of the same language and culture, this grid concept will quickly demonstrate the extreme difficulty and subjectivity of the translator's task, or conversely bring out to the

(a) Precise terms and their collectives

```
Ethyl alcohol (unique)
Propyl alcohol          = n-propyl or isopropyl alcohol
The propyl alcohols     = n- and isopropyl alcohols
The alcohols            = compounds of general formula
```

$$C_nH_{(2n+1)}OH$$

(b) Meaning grid

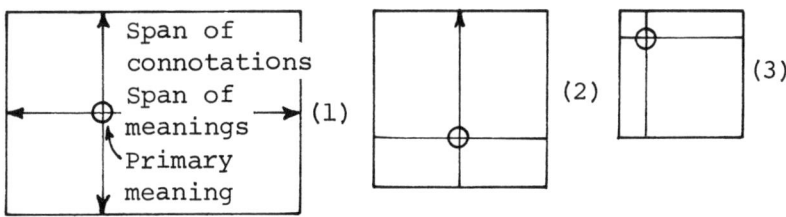

(c) Overlapping grids, same language

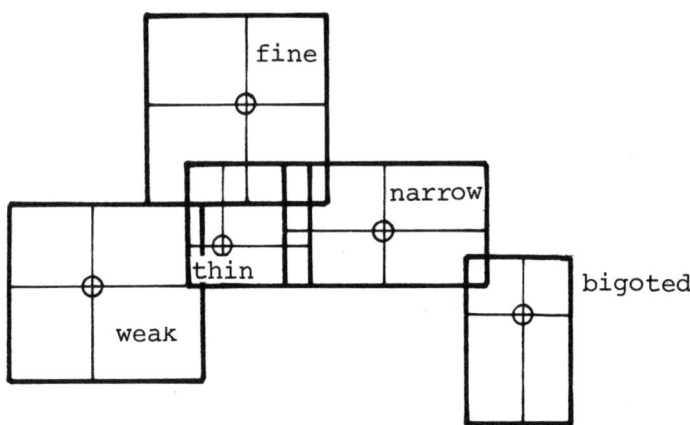

(d) Overlapping grids, two languages

```
        TREU              genuine
  loyal           true      ECHT
        faithful  WAHR    real
    GLÄUBIG             EIGENTLICH
                          WIRKLICH
```

Figure 2.5 Meanings and connotations

non-linguist how easily deviations of emphasis or even errors can arise in translation and lead to misunderstandings between the principals.

2.7   Language and modes of thought

The relationship between language structure, modes of thought and cultural patterns is a three-dimensional chicken and egg problem which has proved the delight of academics of diverse disciplines and will no doubt continue to provide them with sport. Three aspects of this fascinating exercise are however of importance at the practical level where businessman and practising linguist meet.

The first of these is not of itself a language problem and concerns communication between principals, however conducted. It is extremely difficult for an Englishman and a Frenchman to discuss a problem constructively or to move towards one another by negotiation quite simply because their whole approach and mode of reasoning, ingrained at all levels of their respective educational systems, are quite different. The Frenchman and the German go some way towards sharing a liking for dialectic which the Anglo-Saxon rejects, but the widely differing structures of their languages make it difficult for them to move smoothly down a common path. The Anglo-Saxon and the German or Scandinavian appear to get on like a house on fire only to discover that they have at the end of the day formed completely different impressions of what they have agreed. This communications barrier is far more serious than the language barrier itself. Although a good linguist can help, the principals need to make a conscious effort to understand each other's approach and thought.

The second problem arises in the impossibility of translating certain quite simple and everyday concepts from one language to another without making changes so radical that one must talk of a paraphrase rather than of a translation. For example we know of no straightforward way of conveying in another language the full implications and connotation of the expression 'second best'. (Where only part of its full span of meaning is relevant, there is of course no translation problem.) After all, the connotations of 'second best' in American and British English differ considerably, so perhaps the only conclusion to be drawn is that a liking for compromise is indeed a uniquely British trait.

It is, however, in the apparently simple field of prepositions that a complete breakdown in communications is apt to occur and that the linguist, if only he will admit it, meets his Waterloo. It is doubtful if one ever arrives at the full concept imparted by a word in a language other than one's own, but it is fairly certain that one will not achieve this with prepositions. To the layman or the schoolboy linguist, prepositions appear as the least of problems; they are rather simple words which establish relationships between one word and another and whose use is governed by some rather simple rules. In fact their use, or sometimes their deliberate misuse, conveys a wealth of finely shaded meanings, the existence of which, one suspects, even the 'bilingual' only realises through an

awareness that he has missed something. We challenge any native speaker
of the languages in question to give them logical and general rules on when
to use *de* and when *á* between certain verbs and the infinitives they govern,
to give a definition of *auf* that will cover its standard and idiomatic uses, or
to explain at what precise point in the German mind motion ceases to be
motion and accusative gives way to dative. Only a native speaker knows;
and he knows instinctively because this particular minute element forms
part of his culture. English is, of course, even richer in these snags, and one
hears many a fluent foreigner trip on an English preposition.

Perhaps the point one should make from these differences and from
limitations in comprehension is that it is the translator's business to get the
meaning across by whatever means he sees fit, and the principal's to trust
him to do so.

2.8 Literalness versus freedom

The literary translator undoubtedly has a duty to convey not only the
meaning of the original but also to reflect its style, metaphor and allusions
either directly or by means of some parallel established in his mind by a
subjective link of communication at the aesthetic level between the author
and himself. Outside the literary field, there seems no good reason why the
translator should have any obligation to the originator, whether or not the
latter is his client, other than to convey as fully as possible the message
intended.

If the occasion and the purpose of the translation requires close and
evident matching of texts, as discussed in the following chapter, well and
good. Otherwise restrictions imposed on the translator's freedom can only
lead to avoidable loss of information. They should be neither imposed
by the client nor accepted by the translator.

Depending on a number of technical factors the unit of length a
translator chooses as a basis for rendering a particular text may vary from a
single word (or even an element of a compound word) to a complete
paragraph, and even beyond this to an entire section or, in a sense, the text
as a whole. Certainly the message contained in any one section of a longish
text can be expected to influence the translation of other sections.

The respective merits of literalness and freedom are a subject of
professional and academic controversy in which the user will do well not to
get involved. He needs, however, to appreciate that restrictions on
freedom, necessary as they may be, usually result in loss of information, to
understand the principal mechanism which determines freedom or
literalness and to be prepared to discuss this problem with his translator in
the light of the use to which the translation is to be put.

2.9 Matching translation to its purpose

Discussion so far has been mainly concerned with the quality of translation and the areas of choice available to the translator in his effort to convey as much as possible of the information content of the original. The breadth of scope available to the translator in this respect will by now have become clear to the reader, but there remains a further area of choice in the manner of presentation of the message.

As stated above, the literary translator patently has an ethical duty to the original author and a professional obligation to the publisher not simply to convey the meaning of the original but also to reflect its style, metaphor and allusion. *Mutatis mutandis* this duty holds in some measure for the translation of an outgoing person-to-person letter but with this exception there seems no reason for it to apply in the field of non-literary written translation. If it exists at all here, it takes the shape of a restriction on veering too far from the tone of the original rather than of a positive requirement to abide by it.

More important is the need to match the translation to its purpose, and this at once implies that the translator must be briefed both on the purpose of his task and on the background of the recipient or reader. For maximum cost-effectiveness this matching should take place at two levels. The first concerns quality of translation or, more precisely, the proportion of the information contained in the original that in fact needs to be conveyed.

If for instance we consider a typical short business letter on a company letterhead, we find that a large number of the pieces of information contained in this document are purely formal and therefore redundant whatever the purpose, and that the actual message to be transmitted is likely to be contained within 10 to 20 per cent or even less of the total characters on the page. Very often a mere gloss in the margin or below the typed text, giving the gist of the message, will suffice in the way of translation. On other occasions more information, e.g. the address and telephone and telex numbers of the originator, will be needed; and occasionally the original will need to be reproduced as precisely as possible in all its glory for some legal or other formal purpose.

The second level is that of presentation. It is clearly a waste of time for the translator to lavish his powers of expression and he or his secretary their typing skills on a document that is required simply for the information of a few individuals within the sponsor organisation. In the case of a routine outgoing letter, rather more care in the style is called for, and presentation in the typing sense must be at least as good as that practised by the sponsor in his own language. Translations for publication on the other hand call for the full range of the translator's skill and for extreme care over detail. Their presentation in the narrower sense may not be critical, as for instance in the case of a printer's draft, or may call for the highest standards of typing and reproduction, where urgency dictates direct reproduction of a typescript.

The evident need for the translator to respond with some precision to instructions of this kind leads into a general point on translators and translation. The discussion above will have made sufficiently clear that translation is an art and not a kind of numbers game with words and that knowledge of the two languages concerned is really no more than the ante in the range of skills required of the translator. And, quite apart from skills, some of them of a very high grade, the translator will often require to apply professional judgement to the text and situation as a whole if he is to do his job properly. Nevertheless translation is essentially uncreative. It parallels the performing rather than the creative arts. Outside the literary field, and more particularly in the practical world of business and professional activity, the scope for creativity is far more limited than it is in the recording studio or on the large or small screen. To translators capable of producing high-grade results this lack of creativity will often be a conscious or unconscious frustration; the user who wants to recruit and hold a good translator and to get the best out of him, should go to very great lengths to provide him with terms of reference that give as much rein as possible to his latent creative talent. Our personal view is that translation does not constitute a satisfying and therefore full-time professional activity, and concentration on it to the exclusion of all else is likely to produce excessive introspection and deterioration of the very skills and qualities of mind that are needed. Mixed with writing and consultancy, or with university-level teaching, translation of the more challenging kind provides an activity that is at once satisfying and relaxing, in that it is generally somewhat less intellectually and emotionally exacting than these other activities.

3
Commercial translation

The craft-oriented structure of the language profession and, in the UK at least, the lack of language skills among professional men and managers have combined to create both the image and the reality of a kind of mill which reflects the characteristics attributed to these machines by both Blake and the combined efforts of Friedrich von Logau and Longfellow. Every day in every country which trades internationally ream upon ream of translation is slowly and expensively churned out, much of it to go unread either because it is overtaken by events or because it never contained a significant message in the first place. The theme of this chapter, and indeed of other relevant parts of this book will be that the full and formal translation of most commercial documents and correspondence is an activity that is not merely unproductive and expensive, but thanks to the disproportionate delays often associated with it may even be counter-productive.

The development even by small firms and organisations of some level of in-house language resources coupled with the informed use in a consultant capacity of suitably qualified professional linguists can obviate the need for formal translation — and in many instances for any written translation at all — of a very high proportion of the routine documentation that straddles a language barrier. The real need is to limit the amount of translation and to make sure that translation and related activities which are truly essential are carried out quickly, efficiently and cost-effectively.

Not only do the format and formality of letters and other documents vary widely between languages, and indeed between countries sharing a common language, but the entire approach to the problem of conveying a message is also quite different. While this may not be true of engineers and hard scientists, it certainly applies to medicine and gains in importance as a factor as we move across the cultural spectrum through the other learned professions towards the arts. As mentioned elsewhere, French medical literature for instance is couched in such dramatic terms that for the non-French reader, professional or lay, a dark browed, bearded surgeon with scalpel poised leaps out of every page.

Except in the special cases discussed later in this chapter, the translator's task is to choose the form and language that will best convey the message intended by the originators; to do this he may have to take very considerable liberties. We shall be dealing later with some of the aspects of formal and personal letters and memoranda, but a good general example of this point is the problem posed in the topping and tailing in French and German of letters written by English-speaking middle and senior managers. These will typically begin 'Dear Mr Smith' or 'Dear Richard' and end 'Yours sincerely'. Now French convention in the topping and more particularly in the tailing of letters offer a rich treasury of opportunities for flattery and hidden insult, but do not include anything that directly corresponds to this widely used English form. To strike the right note, the translator therefore needs to know whether the correspondents in fact know each other personally, if so how well and — in so far as it cannot be gleaned from the text of the letter — the shape of their relations at the particular point in time. Modern German practice on the other hand offers very little scope for the expression of shades of respect or intimacy, the jump to the use of a first name in writing being a considerable one in social and business settings alike and the inclusion or omission of *Ihr* being the only acceptable variation on *mit freundlichen Gruss* (South Germany and Austria *mit freundlichen Grüssen*) unless you really want to fling a lump of *vorzügliche Hochachtung*.

We thus run into difficulties, or at least apparent deviations from the original, before we get into the text at all. If any but a routine text is to go across properly and convey the originator's full meaning, the translator should be given a free hand to use the approach, language and paragraphing that he believes will best convey the message to a reader whose mother tongue is the language of translation. Similarity of appearance between original and translation in format or in the general lay-out of the letter is not merely irrelevant but counter-productive. Although in fact the letterhead will always give the game away, the impression the reader receives should be that he is reading a letter from an organisation of his own country which takes exceptional pride in the style and presentation of its correspondence.

Just as the reasonably trained and experienced eye can pinpoint the country of origin of an engineering product — a computer, a machine tool, a car or a washing machine — from its general appearance and certain habits of external design that may be in themselves too trivial and elusive to define, so every language, and every country of a group sharing the same language, has typical tricks of punctuation and lay-out. These small editorial points have a disproportionate effect on acceptability to the reader. Frenchmen for instance have a horror of oblique strokes, and extreme care is needed in the use of dashes both in continuous text and in tabulated matter. In English a list or a string of sub-paragraphs is usually preceded by a sign ': —', after which the items or sub-paragraphs may be entered direct or through an identifying letter or number. French, German and a number of other languages end the body of the text with a colon and precede the items or sub-paragraphs with a dash, always if they are not numbered or lettered, and in French quite frequently if they are. Again French uses ordinal numbers for paragraphs. We all know that laxity over details like this and over presentation in general gravely reduces the acceptability of a letter originating in our own country and frequently leads to rejection of the contents or of the writer; similarly we know how we react to an obvious translation sent from abroad with the best of intentions but not fully and correctly anglicised (the state of affairs we shall refer to frequently throughout this book as the 'Japanese camera leaflet syndrome'). It is perhaps less easy to appreciate that others feel exactly the same and respond just as positively as we do to signs that real trouble has been taken to make the communication acceptable to them.

Presentation and editing then unfortunately do matter. Equally unfortunately, most of the textbooks originating in English-speaking countries on foreign-language practices are seriously out of date, if indeed they ever told the full story. If outgoing foreign-language correspondence and documentation is being produced in-house, those responsible for its presentation must have up-to-date manuals from the country of the language, difficult to get and expensive as these may be.

While taking infinite trouble to conform to the practice of the reader's language and country, one must always be prepared to break with it when there is a good reason. For example in most languages other than English it is customary to precede the date on a letter or document with the name of the post town of the originator's address. As long as tax havens remain available to the English-speaking world — and by the look of things they may be history by the time this book is published — this name should be omitted in the case of an 'overseas' company writing and conducting its business from the office of its UK or US principal. Otherwise considerable contractual and possibly fiscal complications may ensue in dealing with a third country.

3.2 Agreements, contracts and matching texts

Great stress has been laid on freedom of translation to achieve the most effective and convincing results, but there are of course occasions when the original and the translation must match as closely and as patently as the structure and vocabulary of the two or more languages allow. Loss of quality and possibly of information just has to be accepted. The requirement for matching texts holds for any document which binds the parties legally or even implies an intention to enter into a commitment. Patents are another instance of the need for matching texts. This principle can often usefully be applied to draft working papers intended for discussion in multi-lingual meetings with the support of simultaneous interpretation.

Most competent translators should be able to produce matching texts if briefed to do so, but the use of a team of translators working together is obviously of the greatest help here. The translators need to know which is the master text, or whether — as is more and more often the case — more than one or all of the languages involved have equal force.

If the effort of translators in producing matching texts is to bear fruit, pagination, presentation and lay out must also match. The numbering of pages, sections, paragraphs should be consistent through all the various language texts. Here courtesy may dictate following the practice of a particular language, otherwise it is simplest to adopt that of the language in which the draft first appears. If possible final typing of the various texts should be held over until the draft in the longest of the languages concerned is complete; otherwise it may be difficult to obtain consistency of layout and page numbering. For working papers in particular it may be worth going one stage further by putting two or more texts physically side by side on the same sheet.

3.3   Treatment of ambiguities

For the reason discussed in the last chapter most texts of any length and complexity will contain a number of phrases or passages whose meaning is not at once clear to the translator. This may be due either to the translator's limitations in knowledge of the language — even if it is his mother tongue — and of the field, or to lack of briefing and a common reference base; or again they may be either intentional or unintentional ambiguities inherent in the text itself. The translator's first task is to decide under which head these obscurities fall.

If he feels them to be due to his own limitations he must of course do everything within his power to clear them up by consultation with colleagues, with the client and if necessary with an expert in the field. Nonetheless if the translator is honest with himself there will usually remain a residue of obscurities of this kind which will shade in to unintentional ambiguities arising from the author's shortcomings.

It is here that one of the major controversies among professional linguists, and one of which users should certainly be aware, lies. The conventional school of thought maintains that the translator's job is to produce the best translation he can, accepting that it contains a few possible inaccuracies of which he is aware (as well, of course, as those of which he is unaware). Indeed for the translation divisions of international organisations such as UNO, the EEC or OECD, who are charged with producing definitive texts in a number of languages, the 'best guess' is often the only solution. They probably do not know precisely who wrote the text or if they do they cannot gain access to him; and since they have ample opportunity for consultation with experienced colleagues and if necessary with experts in the field, there is a very good chance of the 'best guess' being correct.

The other viewpoint, to which we subscribe, is that since the reader of the translation is completely in the translator's hands and since unconscious and unavoidable inaccuracies will mislead him slightly in any event, it is quite unethical to guess. Or rather, that the 'best guess' must be picked out and backed up by a note defining the area of doubt and offering alternative interpretations. Not only do we consider this to be the only ethical course, but we have never yet encountered any reaction from the client other than delighted understanding. In fact the use of notes to cover points of doubt appears to be a major factor in building up the client's confidence. Since some translators may feel that resort to notes of this kind is an admission of weakness, users will be well advised to discuss this point with a new translator and make their attitude quite clear.

We are then left with the intentional ambiguities, another area of professional controversy, and another area in which discussions between client and translator before the event can do nothing but good. It should be the translator's task to reproduce the ambiguity, and indeed in patent work, in many other legal texts and in any document to be used for purposes of negotiation it is his duty to do so while also, in the authors' view, pointing this out to his client and the latter's professional advisers but to no one else. In other texts, unless he is concerned with producing a definitive text at one bite, he should illustrate the problem by a gloss.

Two technical factors make this policy less simple to follow than it might seem. The first is that most texts, including many by both professional writers and writers within the professions, contain so many unintentional ambiguities or loosenesses of meaning that it is extremely difficult to judge when the obscurity is deliberate. This is perhaps one of the points at which the translator acts in the full sense as a professional, applying the full scope of his judgement to the whole situation as he sees it. The second and more serious problem is that it is as difficult to reproduce the precise shade of obscurity and present it in a way that will suitably deceive the reader as it is to present a dry fly to a wily trout — the more so if, as is often the case, there is also a requirement for fully or approximately matching tests. Clearly the translator's duty is to move when he has to in the direction that will safeguard his client's interests even if in doing so he gives the game away or makes things a little too stiff for the other party to accept. Even so it may often be best to ask for the phrasing of the original to be modified.

The authors would in fact go further and maintain that deliberate and nicely calculated ambiguities are an area in which translation as a basic technique may prove inadequate. It is far better for a consultant who speaks the language to draft the document in the language to be used, working from a brief and his background knowledge, and then to back-translate with suitable annotations for approval by the user. This approach carries an important stage further the need, discussed in the preceding chapter, to give the translator the fullest possible freedom except where there are good reasons to the contrary.

3.4   Differences in organisations and procedures

National differences in the structuring of language and of thought were mentioned earlier, and even more marked differences — though not always obviously related to language — are to be found in both official and commercial structures. It could be considered part of the professional linguist's, or at least of the language consultant's stock in trade to understand these differences in organisation and their nomenclature; and he might indeed achieve this if what purport to be the various national patterns were to be more widely found in practice.

The non-linguist needs only to consider the anomalies in his own central, regional and local government organisations and the infinite variety of structures and nomenclatures met with in companies he knows to realise the actual scope of the problem. No amount of textbooks or generalised studies would see him through this maze. Thus while the linguist should have the same broad knowledge of and feel for these organisational problems in the countries of his languages as the manager who uses him does in his own country, he is unlikely to get the answer right first time.

The first difficulty lies in determining the functions of government departments and more particularly the demarcation lines between them — who could *guess* for instance that in France and the ex-French colonies, the *Service des Mines* is reponsible for road vehicles? The problem here is that most working-level civil servants in most countries run in blinkers, and even if the person addressed does not take offence because the matter is not in fact within his sphere he may well have no idea who should really field it.

The next problem is to distinguish between the functions of central and regional government agencies and of unofficial agencies to whom statutory tasks such as the granting of technical approval of a product may be delegated. With all these organisations however there is some pattern if not of logic at least of national habit, and it is not until one moves into the area of trade associations and companies themselves that total confusion really sets in. If two commercial organisations intend to work together to any considerable extent, it will pay for the principals or their intermediary to spend a little time early on explaining each other's organisation chart and in particular agreeing the terms to be used in the languages in question to describe each key appointment.

Here one comes down to the language aspects of the problem. At political level we enter the minister-secretary enigma without leaving the English-speaking countries, but we need to step across a language barrier to run into the full secretary-minister inversion. The same is true in official and commercial circles alike of the terms 'executive' and 'administrative'.

In the UK it would seem that an executive is apt to be junior to a manager while in the States the reverse is true. British and American English only begin to complicate this further by varying use of the word 'director', but again we need to move, this time to the French-speaking countries, to savour the full richness of this triangle of confusion. We know that a *directeur* is not in fact a director but a manager (UK usage), that a non-executive director is an *administrateur* and that the managing director is the *administrateur délégué*. But while the French do have directors performing executive functions the authors would be delighted to hear of any generally accepted and unequivocal way of defining such appointments — although of course the chief executive, almost inevitably a board member, is apt to break any rule that might be apparent by calling himself a *directeur général,* which properly translates as general manager.

Moving across the Rhine and ignoring the unparalleled complexities of some of the older-established academic and professional institutions and commercial organisations, the American if not the Englishman will find structures with which he is not unfamiliar. But even leaving aside the special problems created by West Germany's statutory requirement for two levels of board, we once again run into director trouble. In German *Direktor* is more widely found in official than in commercial circles, and a company director is a *Vorstandsmitglied* ('board member'). Sometimes a managing director is described by the literal translation of that term *Geschäftsführendes Vorstandsmitglied,* but for reasons of economy in breath and secretarial effort if for no others he is often known as the *Geschäftsführer.* (Again 'general manager' or better perhaps, 'chief executive'). This would leave only a single area of doubt if the company secretary, most correctly perhaps known as the *Schriftführer* were not also referred to in many companies and in most trade and professional organisations as the *Geschäftsführer.* To complete this circle, which suggests perhaps nothing more than a ring made of two snakes swallowing one another, the word *Direktor* would be used in an official organisation to describe either the head of protocol or the chief executive.

Perhaps the reader will not yet be so confused that he will forget that so far we have ventured only into three languages(or four if we differentiate between the two branches of English). As we fan out further afield, in particular across the Iron Curtain, the opportunities for, and indeed, the inevitability of, confusion becomes positively Gilbertian.

Superimposed on these organisational uncertaintes are the national, departmental or company peculiarities in procedures and even more in the terminology used in following them. It is clearly out of the question to attempt to deal with these or the underlying structures in general terms, but this section will perhaps serve to emphasise that, just as is the case where no language barrier exists, such things as shipping, export/import and currency control and approval procedures are matters for experts. A translator is unlikely to be able to deal with them adequately and, in view of their tedious and rather menial nature, may well not be prepared to do so. On the other hand he should 'know that he knows not' and have sufficient feel for the sensibilities of both principals to avoid giving offence.

Many of the problems discussed above rear their heads in formal letters, but before one gets down to niceties of that kind there are two more fundamental decisions to be taken — one on style and one on presentation. In the UK most professional and commercial organisations — and thanks to Gowers' influence even Whitehall — have moved a long way from what might call the 'esteemed goodselves' syndrome — further in fact than is often the case in the States and certainly much further than the users of the other main European languages. As in other matters conservatism and a liking for flourishes gains strength as one moves south. However meticulous he must be about format and the niceties of topping and tailing, where the text is concerned there seems to be little reason for the translator to feel himself under any obligation to pander either to the inadequacies of the writer or to the susceptibilities of the more conservative recipient. Language is the principal tool of his trade and his aim must be to write lucidly, correctly and concisely in whatever language he is using. It is generally accepted in the language profession that a translator may properly use his expertise to eliminate in translation the weaknesses of the original and thus partially to offset the loss of information that translation inevitably entails. On the other hand it is open to his client to brief a translator on the particular image that the style of the letter should project, and it is then up to the translator to respond to the best of his ability. There is quite a difficult distinction to be drawn here; perhaps it can best be highlighted by saying that, while a neutral-toned letter should be written in a terse, clean, modern style, archaisms, clichés and bad style are all tools that can be used to serve a particular end.

Almost as important is the question of presentation. This was touched on in the previous chapter and is one on which the originator should if possible be consulted, as there may be factors of which the translator could not reasonably be aware. There are no half measures here. Either letters and other formal documents go out in their English format and layout, only the language being changed. Or the letter must look as like one originating from a high-grade organisation in the country of the language as the layout of the letterhead permits. In practice views on style and presentation are often related. The client who wishes his style to be closely reflected for better or for worse in translation will usually also want to conserve his company's standard layout; another client will want the country and language of origin to be revealed only by the print on the letterhead.

The next problem, again one touched on earlier, and certainly one over which the translator must be left complete discretion, is that of topping and tailing. An originator who writes 'Dear Mr Dupont' or even 'Dear Hans' must not be disconcerted if the translation comes back for him to sign in the form 'Cher Monsieur' or for instance 'Sehr geerhter Herr Direktor'. Equally in the Romance languages he may be invited to sign his name not under some succinct phrase such as 'Yours faithfully' but under what strikes him as a rather ponderous final paragraph. However, topping and tailing, even without the complication of translation, is a matter that can easily give serious offence. If the translator sees any risk of this he should not hesitate to ask his client whether he knows the addressee personally, if so how well, how good their relations are and anything else that will tell him the right note to strike. Equally the translator of incoming mail must be alert to any difference between the degree of formality of the original letter and the reply to it, as this will certainly have significance in anything resembling a negotiating situation. One of the greatest problems in preparing outgoing correspondence in a foreign language is often the typing. Every detail must be correct in accordance with the best modern practice. Accents and other special characters must be typed in by the use of special keys and not dabbed in by hand. Presentation should be at least as good as that of letters the company originates in its own language.

This is perhaps a useful point at which to discuss the various systems that exist for the production by non-linguists or employees with only a low level of language skills of standard or brick-built letters. Some of these contain a code element which enables internal instructions to be passed between offices in different countries or between an executive away from base with considerable economies in telephone or telex time, and this merit holds whether or not a language barrier has to be crossed. Equally, as will be brought out in the discussion on technical documentation in Part 2 of this book, there is great scope for a special-to-company brick system at a rather more sophisticated level, provided that suitably skilled personnel are available to use it intelligently. And these standardised correspondence systems undoubtedly have a value in enabling a qualified multi-lingual secretary to deal with routine outgoing correspondence in a foreign language by using them as a kind of special dictionary.

The authors would welcome anything that cuts down the amount of hack translation, since this would clearly be good both for the language profession and for its clients, but their view is that anyone capable of using such systems for foreign-language correspondence intelligently and without risk of major error is probably himself capable of producing an equally good letter. Many experienced managers will have tried systems of this kind in the single-language context and will probably have found that standard letters always require some little modification and that a brick-built letter reads just like a brick-built letter unless considerable skill and time is used in cementing over the joints. Another limitation of standard correspondence systems which is often not appreciated by those who invest in them is that they make no provision whatever for incoming documents, where translation cannot be ducked and the need for speed is great.

3.6 Person-to-person communications

For routine correspondence at least, most advanced countries accept and practise the convention by which documents are sent out in the language of the originator and translation is left to the recipient. Where the conditions are right this is a very sensible and valuable convention; it saves money and probably time and will usually minimise the risk of misunderstanding. However it quickly breaks down in dealing with third world countries where, apart from the indigenous language, only that of their former imperial masters or economic sponsors is at all widely known. For reasons which will be apparent from the discussion in Chapter 2 it has considerable dangers in the kind of high-level person-to-person correspondence that represents the most important communications link in official circles, the professions, science and technology and commerce alike. The distinction to be drawn between communications of this kind and formal correspondence is not of course simply a matter of whether the format happens to be formal and marked 'for the attention of...' or person-to-person, but whether the message conveyed contains any signals other than those that can be passed on the primary verbal channel. As the previous chapter has shown there is a considerable grey zone here.

Knowing the fate that overtakes letters and documents arriving in a foreign language in government departments, professional institutions and commercial organisations from the largest to the .smallest, we would certainly not be happy to let a letter in which we were seriously trying to communicate with another named individual be sent off in our own language. Admittedly the avoidance of this usually faces us with no problem, but we have spent too much time pulling out of the fire chestnuts of the 'enemy dancing on wet planks, please send 3/4d' kind ('enemy advancing on left flank; please send reinforcements'). It is here that the language barrier is at its most formidable; the hazards it presents and ways of surmounting them were mooted in Chapter 2 and will form one of the principal themes of this book. It is sufficient here to highlight the problem and to re-emphasise that, in contrast to the case of formal correspondence and other impersonal documentation, the translator of a person-to-person letter has a very definite duty to reflect every nuance and implication of the original — which does not of course mean translating it literally and slavishly following its format.

3.7   Translation, paraphrase or précis

Having examined some of the difficulties that may beset active communication across a language barrier unless considerable expertise is deployed, we may now pick up once more the theme with which this chapter opened — the handling of incoming material. There are two very good reasons why anybody having to act on or draw information from communications arriving in a foreign language should have some means of dealing with them at his direct and immediate disposal. Ways of achieving this are discussed later in the book.

The first reason is of course speed of reaction. He may sometimes be able to get back from an appropriate agency a translation of short simple texts by return of post or even the same day by telex, but for documents of specialised content or of any great substance the conventional response-time can best be measured certainly in days rather than in hours — and not infrequently in weeks. An ability at least to pull out the gist on the spot will enable action to get under way while the full translation is being produced.

The second reason has grave implications of both time and cost and must be stated even though, in our view, it could be taken to reflect on some sections of the language profession. A translator's ethic is to translate, and if he receives a document with a request for translation this is just what he will — or at least may — do. If he spends a long time and runs up a considerable fee translating a document that is either irrelevant to the sponsor's needs or completely valueless, he is in no breach whatever of his professional code. Indeed, he would generally speaking be theoretically in breach of this code if he did otherwise.

While this attitude may seem irresponsible to the sponsor, a translator working at three or four removes, none of them specialised, from the person who actually needs the information may not be in a position to do anything else. For instance a neighbour in the motor and engineering business once brought a telex in French to one of us. He was slightly nonplussed to be told that it contained an urgent request for the despatch of consignments of certain specialised breeds of rabbits and pigeons to various rearing establishments in France. When the laughter had died down a suitable reply was prepared and a small contribution placed in the poor box. But had this been a paper of several thousand words and had the recipient sent it to a distant agency for translation, neither the agency nor the individual translator would have had any reason to know that it was totally irrelevant and should in fact have been sent to an organisation of the same name in another county.

These arguments simply serve to reinforce the point made early in the chapter, namely that a very high proportion of routine translation that is conscientiously and lugubriously churned out ought never to have been undertaken at all.

Even where the recipient has or employs under his own hand some level of language skills, these may not always suffice to determine the best treatment of a document. This is where the role of the professional linguist as consultant comes in. Consider for instance the proceedings of an international conference in some specialised professional field or the minutes of a protracted international technical committee. This is likely to be a very massive document, and its formal translation in full would call not only for a massive, and hence time-consuming and expensive, translation effort as such but also in the usual way of things for an above-normal typing effort. When asked to examine, or more usually at first to translate documentation of this kind, we have usually found that about one third of it is procedural, with no value except perhaps the names and appointments of key personalities (and much of this is often repeated in proceedings covering say, a committee and its working groups); and of the rest one-third might be outside the sponsor's particular sub-field, one third old hat (here the sustained link between the language consultant and his user is important); and the rest consists of presentations and discussion which although of interest can be fairly heavily précised. A few minutes' study by a suitably skilled and informed person has cut the magnitude of the task to perhaps 10 per cent in terms of length and time. Even if the reduction in fee is not quite proportionate, experience suggests that direct savings of 50-60 per cent in cost and time can be achieved. If oral briefing rather than a written précis is acceptable, the saving can of course be greater still.

For documents such as conference proceedings, or for bunches of scientific papers or correspondence that have no distinguishable coherent format to speak of, a consultancy approach is the only effective solution since little pieces of meat often have to be picked out of a procedural stew. But for large coherent documents such as books, technical periodicals or special reports, e.g. strategic planning reports or project studies, an alternative approach that makes rather less demand both on the broader skills of the linguist and on the closeness of his relationship with the sponsor will often serve nearly as well. This is a technique which can best be described as 'filling in a skeleton'. Taking this book as an example, stage one might be the translation of the chapter headings, stage two of the section headings within certain chapters selected by the sponsor, stage three the précising of sections selected from these, and finally the translation in full of a few selected passages. This selective translation is a time-consuming process but the savings in cost as against translation of the whole may lie in the 90 per cents with no loss of effectiveness, and the translator will be briefing himself and thus becoming more perspicacious and effective as the sequence proceeds.

Another saver of time and money, of which the user who is not a professional linguist is most unlikely to be aware, is agreement not simply to an 'information only' translation which is in effect a full and accurate but unpolished and perhaps not fully researched translation, but to a paraphrase. Many formal texts, ranging from say a company's general conditions of sale to a country's regulations for the transport of dangerous loads, are written in a formal, complex, quasi-legal style that makes translation in the accepted sense of the term an extremely time-consuming process if the result is to be unambiguous or indeed intelligible. If the text in the language of translation is required for internal and information purposes only, a paraphrase by an experienced translator with good subject knowledge will save a great deal of time and money and should, in this particular case, avoid the possible loss of information through obscurities. Naturally the linguist given such authority will wish to focus attention on certain passages that strike him as critical, probably offering true translations of high accuracy backed up with interpretative notes. He will be all the better in a position to do this if he is released from the onus of reproducing the turgidity of the original as a whole.

Whether it is a matter of giving the gist of a routine letter by a quick manuscript gloss or of preparing a substantial report on a massive bunch of documentation, précis, paraphrase or selective translation will almost always provide the most cost-time-effective solution unless the text is required for publication or for contractual or other legal purposes.

The reader will by now hopefully have digested the message of this chapter, but it is such an important and to some extent an unusual one that it may be worth summarising. The convention of sending out formal and routine correspondence in the language of the originator is an eminently sound one, provided that there is reasonable certainty that the recipient will be able to get it translated quickly and competently. It becomes more and more dangerous as one moves away from areas of routine into person-to-person communications and specialised or technological documentation such as manuals.

There are certain particular circumstances which justify full formal translation of a document into the recipient's language. It may be required for some legal or similar purpose, in which case the problem of matching texts and master texts must also be taken account of. It may be required for publication, but here some form of editing going beyond translation as such will almost always be required at some stage, and this can often best be done by the translator. Patent documentation constitutes texts which have legal force, which will be subjected to frequent hostile examination in great depth by experts and which are of a quality suitable for publication. These perhaps represent the most exacting of all non-literary translation tasks, and they must wherever possible be undertaken by the select body of translators who specialise in such work and have at their disposal not only their own considerable talents and experience but also the advantage of an international net of colleagues whom they can consult freely.

With these exceptions, formal translation is hardly ever the best answer to commercial translation problems, and may often be unviable in terms of time and/or cost. The recipient of foreign-language documents who is completely unable, either with his own resources or those of his staff, to discover even its gist needs to be rather careful over his approach to the commercial translation market. Some freelances and most reputable major agencies are usually agreeable to acting in a consultant capacity to the extent described above if they are invited to do so.

4

Technical translation

4.1 Verbal and mathematical or symbolic languages

Following the convention of the language and many other professions, the
authors have deliberately misused the term 'technical' to signify 'scientific
and technological'. Other fields that would be covered by the true meaning
of the word technical are commonly referred to as 'specialised'.

Scientists and engineers have no less love of controversy than their
colleagues in more abstract and subjective fields — if indeed anything can
be more abstract than modern physics — but there is perhaps one thing
over which most of them, together with the majority of informed laymen
would agree. It is that in these fields verbal language offers at best a crude,
clumsy and imprecise means of communication. The true language of
mathematics, science and technology is the language of symbols, curves
and, where appropriate, drawings. Two engineers of quite different
backgrounds and speaking not one word of one another's language have
often been seen communicating with high speed and precision with the aid
of an engineering drawing shared between them and a pencil and the back
of an envelope each. Had they spoken the same language they would
doubtless have used it, but would probably have achieved their aim less
quickly and effectively.

There are certain major fields, most notably perhaps organic chemistry and botany, with its Latin nomenclature, where the scientific verbal language does in fact represent a code, an alternative to or substitute for symbols. At the elementary level of inorganic chemistry for instance most schoolchildren will know that 'ide' as in 'sulphide' means a compound containing two elements that also combine to form an acid or salt but no oxygen; that '-ous' as in 'nitrous' means an acid or salt unsaturated with oxygen and that '-ic' as in 'phosphoric' implies the fully oxidised compound. An organic chemist can reconstruct the short, the structural and even the spatial formulae of quite complex compounds from their names. (Here one inevitably recalls Paul Jennings' famous compound 'bicycltricyclpolyputaketlon', which is not in fact a plastic used for forming complex surfaces of rotation but a phonetic representation of his parrot's utterance 'Bicycle, tricycle, Polly put the kettle on'.) And the botanist's code, on which the whole system of classification of that science is based, is a verbal one in which the level of classification is given by the sequence of words and by the use of upper and lower case initial letters. Not only does this gain precision through the use of a dead language, but the structure in so far as it exists bears about as much relation to that of Latin proper as menu French does to the language recommended by the *Academie Française*. One could say of it, and probably of the nomenclature of chemistry and pharmacy, that these are verbal codes but not linguistic ones.

Most other fields, too, even the more mathematical, have a common usage in the verbalisation of symbols for use in transmitting these orally. For instance, we say 'three squared' or 'x to the nth' or the 'chi-squared test'. Corresponding expressions exist in every advanced language. These are no more than conventional, objective mechanisms for transmitting a visual signal on an audio channel. The need for written translation does not arise and interpreting is simple and unambiguous as long as the interpreter knows the conventions.

The problem even within one language begins to arise when the individual moves away from this visual language of symbols, figures and drawings and starts to verbalise. He moves out of a concise and precise medium which he uses to formulate his thoughts as well as to express them into one which is imprecise and inappropriate in itself and in the use of which he may well be less than expert. On the other hand there may be very good reasons for making this transition — to communicate with a layman perhaps, to make a long oral presentation acceptable to the listener or simply to describe mechanisms, phenomena or procedures that cannot be fully covered by symbolic or other non-verbal means. Thus technical writing and consequently technical translation are at best nothing more than necessary evils.

4.2   Single-language terminology

There is the story — make it come from where you will and add dialect to taste — of the yokel who, when a motorist asked him the way, answered: 'If you want to get there, don't start from here' — and this might well be found graven on a technical translator's heart. For many of the documents he is asked to render are intelligible only to the author, and not always — experience indicates — to him. The first difficulty lies in a law which might rank with the Murphy-Klipstein laws on the behaviour of inanimate objects, to the effect that no-one's own work is specialised. To the engineer nothing is more instantly comprehensible to any man of intelligence than the working of the brainchild he has brought into the world, except it be the bunch of neologisms and adaptations he has coined to describe it. The second difficulty is that the days of the polymath are now passed and scientists and engineers, particularly in their creative youth, are frequently anything but masters of language. Apart from the sheer misuse of words and ambiguities of construction, a particular hazard in English is the use of nouns as attributives. Faced with a string of six or seven of these without any of the aids one expects to get from the rules for compounding in German, one is completely at a loss to discover, in the words of the limerick, 'who does what and with which and to whom'. It is sometimes difficult even to determine to which of them a true adjective or dimensions dropped casually into the morass applies.

The hard sciences have a splendidly rigorous terminology, while in the soft the term used depends on the author rather than on the context or the meaning required. The younger branches of engineering, developed from modern physics and physical chemistry mainly in the English-speaking countries, stand out for consistency of nomenclature and for the borrowing by other languages of the English term originally coined. But in the more traditional branches such as civil, mechanical and heavy electrical engineering, inconsistency of terminology is so prevalent even within the same drawing office as to make verbal descriptions a wholly inadequate basis for translation. The translator must get down to the drawings and if possible to the hardware itself. The designer of a new machine or device is perfectly entitled within rather broad limits to select or coin whatever terms he likes to describe it, and it is up to the translator — or for that matter any other reader — to use visual aids and his trained powers of deduction to understand the description. But there is very little excuse for the main chassis members of identical material and section of three variants in a batch of closely similar platform semi-trailers to be labelled respectively 'I-beams', 'H-beams' and 'Joists' — especially when the associated specifications call them simply 'main longitudinal members'. This is perhaps a striking example, but it is by no means an uncommon or an extreme one.

Another pitfall for the outsider, whether or not he is a translator, is the unconscious use in drawing legends and in specifications of what amounts to a private shorthand. This frequently involves either the use of a word in a meaning completely different from a generally accepted one (*cf.* the discussion in Chapter 2 on family language and subjective overloading) or the use of a single word from a long phrase. Again one is forced to rely on visual aids to interpretation, deduction and even a process of elimination

('We've identified everything else that ought to be there, so "carrier" must be the spare wheel carrier.').

Clearly in these more traditional fields there is a need to standardise terms at national or language group level. But if effective translations are to be produced without the translator having to sit in the author's pocket there is a far greater need for discipline at grassroots level. Chief development engineers, designers and draughtsmen must impose on their staffs a four-pronged working discipline. First, there must be a common effort to use as far as possible terms drawn from established reference works and textbooks and/or approved by the appropriate trade association or professional institute. Second, drawing conventions must be standardised (this is usually the least of the problems, those concerned being trained in engineering drawing but not in the use of language). Third, they must agree on a name for a particular component, assembly or function and use it consistently throughout all legends, specifications, manuals and parts lists. Fourth they must exercise the same discipline as the good technical translator in carefully assigning a term to a particular component, assembly or function and then reserving that term for that use alone. For example a packaging machine will have a product feed, which may be in two distinct stages, and two separate feeds of wrapping material. These could be distinguished, for instance, by naming them respectively feed, infeed, wrapper feed and label feed. In contrast to the great richness of the English language as a whole, English would appear to be less rich in potential engineering terms (apart from sheer perverse variations such as were mentioned above) than the other main technological languages. This is perhaps partly due to the low place use of language — mother-tongue and foreign languages alike — has in the educational systems of most English-speaking countries, and also to a turn of mind that, as discussed below, will flog a familiar term to death rather than coin a new one.

One knows from experience with the hard sciences and, for instance, with electronics that consistent terminology is readily attainable and that given it accurate and unambiguous translation can be achieved with a relatively low level of subject knowledge. Surely it cannot be economical for the senior engineering disciplines to pay so little attention to nomenclature that an accurate and clear translation can only be achieved by a qualified engineer working on site.

4.3. Specialised and dialect variations

Some of the specific problems that arise in the traditional engineering fields are worth examining in more detail. The first is to accept that there is no right and wrong answer; to be effective a translator must determine the particular phrase that the intended readers are using at the time. To take another example from vehicle engineering, a platform semi-trailer is a fairly basic and highly standardised object. It is therefore interesting to compare the list of terms in Figure 4.1 which has been taken from legends of the drawings of two virtually identical semi-trailers produced by two leading French manufacturers. Perhaps the most surprising thing is that the trailer in both cases was designated *Semi-remorque plateau*.

The next difficulty is the differences in convention that exist between fields in one language but not in another. Taking again a very simple example to illustrate a point with the most complex implications, it is apparently quite in order for an English vehicle engineer to talk of an 'H-beam', while his compatriot in the construction field who does so is likely if not to be hurled instantly from the highest scaffolding at least to become the subject of a Howard Bateman cartoon. The French on the other hand, both in their standards and in practice, are quite content to refer to this section as a *profilé en H*. The Germans have a word for it too, only this happens to be *Doppel-T-Träger*. When one throws in differences between English and American usage, particularly prevalent in the vehicle engineering field, the translator is clearly in a no-win situation.

Superimposed on this problem of what one might call specialist variations is the problem of dialect. This may be of no great significance any longer in England but is certainly so among our French and German speaking Common Market partners. Where technical translation is concerned, this problem is perhaps seen at its best in the field of agricultural machinery and the associated procedures. Somewhere in each of these language areas there must be a kind of centre of gravity where model farmers use a generally accepted nomenclature. But it is not easy to find this node, particularly as it will vary with the type of machine and the kind of crop. It is quite certain that a leaflet written or polished by a Breton will be quite unacceptable to an agent operating in Belgium or Provence — and vice-versa, and equally that text optimised for the North German Plain will gain little acceptance in Bavaria, to say nothing of Austria and Switzerland. These areas in which comparatively modern technology and ancient professions and crafts impinge on one another are

ENGLISH	Manufacturer A	Manufacturer B
Upper rubbing plate/apron	*Plaque supérieure d'attelage*	*Plaque frottante*
King pin	*Axe d'attelage*	*Cheville ouvrière*
Side raves	*Longerons extérieurs*	*Rives de bordure*
Rear suspension	*Suspension arrière*	*Train roulant*
Deck	*Pont*	*Plateau*

Figure 4.1

apt to present the translator with a far more difficut problem than the most way-out concepts of aerospace, computer technology or nuclear physics.

Finally under this head a word about neologisms, not only for their own sake but because they will bring out many of the problems that exist in technical translation between English, French and German. Fortunately since all other languages including Russian are apt to borrow heavily from one of these three, the problem is less widespread than it otherwise might be. First of all one has got to be clear that there is an unbridgeable comprehension gap. Even if he speaks French fluently and has worked for several years alongside a Frenchman of similar discipline, an English civil engineer will never know exactly what picture the Frenchman has in his mind when he uses, say the word *lisse* or why he prefers it in the case in question. The discussion in Section 2.6 on meanings and connotations is highly relevant here. But it would seem that the Englishman, the Frenchman and the German have completely different approaches to the coining of neologisms when these are needed. By and large, as was mentioned above, the Englishman will take the traditional expression that most nearly meets the need in terms of appearance or function — one cannot say which — and transfer it without qualification. The Frenchman will put on his Cartesian hat and derive a term from first principles. Thanks to the superb facility of the language for compounding words according to clear-cut rules, the German has an easier problem. The difficulty for the translator is plain to see, and once again the only solution for it is to get away from the words and back to the visual or material reality.

The problem of translating some concept that is new in principle or detail for the first time into another language in such a way that it will be as intelligible to the reader as was the original can never be an easy task, if only because when the reader's credulity is stretched he may tend to blame the translation. But in a continuous text illustrated by diagrams or photographs, where the translator has an opportunity to use descriptive translations and to define his terms, he can be reasonably confident of getting the concept across if he himself has understood it properly. When however, as may happen in the case of a prefabricated building system, unfamiliar concepts have to be put straight into the kind of abbreviations that will go on drawing legends, parts lists and flow-charts, the translation is unlikely to be wholly successful unless each term is related to its appropriate hardware by means of a drawing or photograph.

4.4 Units and conventions

Metrication in the UK and the increasing use of the metric system in those English-speaking countries which have not already adopted it have unfortunately not gone quite as far as the layman might hope and think towards simplifying the statement of dimensional quantities. Most countries which have traditionally used the metric system make use of the full range of units, e.g. millimetres, centimetres, decimetres and metres, and frequently mix in metricated versions of pre-metric units as *livre* = *Pfund* = 500 g or *Zentner* = 100 kg. The Système International (SI) which should normally be used in all documents intended for translation, and all translations, contains for example only two units of length greater than the millimetre (millimetre, metre, kilometre) and is simplified in many other important respects. There are sometimes good reasons for using units of 'national' metric systems, and some of these will be discussed in Part 2; but if they are used in the scientific or engineering contexts there is a risk not of a misconception — as would be the case with a Frenchman working in Anglo-American units — but of 'slipping a ten', which can be equally disastrous. Oddly enough the greatest risk of confusion arises over 'tons'; apart from the long-standing problem of the US short ton (2000 lb) and the British long ton (2240 lb) there is no reason why we in England should not continue to use the word 'ton' in everyday parlance to mean 1000 kg, just as the Germans have retained the *Pfund* and the *Zentner*. But when we are talking in legal or engineering terms, we shall have for some time at least to continue to write 'tonnes' and — ridiculous as it sounds — to say 'tunnies'.

It is important to note that in certain fields where they are already internationally accepted Anglo-American units will continue to be used. Among these are the British and American threads, some of which have in fact been widely adopted in metric countries, and wheel and tyre dimensions. It is however often useful to give in brackets a 'nominal' metric approximation either to the identifying dimensions or to any dimension, such as wheel offset, which the metric-oriented reader may require to visualise. The problem of converting and of quoting conversions is never quite as simple as it seems, but as this is a question of engineering philosophy the discussion of it is left over to Part 2.

The more modern branches of the sciences and their related technologies have grown up with the metric system so that no conversion problem arises. The translator should however appreciate first that it is extremely difficult for an engineer trained in the Anglo-American system to visualise a metric quantity, and vice-versa. Further civil and mechanical engineers forced to work in an unfamiliar system of units or to carry out conversions may very easily make mistakes, the most probable one being perhaps the inclusion or omission of a g, the acceleration due to gravity. Should a complaint or a claim arise from the appearance in a translation of an error of this kind, it is often very difficult to determine responsibility. What is quite certain is that all conversions between the two systems of units should be independently double-checked.

Even during the period of transition to SI and consequent settling down, there are rather few problems of convention. The principal one, which must be carefully explained to anyone concerned with typing foreign-language texts, is that in almost every language other than English the decimal point is represented by a comma, the period being traditionally used to mark off thousands, millions, etc. Modern internationally agreed or at least accepted scientific and engineering practice is to write metric quantities — and indeed all figures appearing in texts where metric quantities are quoted — with a comma for the decimal point (period in English) and a space between each trio of figures moving left and right from the decimal point. Where money is concerned however it is still customary to insert the traditional full stop (comma in English) as indicated above, and there is some confusion over whether the outermost figure in a four-figure group left or right of the decimal point should be separated.

The danger of errors of substance apart, correctness over the full and abbreviated names of units and the setting out of quantities is important as a point of presentation. Although the British pay more attention than most to details of this kind, the credibility of a document in anyone's eyes cannot but suffer from obvious lack of attention to detail. The technical translator should be able to get all these points right in the first place and, if given a chance to proofread, make sure that they stay right.

4.5 Regulations and standards

Frequently as inexperienced exporters may do it, it is clearly folly to move into a market without having acquired, studied and at least attempted to comply with all relevant regulations and standards. The practical and managerial aspects of the difficulties that are apt to arise in this connection are discussed in detail in Part 2. Over and above these there is the language-technical problem of how to get the contents of massive standards and regulations which are not available in English across to non-linguist designers, consultants and other specialists. One must start from the premise that full formal translation will usually be prohibitive in cost and, even more important, in time. Experience suggests that it is often disastrous for engineers with a limited knowledge of the language in question to attempt to decipher regulations and standards with the aid of a dictionary. Not only may they quite simply miss key points and get things wrong, but they may subconsciously put the interpretation that suits them best on the confused and confusing picture that the text produces in their mind. We know of two instances where this actually occurred; one misinterpretation came to light before production and simply led to a mild touch of the *maladie anglaise* — doubling of the delivery time; but in the other a complete run's worth of production units had to be drastically modified.

While a suitably qualified language consultant can help a great deal, it is really neither safe nor fair to throw the entire responsibility for conformity of the design onto him unless he is also a fully-fledged consulting engineer practising in the field in question and familiar with the country concerned. Paraphrasing or selective translation of the kind discussed above may provide a solution, but even these may prove rather too circumstantial. The best solution may well be not to use direct written translation at all but to hold a briefing meeting at which the linguist presents the requirements clause by clause to the specialists concerned and important points are discussed and clarified on the spot. If full minutes of this meeting are taken, they will provide exactly the guide the designer requires. (This briefing meeting technique is a very useful one and will be discussed in another context in Chapter 14.)

4.6 Drawings, tables, etc.

The handling of all types of graphics and of tables containing large quantities of figures should be planned in such a way as to avoid redrafting or retyping. Apart from the obvious problems of cost and time, each stage of manual reproduction reintroduces the risk of error. The need is therefore for translator and typist or draughtsman to get together and agree on a layout and procedure that will enable the legend or wording in the various languages required to be dropped in using a collage technique and/or whatever electromechanical reproduction facilities are available.

If some good reason such as geographical separation prevents translator and client working together in this way, it is probably best to pass the whole task over to the translator, authorising him to make use of a suitable service firm, e.g. of technical illustrators, in his location. This will however be more expensive and increase the overall risk of error. It may lead to practical problems at the final stage if the service firm is unable to produce masters that match the client's reproduction facilities.

The basic technique is thus to produce a master containing all non-language elements (graphics and figures). The English legend, headings and text can either be included on this and subsequently masked off, or put on an overlay. The foreign-language texts as they become available are then put onto other overlays, which must also of course mask the English text if this is on the master itself. Since the foreign-language texts will seldom be available when the basic master is prepared, it is essential to follow the linguist's advice on the space that will be required for the 'longest' of the languages in question. This procedure may sound complicated, but it is well within the scope of any organisation that possesses a drawing office.

Here again presentation is important, particularly in a document that is intended to build up or maintain credibility and acceptability. Shaping up legends, headings and notes so that they are not only linguistically correct but presented in the style of the language should be within the scope of an experienced a technical translator particularly if he is working closely with the client's or a subcontractor's draughtsmen.

Engineering drawing conventions present far less difficulty than one might expect. Conventions are fairly well internationalised, particularly among the established users of the metric system, and differences arising from the Anglo-American and metric system of units are well covered in a number of publications (such as for instance those put out by the British Steel Corporation). In addition to copies of standards or leaflets, it is always advisable to try and give the draughtsman some specimens of drawings made in the countries concerned to give him a feel for style and presentation. Given suitable support and encouragement, the younger draughtsmen-designers at least learn remarkably rapidly both to work in slightly different conventions and to letter up foreign-language legends quickly and accurately. In fact they are apt to become over-enthusastic and must be heavily briefed not to try adapting and recombining the phrases of foreign-language legend already available to them without reference to the technical translator; otherwise the result will at best be unprofessional and may be wholly disastrous.

4.7 The need to visualise

After exposing the problems inherent in technical translation and describing techniques for dealing with some of the tedious but important detailed aspects, it may be helpful to broaden the discussion again and give the users of technical translators rather more insight into the problems that face the translator. Earlier, when speaking of translation in general, we said that words were no more than tools, and we have seen above that in the translation of scientific and technological texts they are often little better than blunt instruments. Whereas in other forms of translation the words of the original do serve to conjure up in the translator's mind the concept or image which will serve as his starting-point, in technical texts they are very often no more than labels or signposts that will lead him to and identify for him the visual or numerical representation, or the piece of hardware with which he is concerned. If the reader accepts the hypothesis put forward at the beginning of this chapter, namely that verbal language in these settings is often no more than a code, he will appreciate too that the more heavily codified the language of the original, the easier the translator's task and hence the better, faster and more cost-effective the result will be.

On the other side of the coin is the translator's professional duty only to work in fields in which he can conceptualise and reconstruct, or even in most engineering fields actually visualise. And the person commissioning him will do well to make sure in initial discussions that he does in fact have this ability. If of course the client, preferring the devil he knows and more particularly the devil who is available, chooses by mutual agreement to stretch a translator ouside his normal field rather than turn to a new one, this is a fair management decision. Experience suggests that it would not always be an unwise one.

4.8 Subject knowledge and briefing

While it is clear enough that the technical translator — and for that matter the interpreter working in scientific and technological fields — needs to conceptualise, synthesise and in the case of macro-hardware to visualise, it is far from easy to say just what depth of knowledge or qualifications he needs to do this. While some measure of subject knowledge, or at least basic numeracy is essential, it would be quite wrong to suppose that extensive experience or high qualifications are a guarantee of the requisite ability. Many able and experienced engineers who have specialised, as all must now do, in one or more narrow fields are often quite incapable of grasping concepts outside this field. Even if they speak the languages concerned, they may not have sufficient command of language to make good translators.

The talent to be looked for is thus a special one and may perhaps be seen as twofold. The first and more superficial need is the ability to learn new facts quickly and accurately and memorise them together with the associated terminology. The second, technical awareness, and more particularly the ability to conceptualise, are comparatively rare and are not easy to detect by normal testing or interviewing techniques. The types of test most likely to pinpoint them are to be found in the AIIC (*Association International des Interprètes de Conférence*) test battery and in certain batteries of intelligence and aptitude tests, e.g. the matrix test.In any event the application and interpretation of such tests is a matter for experts, and the person selecting a technical translator must rely on such evidence as he can elicit in normal discussion of the subject and/or of the texts and graphics in question. An almost equally important characteristic to look for is the ability to collaborate with specialist and junior staff.

Briefing and reference back to sort out queries is of paramount importance. Ideally the technical translator should be given the opportunity to go over the work he is going to handle with the specialist concerned and to spend enough time in the laboratory or on the shop floor to familiarise himself with the hardware. Since he will not absorb 100 per cent of what he hears and sees, he must be assured continuing access to all specialists concerned. And as mentioned above if, as they almost always will be, tables and graphics are concerned, he must have an opportunity to work out the solution in detail with the secretariat and the drawing office.

If necessary all these things can be achieved in some measure by remote control, but there is little doubt that the cost will usually be higher, the time longer and the result less satisfactory.

4.9   Drafting of documents intended for translation

However well the translator does his job, the quality of the result will depend in very large measure — and this is perhaps truer of technical translations than in any other field — on the quality of the original. The onus thus lies on the originator not only to pick a good translator, brief him properly and give him every support he may require, but also to produce a text that is comprehensible and therefore translatable. From the discussion in this chapter there emerge certain guidelines that are straightforward enough in themselves however difficult they may be to apply.

The first is to accept that verbal communication is a poor medium in scientific and technological fields at the best of times, and therefore to cover as much as possible by visual representations ranging from photographs through engineering drawings and graphs to mathematical symbols and expressions. When these possibilities have been stretched to their limit, the next resort is the use of words as a code rather than within their normal linguistic framework. Then comes the point when verbal language in the normally accepted sense of that term must be used. Here the first principle must be consistency; each component, subassembly and unit must be assigned a noun by which it will be designated and a verb which will describe its action within the mechanism or its operation as a whole. Once assigned, this terminology should be used whenever the element or its action is referred to. Nouns as far as possible should be unique (within the framework of the text) although it may sometimes be necessary to compound or qualify them to produce a unique term. Verbs and their derivatives can seldom be uniquely assigned, but they can be consistently used. For instance if the feed arrangements for a small product include two stages at which the product is moved or kept in motion by shaking it, one might distinguish these as the 'vibrator' and the 'agitator'. For clarity it is then essential that the vibrator always 'vibrates' the product and the agitator always 'agitates' it.

But the most heartfelt plea of all to the originator is to ensure that the texts are well written. Organisations that do not employ or commission a technical author should make sure that some filter is provided between the designer, who even if he normally writes well is unlikely to write clearly about his own brainchild, and the end-reader. If, as the authors recommend, the translation is being done by a team, one of whose members has the mother-tongue of the original, it may well be feasible to combine final editing of the original and translation in one operation.

5
Promotional literature and copywriting

The production of foreign-language promotional literature is perhaps the most challenging, and certainly the most subjective and therefore controversial area of commercial language work. This chapter considers some of the broad language-technical factors. These are developed further and related to managerial problems in a later chapter.

Perhaps the first point about which all concerned with an exercise of this kind should be clear is that it is not really meaningful to talk about 'translation' here. The task is quite simply one of copywriting. Just as the PR or advertising consultant takes the information provided by his client in the form of a draft, develops this by interrogation and discussion, shapes and slants the ideas draft to take account of promotional factors, decides upon visuals and design, and only then starts working up the final copy through a series of drafts, so the linguist. The only differences between his task and the initial copywriting are that the visuals and design are predetermined and the base text is less raw, having already been worked up by a professional. Thus linguists working in this field need copywriting flair, which translators may or may not possess.

5.1.1   *The living language*

Non-literary translation tends to use the standard or 'mandarin' language, avoiding jargon as far as the original allows and most certainly steering clear of slang. If for some reason slang is used, it is often better to retain well-known expressions in the original language rather than offer their equivalent in the language of translation. Quite apart from the fact that a rather cold, standard language matches the frequently all-too-depersonalised circumstances in which translations are carried out, the language and terminology departments of large international organisations, who tend to be trend-setting in many spheres, naturally — and for their purposes properly — seek to develop a standardised and to some extent internationalised language, e.g. Euro-French, which may differ quite widely even from the standard language of the country that gave it birth.

Copywriting is a completely different matter. It calls for the living language spoken at the time by the target socio-economic group. Naturally time scales differ. Television advertising has got to use the catch phrases of the moment or indeed create new household words by copy which is perfectly attuned to the mood of the moment. On the other hand a major profile-type brochure put out by a government department, a local authority or a large commercial organisation, may need to have a 10-year life. While this requirement will bring the language to be used closer to contemporary 'mandarin', it must be contemporary at the time it is written and not already dated by two or three years.

It at once becomes clear that the man we are looking for to write this copy is not some introspective translator tucked away in some rustic nook or academic cranny, or even living outside his own country, but a professional writer who, wherever he may happen to live, is swimming on and with the living tide of his mother-tongue.

5.1.2   *National attitudes*

Perhaps the most fundamental of many factors which tend to make copy diverge from language to language is national attitude. This must be considered at two levels — the national attitude as such and the target nation's attitude towards the country sponsoring the promotion. Where attitudes conflict, as they very often do, it is a nice choice whether to adopt an approach based on the target country's view and thus gain sympathetic hearing for the (hopefully) demonstrable advantages of the product; or whether to sell the contrast. This will of course to some extent depend on the second aspect of this problem, the attitude of the target market to the originating country. Unfortunately the two overwhelming arguments 'British is best' and 'the Dollar is almighty' have lost much of their validity, while the adverse reactions that those good old days produced in 'lesser breeds without the law' remains. The Anglo-Saxon exporter is therefore faced in most markets with a two-level chauvinism — nationalistic, and anti-imperialistic or simply anti-top nation. One cannot generalise on how he should seek to overcome this opposition or to turn the weaknesses of his own society into marketing strengths; but there is an acute need to be aware of the problem.

There is yet a further twist to this rather complex story, worth stressing although it is one that applies equally in the home market. This is the often diametric opposition to be found in every society, every group and almost every individual between public and private attitudes. Are you going to sell your product as an aid to moral uplift, education and gracious living, or as a means of getting more money and more sex? The international facet of this aspect is that the public acceptability of private attitudes varies immensely from society to society. In Germany — as, one is told, in Yorkshire — making money and demonstrating the possession of it is in every sense of the word a respectable goal, just as a full and highly satisfying sex life is in many Scandinavian circles. Moving south, east or west, one is forced to present these goals as improvements in the quality of life which will benefit not only those who enjoy them but society as a whole.

5.1.3   National PR techniques

While national PR techniques are necessarily in some measure related to the national attitudes discussed above, they also vary quite independently of any other identifiable factor other than perhaps the history of PR in the country concerned. The problem can be reduced to manageable proportions because in virtually the whole of the third world and the Comecon countries sophisticated PR and advertising techniques as we understand them do not exist at the commercial level. They are powerful tools reserved for the promulgation of government policy.

One has become hesitant of claiming any more world bests for the UK, but the slightly dubious honour of a world lead in PR, promotional and advertising techniques is perhaps one to which she can still lay claim. Probably because of the common language and the deep-rooted similarities of culture, the UK has taken the body of technique and practice evolved in the States and developed it to suit the rather less brash and more sophisticated needs of Europe — or at least of her own culture, for quite apart from problems of the language barrier British PR proposals seem to find little acceptance and operations little success in other markets. (One is not talking here of course of major groups which specialise in international operations.)

Perhaps the approach closest to our own is to be found (apart obviously from the old Commonwealth) in the Scandinavian countries and in an internationalised and highly sophisticated form in Switzerland. Italy seems to prefer a very soft sell, often so indirect that the visuals at least strike us as virtually irrelevant. There does not appear to be any typical French approach—this is perhaps one respect in which her claim to bridge the Nordic and Mediterranean cultures is open for all to see. Germany delivers heavily telegraphed punches straight from the shoulder to the belly or below the belt. Holland and Flemish-speaking Belgium aims a bit higher and softens the blow with a jovial smile, moving towards Scandinavian trends.

Not all will agree with those sweeping assessments; there are perhaps equally striking differences within the approaches used for consumer goods, consumer durables and trade or capital goods. It is sufficient to make the point that these very wide differences in technique compound the differences in national attitude discussed above.

5.1.4 Income groups and living standards

A copywriter used to writing for his home market will work with a number of tacit and perhaps unconscious assumptions about the make-up of the various socio-economic groups, or to be more precise the social and cultural make-up of a given income group. In fact these assumptions are rather unlikely to be valid across national boundaries because most advanced societies, to say nothing of the less developed ones, tend to have one or more characteristics which impose a pattern. In the UK for example the distinction between public, grammar and secondary modern schools imposes differences in cultural and social attitude which are becoming less and less closely related to earning power or disposable income. Thus they tend to produce vertical slices running down through a number of income groups. In France and the States, although the one has an academic and elitist educational system and the other a more practical and egalitarian one, the grade school, high school and college cutoff points match earning power more closely. Again, to carry the point further, the level of financial reward of various sectors of the professional classes of western Europe is almost reversed east of the Iron Curtain with North America lying mid-way between the two. As a result the highest brows, found in the UK mainly in the lower B and well down into the C1 groups, move progressively upwards as one passes through western Continental Europe to North America to sit firmly among the As when one doubles back across the Iron Curtain. It is probably only within the student sub-culture that assumptions based on one society can be extrapolated to another; 'Teach the world to sing' not only hit the top of the charts but also sold a great deal of Coca Cola.

Superimposed on the secondary differences between societies are the straightforward differences in national or racial taste. It is not unusual to see an obviously poor Chinese couple desperately but happily staking their last few dollars at the more expensive tables of a casino, or a French artisan surrounded by his large family over Sunday lunch in the best restaurant his small town can offer—indulgences which would be regarded with horror in Anglo-Saxon societies. Both statistics and current political pressures in many countries show that wildly different proportions of income are spent

under various heads in societies that appear to be rather similar. And the
spread through the upper divisions of the prosperity league table shows
that the difference in average income per head between, say, West
Germany and Portugal is more than enough to make the necessities of a
given income group in the one wayout luxuries for the equivalent group in
the other. This factor alone is almost sufficient to rule out strict translation
as a means of producing foreign-language copy, though it does not of
course preclude the international use of slogans in the original language to
promote product or brand image.

5.1.5   Importance of appeal to women

One of the most subtle problems, to which again one can do little more
than draw attention in general terms, is the relative influence of husband
and wife on spending decisions and selection of options both within the
family and — less obviously — in professional and business life. Again this is
one of the major preoccupations of copywriters working within their own
market, and again they may be unaware of the great differences when
national, let alone racial or cultural boundaries are crossed. In fact this is
really a compounding ingredient of the difficulty discussed in the previous
section.

There are two fascinating contradictions here. One is that in emerging
from apparent submission in the cloister and at the hearth either towards
seeming matriarchy as in the States or into professional and other earning
activities, women have in fact traded off a great deal of real if latent power
for the appearance of influence. It could be that it is in societies which have
shown the least advance in the status of women, and most particularly
perhaps in Muslim societies, that the copywriter should address himself to
the woman, while in Germanic and Anglo-Saxon markets it is the man's
view that in fact holds sway. The second is that in the more traditional
societies decision discernibly associated with women are creative and far-
sighted, the men having a more negative attitude weighed down by
immediate practical factors, while in the 'liberated' societies either the
converse is the case or at least the wife joins her husband in focussing on the
short-term and material.

One area in which the influence of woman seems to be particularly
strong and to operate in the rather contradictory ways touched on above is
that of movement of her home and her children, either for short periods on
holiday or for a 'tour' of several years. One must admit with some shame
that there is — or was up to 1973 — a quite discernible pattern of young
professional men and managers moving to England with their families only
to return home prematurely because loneliness and non-acceptance
reduced the child-bound wife to a nervous wreck. Language barriers are,
of course, often a contributing factor in such cases.

Even where it is only a matter of light slanting or emphasis, the
distribution of appeal between men and women may well determine
success or failure. This is an aspect of promotional planning and writing

that calls for a gap to be bridged by a translator—or rather a copywriter—who is familiar with attitudes in the country of the original, while remaining fully aware and sensitive to social trends in the society of his mother tongue.

5.1.6 Foreign views of Britain

It is really rather humiliating to discover that foreigners — and even citizens of the third world — dislike and despise the British just as wholeheartedly as we do them. Since the British Empire dissolved in the eddies of the Second World War, it is perhaps the Americans who have learnt this lesson more slowly, painfully and publicly. What adds insult to injury for the White Anglo-Saxon Protestant (WASP) is that it is often not the obvious weaknesses in his society — such as violence in the States or the economic maladies of Britain — that evoke these reactions, but the qualities he has always regarded as strengths. A young Italian for example was deeply shocked to see his English host look at his watch to make sure that it was 6 o'clock before pouring himself a dry martini. This seemed to him a kind of prostitution—'You Englishmen are all born with a clock in your head'. It may well be true that, in their successive periods of becoming and being top nation, both Great Britain and the States fostered characteristics and values wholly at variance with the real nature of their own peoples as well as calculated to arouse fury in others. What for instance has the stiff upper lip and high-sounding morality of the Victorian era and the two World Wars to do with society from the highest to the lowest as Shakespeare or the Restoration authors depicted it? And in any event power backed up by military and economic sanctions evokes not respect but resentment turning to rebellious fury once the sanctions are removed.

Thus where many people all over the world use some form of the English language as a *lingua franca* the fact that it is the language of two successive super-powers makes it an object of resentment at cultural and political levels.

The Briton or American trying to project an image or promote a product abroad is faced with a situation so adverse that he can only begin to conceive of it by examining his own attitude towards, say, the Japanese invasion of his own market. Britannia and John Bull, Liberty and Uncle Sam do not look quite the same in *Le Canard Enchainé, Simplicissimus* or *Krokodil* as they do in the *Sunday Times* or the *Daily Telegraph*.

It follows that the first task in preparing English copy for re-writing in a foreign language is a destructive one — the removal from it of all expressions of and assumptions based on those attitudes which will be offensive to the intended reader.

Equally at the more practical level — and this applies perhaps to Britain rather than to the States — people from, say, France, Germany or Scandinavia may be struck by the same genuine fear of standards of hygiene, medical treatment and schooling that we see so vividly reflected in the English language novels and travelogues of the 19th and early 20th

centuries. Such feelings are of course particularly strong where mothers
and their children are concerned. Unfortunately this is very much a
question of 'her best friend wouldn't tell her', and one needs to have a very
close and relaxed relationship with one's friends from abroad to be told
exactly what they think of the Anglo-Saxons. Yet this knowledge is an
essential tool of the trade for anyone who is attempting to project a
national, commercial or product image across a language barrier or for
that matter into the English-speaking countries of the third world. Here
again there is the need for a human bridge — a person who knows both
points of view, can regard both of them dispassionately and can decide
when the unacceptable attitudes of the original must be discarded and
when and how they can be turned into strengths.

5.2 Technical factors

The technical problems that bedevil the production of multi-lingual
promotional literature are perhaps better seen in the context of a project
and are therefore discussed in a later chapter. The purpose of this section is
to give a preliminary airing to certain factors related to the language being
used rather than to the practical setting.

5.2.1 Language lengths

A non-linguist listening to a speaker or the radio in a foreign language
often gets an impression of long-windedness; oddly enough this may be
perfectly correct. Let us take English as a reference base, scoring it at 100,
and 'ideal' translations of an English text into various other languages.
Statistically German will score 133 on length, with Russian fairly close
behind it; French comes out statistically at 125, with the other Romance
languages tapering off from there. Ideographic languages and those such
as Arabic which use a special script cannot of course be compared in this
way. They impose quite special problems of layout which must be
considered in context.

Coming back to the European languages, the problem posed by this
length variation will be obvious; but as so often statistics do not tell the
whole story. Because of the respective structures and characteristics of the
languages, many technical texts will tend to come out only a little longer in
German than in English (because of the German use of compounds) but
very much longer in French because the description of a component will
often require a series of qualifying prepositional phrases. Further the long
words of German and Russian are subject to the same kind of rather strict
rules on hyphenation that exist in other languages, and this may mean that
a great deal of space is wasted in a narrow-column layout.

Experience suggests two rules. First that in allocating space to an as yet
unwritten piece of copy it is advisable to allow 50 per cent more space for
each foreign language than for the English. A little extra white space often

improves the design, while overcrowding is always disastrous. And because a major element in the difference in language lengths is the average number of characters per word, word counting is not a good enough check. The texts in the various languages must either be checked out by someone skilled in using a printer's rule or resort must be had to the tedious business of character counting.

Provided that the sponsor does not insist too much on a literal or full translation, it is usually possible to 'write to length' and even to write to a detailed character count to fit an already established design. In fact the latter is a fascinating task not unlike the solving of crossword puzzles or the composition of Latin verse and tends to produce very good taut copy; in one's more cynical moments one feels that it may in fact be the most effective way of producing a multilingual leaflet. But these exercises are not 'translations' and in fact go right against the grain of the translator's ethic and training. On the other hand they are right up the copywriter's street, because he is having to do this all the time to trim his copy to the space available.

5.2.2 Style and slanting

If we think in terms of copywriting in the foreign language rather than of translation, it at once becomes clear that the person producing the foreign language text is under no obligation whatever to adhere closely to the style or angles of the original. He must in fact be free to adopt whatever style and to a large extent whatever angle he thinks will best appeal to the target readership in the language concerned. The only reasonable constraint is the need to attune the text not only to the readership but also the sponsor company's image. This is particularly so when product appeal in the market in question depends largely on a tradition of excellence or more simply on snobbery, and where this element dominates it may even be preferable to forget about the readers' susceptibilities altogether and reflect closely the style of the original.

In the second and early third quarters of the century, when advertising seemed to depend for success on gimmicks and extremes, these aspects of style and slanting must have posed extreme problems, and certainly they frequently led to disaster. Fortunately modern trends in advertising and promotion, under the influence of both legislation and professional opinion, are moving much more towards the down-to-earth and factual or towards the literally 'fabulous' where Aesop, Hans Andersen and many others have created a cast of internationally known stock characters. Since in any case it is good policy to build up credibility in foreign-language markets by striking a rather restrained note, there is in this respect a tendency for foreign-language copywriting to move back closer to the process of translation.

It is perhaps surprising that many advertising and PR consultants seem to regard the choice between single-language editions of promotional literature and a polyglot production to be based simply on cost and expediency. A little thought and effort to look at the problem from the foreign reader's point of view reveal that there are important and perhaps crucial psychological factors. Experience suggests that a polyglot leaflet usually distracts the reader totally and for a considerable time from the purpose in hand. If he is a linguist he will look first at the language he can just read but knows least well and work back from there to his own language, making the study a kind of improvised test. When he gets down to the languages he knows well and has understood most of the text, he will begin comparing the text to see whether he thinks the translations are accurate. The non-linguist appears to play a game of spotting English-looking words in the foreign-language texts. In both cases by the time the reader gets round to considering the message he will have lost interest.

Single-language editions avoid all these distractions and, even more important, make the reader feel that the message is addressed specifically to him — that he is the consumer the writer had in mind and not just some small fly in the international ointment. On the other hand for certain products the flavour of internationalism, with all that it implies, can be a very strong selling point. Where this factor applies, it is up to the designer to make the best of both worlds, for instance by going for single-language editions for the copy and introducing verbal and other pointers towards internationality in the heads and visuals.

5.2.4 *Printing problems*

Ideally the person typesetting should have at least a reading knowledge of the language he is working in, but this is very often not the case. Working literally letter by letter is slow. More important, it is extremely tedious and thus liable to produce errors. The significance of accents and other special characters, or of peculiarities of punctuation, is not understood and they therefore tend to be ignored. But it is with hyphenation that the crunch really comes. The linguist cannot give guidance in advance because he does not know where the need for word splits will arise. It is both physically impossible and ridiculously expensive for him to peer over the setter's shoulder during setting. There are various national and international guides on this topic which printers should have, but they are very difficult to understand where the reader has no knowledge of the language and constant reference to them would be impossibly tedious. It is therefore probably best to accept that the galleys will come out full of horrors as far as word-splitting is concerned and the linguist must sort it out at this stage.

The only constructive expedient known to the authors is for a multilingual secretary to type the printer's draft with the same number of characters per line as will be used in setting. This however is time-consuming and therefore expensive, and is probably only justified when the design has already been established in detail and the foreign-language texts have to be written to a predetermined line-by-line character count.

5.3   Direct translation or rewriting?

This has inevitably been a rather tentative and superficial exploration of a subject which is a major one in its own right, and the same is largely true of Chapter 16 which deals with the managerial and practical aspects of the problem. However, the space this chapter takes up and the time the reader devotes to it will probably be justified if he takes away one single message.

With rare exceptions 'translation' is just not a meaningful term to use in conjunction with the production of foreign-language promotional literature. Just as in the more liberal and heretical circles of the Army an order is said to be a good basis for discussion, so for the linguist original copy in one language is no more than a good excuse for writing something in another.

Professional translators may sometimes lack the boldness of mind required — if they ever had it it will have been beaten out of them by their more conventional clients. Authors are often reluctant to accept the constraints on length and style that work of this kind imposes. One therefore needs to look among professional copywriters, journalists and script writers of the mother tongue concerned. But they of course may have difficulty in appreciating the nuances of the original and may well lack the requisite knowledge of the background against which it was written. Thus the language aspects alone, to say nothing of the problems highlighted in Chapter 16, makes the use of a close-knit and largely co-located team a prerequisite for success in the production of foreign-language promotional literature.

6

The nature of interpreting

It is perhaps very difficult for anyone who has not worked as a professional linguist to realise that translation and interpreting are two different arts and that an individual who excels at one will seldom be particularly good at the other. It is true that this distinction is highlighted and formalised by the structure of the language profession, but while translation is deliberate and analytical, aiming at precision, interpreting, like the performing arts it closely resembles, is dynamic and often calls for improvisation. The difference can perhaps best be brought out by considering first the technical aspects.

6.1 Characteristics of spoken communication

In our discussion of the nature of written translation in Chapter 2 (see Figure 2.2) we touched on the question of primary and secondary verbal, aural and visual channels and their relative importance. We found that in formal translation of typewritten texts the primary verbal channel was the only one of great importance, with some support in the shape of nuances from the secondary verbal channel. We also considered (see Figure 2.3) the importance of a common reference base between the correspondents, the need for the translator to share in this, and the problems presented to the translator by the heavy subjective overload of words and phrases used between correspondents who knew each other well. Family language is an extreme example.

In direct face-to-face communication between individuals who know each other intimately the primary verbal channel can and in fact sometimes does drop out completely, the entire message being conveyed by visual channels, e.g. the exchange of a glance, supported perhaps by some non-linguistic utterance such as a grunt. Moving from this extreme case to the more normal business and professional situation, we can now see that if no language barrier is present the primary verbal channel is of comparatively little importance, providing at most a statement of the theme which is embroidered and varied by expressions of the eyes and face, by gestures, by intonation and by tone of voice, all these being of course backed up by the secondary verbal channel (allusions, etc.) which is in turn reinforced by association with the aural and visual channels.

We also found that in written communication through a translator there was no immediate feedback and the process was therefore essentially a divergent one or open loop. The translator takes, consciously or otherwise, a series of decisions on interpretation of phrases and on nuances, and if these happen to take him further and further from the original writer's intention, no-one will be aware of this until a written reply is received. One of the compensations for the many difficulties of the interpreting process is that there is constant and immediate feedback and the situation is thus essentially a convergent one or closed loop. Errors will tend to be corrected without interruption of the process and a major divergence, if it occurs, will be instantly obvious.

Given a skilled interpreter and principals used to working through one, loss of information occurs less through failure to pass on the full content of the message conveyed from speaker to interpreter on all these channels than in the impossibility of presenting all this information in its original synchronised form. This together with the risk of imperfect interpretation makes the primary verbal channel, i.e. the actual message content of the words spoken, much more important when working through an interpreter than it would be between two people with the same mother-tongue.

6.2   Synchronisation of primary and secondary signals

The synchronisation problem is probably at the root of the highly subject-ive opinions held and expressed on the pros and cons of the two main interpreting techniques — simultaneous and consecutive. Apart from the feeling of loss of rapport which many people — particularly perhaps older ones — consider to be a basic failing of any electronic channel, simultaneous interpreting can in the nature of things never quite live up to its name. Neurophysiologists at Oxford and elsewhere* have done a good

*This work was informally reported in a lecture given during a course entitled 'Recent Devel-opments in Science' held at Brasenose College in the mid-sixties for members of the Armed Forces.

deal of work on the disruption of sensory circuits by the introduction of delays, and in particular on the effects of phase displacement of multiple signals, and have found that under experimental conditions these may have rather extreme effects. Only audio channels are available to the interpreter in this situation, and it is probable that any attempt on the listener's part to watch the speaker and so receive visual signals no longer synchronised with the verbal message will do more harm than good. When one considers further that when working from some languages, particularly German where the verbs may come at the end of a long sentence, the interpreter is faced with the choice of guessing or allowing a time lag that may be both irritating to his listeners and irrecoverable, it does seem that there is considerable objective foundation for the prejudice many feel against simultaneous interpreting.

The exception is that a first-rate interpreter who has been given a copy of the script of a lecture or presentation may often be able to achieve virtual simultaneity — a kind of live dubbing.

Where it is not impossibly time-consuming, consecutive interpreting has enormous advantages. First of all, if the listener has some small understanding of the speaker's language, he gets two bites at the cherry, and many people find this extremely helpful, particularly in the presentation of complex scientific or technological matter. The good consecutive interpreter is in effect an actor who re-enacts on all channels normally available in spoken communication a script received by and registered in his mind. Ideally he can reproduce the message completely in the other language, even to re-pointing detail on any visual aids. The only limitations here are on the one hand the skill of the interpreter, and being a professional he may well be able even to improve on the original; and on the other the requirement, imposed by the time factor and the dynamics of the situation, to summarise rather than to reproduce in full what has been said. Thus, although simultaneous interpreting is a far more difficult skill to acquire to an acceptable level, there is certainly much in what experienced conference interpreters say when they claim that good consecutive interpreting is at once a more challenging and a more satisfying task.

6.3   Interpreting techniques

This is perhaps a convenient point at which to define and to discuss briefly the three basic interpreting techniques.

6.3.1   Simultaneous

In simultaneous interpreting, as its name implies, a team of interpreters renders the speaker's words into whatever number of languages are required as soon as possible after he has uttered them, each member of the team speaking at the same time. The audience is provided with multichannel listening equipment on which each member selects whichever language channel he wishes, including the original if the situation is such that some form of PA would normally be needed. Whether or not they are in a booth or a soundproof room rather like a projection room, the interpreters can seldom be seen clearly by those whom they are addressing and can therefore communicate only on verbal and aural channels.

6.3.2 Consecutive

In consecutive interpreting no equipment is required other than a public address (PA) system where the circumstances are such that this would be needed in single-language working. Where necessary the speaker can continue for up to five minutes, or with experienced interpreters up to ten minutes or more without interruption. At a break point agreed in advance or signalled, the interpreter reproduces what the speaker has said. Ideally he should be as visible to the audience as the original speaker; where people are sitting round a conference table he should have a seat at the table, and he should stand beside the lecturer on the rostrum. If visual aids or models are in use, he can point or handle these just as did the speaker himself. The one exception is film; it is next to impossible to interpret this 'simultaneously' and pointless to do so consecutively, so that a pre-recorded synchronised tape is the only effective solution.

6.3.3 Whisper interpreting

This technique is greatly liked by many users. Others, particularly at the highest political level, may not accept it, and even the most experienced interpreters dislike it to the point where they often refuse to do it. The method consists essentially in simultaneous interpreting without the use of equipment, an interpreter sitting just behind and between each group and giving a simultaneous translation in a low-pitched voice.

The problem is of course interference. General professional opinion is that this limits the use of the technique to two languages or three at the outside, and to groups in each language preferably of two and certainly of no more than three — say six people in all. We, however, contest this view strongly, having used the technique with complete success with five languages and language-groups of up to six and a much larger group with the language of the chair as their mother tongue.

The secrets are first of all to have a large room with plenty of space between groups, using a PA system to amplify the speaker's and/or the chairman's voice, and to accept that some consecutive interpreting into the language of the chair may be necessary. This kind of interpreation admittedly provides a level of communication lower than simultaneous with equipment or good consecutive. However in the normal situation where all the delegates have good subject knowledge and many at least a smattering of the language of the chair, the efficiency is acceptable. The direct advantages are a saving in time and cost and the ability to work in a number of different locations. But even more important are the psychological benefits of excellent dynamics, an atmosphere of intimacy and knitting together and hence a rapport of a kind completely unobtainable with simultaneous interpreting equipment. There can be little doubt that whisper with a judicious admixture of consecutive is a preferred technique for the typical professional or commercial gathering numbering up to about fifty, particularly when there are several different venues — provided that interpreters able and willing to work in this way can be found.

6.4   Literalness versus freedom

Experience suggests that interpreters gravitate towards the extremes of the literalness/freedom spectrum far more than do translators, and that the choice of extreme depends far more upon the particular interpreter than on the circumstances or the nature of the subject. Probably the dynamics of the situation require an individual to use a processing unit of the particular length that best suits him, while the translator with more time can afford to tune in to the cycle that he feels best meets the need. This tendency is perhaps most marked in simultaneous interpreting, where for no very apparent reason one interpreter will give the nearest thing to a word-by-word rendering that makes sense in the other language, while another, accepting a rather longer lag on occasions, will take complete sentences or even paragraphs as his unit. There appears to be little to choose between the validity and acceptability of these two varieties.

The consecutive interpreter is always faced with the conflict between giving a full and faithful rendering of what has been said and compressing it sufficiently to maintain the dynamics of the situation. He is thus forced to act in the true professional sense and make a subjective judgement on what detail to omit, which passages to résumé and which to give as nearly in full as he can. He will therefore tend to use literalness as a means of emphasis, staying as close as he can to the speaker's utterance when he slows his pace and modulates the pitch of his voice to stress a key passage.

This dilemma highlights the main drawback of consecutive interpreting to large audiences. If an interpreter is working between two groups of, say, two or three each, he will quickly learn how much of the other language the weakest individual in each group understands and therefore the extent to which he can safely abridge his interpretation. Even if he can do this with a large audience, the span of abilities is likely to be so great that no one course can conceivably satisfy all its members.

6.5   Characteristics of an interpreter

No one person is likely to make a good interpreter and a good translator.

The one art calls for a bold, extrovert exhibitionist and the other for a cautious, introvert perfectionist. Interpreters come at all levels of skill but, provided these are adequate for the technique and purpose in hand, neither the level of their languages nor the depth of their subject knowledge are likely to be the main factor in determining success or failure. The key requirements are that they should inspire confidence in both parties and that their attitude and manner should be such as to draw the parties together — just as talking to each other in a common language would — and foster mutual confidence between them.

To inspire confidence the interpreter needs to be self-confident as opposed to hesitant, but to be prepared upon occasion — especially in informal meetings — to flatter his audience by occasionally appealing to their greater knowledge. More important still are both integrity itself and the appearance of integrity. While one seldom comes across a 'bent' interpreter in the full modern sense of that word, one does surprisingly often find an interpreter who deliberately or otherwise bends what has been said. There are in fact two real and difficult ethical problems underlying this tendency.

The first is that the interpreter's task is to convey one party's message to the other as accurately and completely as he can, and to do this he needs and can reasonably expect to be given considerable freedom. If however he himself has slightly misunderstood the tone of the message or some slant or nuance in it — or even perhaps if he has strong personal views — his interpretation will produce the same kind of divergent situation that we find in translation. This is not important at the practical level because, as was said above, interpreting unlike translation is a closed loop system stabilised by negative feedback and is therefore inherently convergent. But divergence may be quite disastrous if it is detected by either of the parties and taken as deliberate misrepresentation. Thus if he is to rise above the level of being a pure word-box and actively inspire confidence and good relations, the interpreter's assessment has to be right often enough for his lapses to be taken as genuine errors.

In situations where the interpreter's sponsor is impartial, as in a court of law, a major international organisation or a major scientific conference, the interpreter's duty is clearly to interpret what is said to the best of his ability regardless of the consequences; and the professional code of AIIC (*Association International des Interprètes de Conférence*) is very clear and strict on this point. At the other extreme of international negotiations at political, official and working levels it must surely be the patriotic and professional duty of an interpreter to act in whatever way will best serve the purposes of his delegation. He should certainly for example cover up a slip of his principal's tongue involving a breach of security and pass on anything he learns from the other delegation's interpreter or from overhearing caucus-type conversations and asides.

The typical commercial situation lies somewhere between these two extremes and it is not easy to know what attitude should be expected of an interpreter subject to the AIIC or a similar professional code or what line he should take. In other cases where a professional man is retained by a

client to serve his interests, such as accountants or lawyers, the professional
codes permit and indeed encourage wholehearted and active support of
the client's case within certain rules of conduct. A business man who
engages an interpreter as a professional expert — at what will probably be a
very professional fee — is likely and indeed entitled to expect the same kind
of support, or at least the avoidance of actions which, while according with
the interpreter's code, will cause his client acute embarrassment.

This dilemma is so difficult to resolve and so destructive of clients'
confidence in interpreters and hence readiness to employ them that there
seems to be a need for a dual code, insisting on impartiality when paid by
the impartial but giving reasonable scope for slanting and advocacy when
employed by an interested party.

In any event the relationship between a principal and his interpreter is a
highly personal one, and the opportunity open to an interpreter to take
positive action to create and maintain good relationships may often be
limited by his employer's attitude. The attitude of Olympian detachment
which many interpreters seem to prefer is perhaps appropriate and even
inevitable in large conferences, but at smaller meetings where real business
is done it is unhelpful, if not unacceptable. The principal and his
interpreter are very much a team and must learn to work together and
complement each other's strengths.

6.6   Matching interpreting to its purpose

Having spoken of the need to match an interpreter to his principal, we can
now go on to the broader problem of matching techniques and levels of
skill to particular requirements. To approach the problem by bracketing it
is clear that, on the one hand, the very small proportion of large meetings
or conferences at which any real business is to be done or decisions are to be
reached calls for the very highest interpreting skills, capable of getting
across the full content of a personal message in a hideously depersonalised
and electronic environment. Such an interpreter would however be wasted
if not indeed useless for maintaining communication between a foreign
installation engineer putting in a new machine and the purchaser's
maintenance team. Here such messages as cannot be conveyed by signal
can be put across by an enthusiastic and averagely intelligent schoolchild.

The theme that will reappear in the next chapter and in Part 2 is the
supreme importance of the interpreting task in the small committee-type
or informal meeting where negotiation actually takes place and decisions
and agreements are reached. Businessmen who do not realise the nature of
the problem are often content to pick up an interpreter on the spot for
discussions of this kind or to take a chance on accepting the opposition's
interpreting facilities. We believe that this is the one occasion when they
should seek out in advance and take with them, more or less regardless of
expense, the best and most experienced interpreter they can find, one who
is capable of performing to equal effect in any of the three interpreting
techniques or of switching quickly between these.

The profession likes to draw a distinction between 'conference intepreters', capable of all techniques, 'consecutive interpreters', capable of high-grade formal and specialised consecutive interpreting, and *ad hoc* interpreters whose skills are limited to informal consecutive interpreting, guiding and escorting and the like. While there is no objective distinction whatever between 'consecutive' and *ad hoc* interpreting, it is true that for a very high proportion of the interpreting tasks that industry requires it is unnecessary to go to the great expense of using fully qualified interpreters. Interpreting is a particular skill which needs to be developed by training and is possessed by only a limited number of linguists, but there is a vast range of interpreting-type tasks that can be carried out satisfactorily by anyone with a reasonable knowledge of the subject and of the two languages, such as a multilingual secretary. For many small business meetings other than those of crucial importance the host's multilingual secretary is probably the best possible interpreter. She will more than make up for any lack in language and interpreting skills as such by her knowledge of the subject, the background and personalities and by the fact that at least one of the parties has complete confidence in her.

But the choice of interpreter will to a large extent be governed by the technique to be used. Cost alone, as discussion in subsequent chapters will show, would make it absurd to use simultaneous interpreting where it is not essential, and at the risk of putting forward a conservative British view, the authors believe it to be the weakest of the three techniques. However, whisper is traditionally limited to groups of two or three in at most three languages, and it may be difficult to find good interpreters willing to use this technique. And consecutive, while ideal for two languages, and feasible for three with first-rate interpreting, becomes hopelessly unwieldy when more than three languages are required.

A useful expedient for meetings held in two or three languages with a high content of papers, presentations, etc., is to use simultaneous for these, where good preparation can achieve something very like a dubbing effect, and go to consecutive for discussions.

For the small bilateral working group, where the members of the delegations, interpreting team and secretariat generally remain unchanged over a number of meetings, the ideal is probably to use conference interpreters, to work with consecutive interpreting for the first meeting or two until everyone has got to know the others and weighed them up, and then if relations are good switch to simultaneous to speed up work. It is always possible to revert to consecutive for particular discussions if members wish, and the flexibility gives a good, business-like atmosphere. The important lesson here perhaps is that interpreters and secretariat are just as much members of the team as, and even perhaps more important than, the delegates themselves.

7

Simultaneous interpreting

The complex administration of a multilingual conference is mainly a management topic and will be discussed in Part 2. The purpose of this chapter is to give some idea of the basic parameters and cost, and to broadcast a warning that there is a good deal more to the successful operation of the simultaneous interpreting technique than just booking interpreters and equipment, warning delegates and hoping that all will arrive in the same place at the same time.

7.1   Conference interpreters

Conference interpreters are the cream of the language profession and claim to be the smallest and most select profession in the world. They are likely to be AIIC members (*Association Internationale des Interprètes de Conférence*). They may be employed either by international organisations or by national civil services (as for example in West Germany), or they may be freelances belonging to one of AIIC's national pools. AIIC freelances are subject to the rather strict code of professional ethics mentioned above, to a set scale of fees and allowances that puts them in the same price-bracket as a middle to senior consultant, and to a set of rules on hours and numbers which, while wholly justifiable in terms of the very high professional standard that this organisation sets itself, are not always very constructively presented and applied and combine with the fees to give conference organisers an unfortunate impression of restrictive practices.

As was stressed in the preceding chapter, conference interpreters probably best justify the very high cost of using them less in major conferences than as individuals or small teams working in support of small delegations.

There are in the UK for example several simultaneous interpreters of acceptable standard who are not members of AIIC and are not therefore bound by the AIIC rules on cost and number. They will have come up through one of the continental schools or the 'advanced' or 'applied' language degree and diploma courses that are becoming increasingly common in the UK, and thence via one of the major international organisations, typically going freelance on marriage or returning to freelance professional work after raising a family. They are available through interpreting bureaus — often and perhaps in this case correctly known as agencies — at rather less astronomical fees.

Since one of the AIIC rules is that any interpreters working at a meeting at which an AIIC member is present, whether or not members of AIIC, must be paid at AIIC rates and work to AIIC conditions, a choice has to be made one way or the other. The otherwise more attractive alternative of engaging AIIC interpreters as consultants/leaders and filling in with those less highly qualified is not available.

The moral for sponsors and organisers of conferences and large meetings is that the conference must be planned *ab initio* to make the most cost-effective use of conference interpreters. This calls for the services of an AIIC interpreter experienced enough to act as a consultant or of a language consultant familiar with AIIC procedures. (As AIIC coordinators are apt to change or to move house, it is best in the first place to contact the Institute of Linguists or its equivalent in other countries.)

7.2 Equipment

Simultaneous interpreting calls for rather complex and expensive if not particularly sophisticated equipment, and this is available on hire from a small number of specialist firms; consultant interpreters and linguists can advise on these. For smaller meetings with a maximum of say three languages and 25 delegates, it may be possible to reduce both costs and the depersonalising array of hardware by using the 'topless' (boothless) equipment now available and/or an induction loop and free hand/head sets. The more traditional paraphernalia can be rather alarming and has the added disadvantage of isolating the interpreters from the rest of those present. If required, even in temporary installations, tape-decks for playback and recording for later transcription can be incorporated, and control facilities for visual aid equipment can sometimes be wired in.

The equipment is usually set up the day or evening before it is required by a team from the hiring company of whom at least one member stays behind throughout the conference to operate and service the equipment. Even the more modern types of equipment require fairly expert operating to maintain the best possible level of communication, and it is essential to gain the engineer's wholehearted collaboration by ensuring that he has the facilities he needs, by putting and keeping him in the picture and by consulting him over technical problems that arise during setting up and in the course of the meeting itself.

The only predictable thing about the cost of hired equipment is that it will be high, and this is no reflection on the companies that hire it out. The capital cost of the equipment is substantial; its weight and volume makes transport relatively expensive; setting up and maintenance in a whole variety of situations inevitably has a high labour content and involves unsocial hours, and the high proportion of one-night stands together with the likelihood of misuse by inexperienced delegates makes the rate of wear and tear extremely high. Factors internal to each hire company, such as the relative location of successive meetings, cause a wide variation in quotations. Experience suggests that for identical requirements at the same time and place fees quoted may vary by as much as a factor of 2 or 3.

As a rough yardstick, equipment hire — or the equipment element in the hire fee for a permanently wired conference room — is likely to cost about the same amount as the team of interpreters who use it. This suggests that it is not cost-effective to economise on either but better to go for the quality that will produce first-rate results. More constructively it redoubles the need to plan the conference *ab initio* in a way that will achieve economies in both human and material language resources and will make the best possible use of those that are provided.

7.3   Secretariat and transcription

A large proportion of the considerable administrative task of organising and running a conference will devolve at secretarial level. (This aspect will be further discussed in Part 2.) It has a high language content because of the need to prepare all the advance documentation. It is the conference secretariat proper that is discussed here because its method of working is closely related to the interpreting technique and equipment used. The first point to make is that, with the best will in the world, interpreters cannot under any circumstances whatever combine any form of recording activity with interpreting. There is a widespread misapprehension about this because interpreters take notes, but the type of notes they take are highly specialised and individualised and in no way form the basis of post-meeting reconstruction of what was said. It is feasible to use stenographers working in shifts, taking down from whichever language channel they prefer and then transcribing. But the team needed is a large one and the quantity of paper resulting is almost unmanageable. Another expedient is to use an executive secretary trained as a minute-taker, but her task becomes almost impossible unless the interpreting is exceptionally good and more particularly the conference is exceptionally well controlled.

Probably the most cost-effective technique, though by no means the cheapest, is to have a team of minute-takers working in shifts and concentrating solely on picking out the main points. They can safely do this if they are backed up by a complete tape record of the proceedings which they can take away at the end of the shift and play back to build up their minutes. This will involve the inclusion of a transcription tape deck in whichever language channel is appropriate on the simultaneous interpreting equipment and also the availability of a compatible tape recorder for playback by members of the secretariat.

7.4   Stress and teamwork

The AIIC rules lay down, roughly speaking, that interpreters must be paired for each language combination and that their working day must be limited to an overall duration of about 7 hours which must include one long and at least one short break and a maximum of 6 hours in session. Although these restrictions may be unwelcome to conference organisers, they may serve here to drive home the point that a multilingual conference represents a very high stress situation for all concerned with its operation — chairmen, administrators, interpreters, secretariat and equipment engineers alike.

Administrative crises must be kept outside the conference rooms, but within them chairman, interpreters, engineer and secretariat must work as a team, and however distinguished he may be, the individual who hopes to chair a successful multilingual conference should to go considerable trouble to discuss and agree methods with the other members of this team. Though not all interpreters like having linguists among the delegates — and sometimes one must admit the reason for this is not hard to hear — they will probably welcome a chairman with some competence in at least some of the languages concerned, first because he may have rather more understanding of their problems and second because he can gain and hold control of the conference temporarily should — as is not infrequently the case particularly with temporary installations — the equipment break down. It is very difficult for anyone who has not actually seen this happen at a fairly large meeting to realise the truly Babel-like chaos that rapidly arises and takes a long time to sort out. Without their equipment the interpreters are helpless unless the meeting can be kept under control for long enough for them to move out to a point where they can continue consecutive interpreting at least of soothing words and essential instructions.

7.5   Conduct of the meeting

In any meeting, large or small, it is desirable to control it firmly enough to ensure that not more than one person is speaking at any one time. In a

multilingual conference using simultaneous interpreting this is vital. It is
vital for two reasons, the relative importance of which depends to some
extent on the type of equipment in use. The first problem is that in systems
where the engineer or a nominated interpreter controls the microphones
on the table, anyone who speaks without having signalled for his microphone to be switched on puts no signal into the interpreting system,
although he may interfere with an adjacent mike that is live at the time. If
the delegates themselves have control of the table microphone nearest to
them and two switch on and start speaking at once the resulting chaos is
even faster and more dissatisfying. The second problem is that if two inputs
in different languages reach the interpreters it is fairly certain that the
teams working out of each of the languages will start speaking at the same
time, so that in all probability, since interpreters control their own mikes,
some channels will have two signals on them at the same time.

With this sort of thing happening in what, as has already been
emphasised, is a high stress situation tempers rapidly begin to fray, the
interpreters start complaining or, justifiably enough, trying themselves to
restore control, and the service engineer becomes confused, the more so as
these situations often lead to a complaint from the chair that the
equipment is not working. (One of us was present at a meeting in which the
engineer put paid both to the disorder and to the resumption of
proceedings by walking out.)

Any time and effort spent by the organisers on facilitating good control
of the meeting and collaboration of delegates with the chair, the
interpreters and the equipment engineer will be amply repaid. It is almost
certainly worth having instructions, which must of course take account of
the particular features of the room, the equipment in use and the form of
the meeting, prepared in all the languages concerned and:

1   Included in the programme or some document the delegates will have
    fairly constantly in front of them.
2   Mounted on millboards and placed at frequent intervals round the
    conference table.
3   Read out by the chairman (and in other languages by the interpreters
    concerned) at the beginning of the opening session and of any other
    session where the form of the meeting or other circumstances have
    changed or where new delegates are present.

There are a very few occasions, most notably perhaps in small working
level meetings when the drafting of matching texts is in progress, when it is
useful to hand control of the meeting over temporarily to the interpreters,
who can then confer in their booths and put their versions out
simultaneously on the various language channels. But with this one rare
and perhaps questionable exception, control of the meeting must remain
with the chair. Because it effectively depends on the switching on and off of
the mikes on the table, it can very easily pass to the equipment engineer,
who is not the person best qualified to exercise it. Therefore in discussion
or question periods when there is any reasonable prospect of two people
signalling they want to speak at the same time, the arrangement must be

that the service engineer does not act until he receives a signal from the chair — in effect pointing out the microphone to be switched on.

This chapter has to some extent deliberately laboured the high cost and the considerable administrative and executive difficulties of arranging and conducting a successful multilingual conference. It would be wrong however for the reader to take away the impression that these are insuperable. Multilingual conferences are perhaps the supreme example of the language barriers being a fence which will bring down bad or badly-ridden horses but show off the good ones to best advantage.

8
Consecutive interpreting

The nature of the simultaneous interpreting function and the parameters of the situation, and more particularly of the equipment used, impose severe constraints on flexibility of operation and on the way in which the considerable talents of conference interpreters can be deployed. The classical technique of consecutive interpreting is by contrast completely flexible — ranging from the formal section-by-section interpretation of an address or the full and immediate interpretation of a discussion, through situations in which the interpreter acts as intermediary, to those in which discussion is conducted mainly between the principals in one of the languages concerned and the interpreter only steps in when difficulties arise or when his skills are required for specialised tasks such as the drafting of an agreement with matching texts.

While the laymen's preference for one technique or the other will probably be dictated by his reaction to the presence and use of electronic equipment, it is worth noting that most conference interpreters, particularly the most skilled and experienced, regard consecutive interpreting as the higher and more demanding branch of the art. While some say that the British preference for consecutive interpreting is a prejudice, there do seem to be rather strong indications both from practitioners and from their users that this preference is based if not on hard fact at least on sound psychological ground. Our view is that, quite apart from the remarkable savings in cost, consecutive interpreting is the superior technique in situations where it can be used, and that the right question to ask is therefore: 'Must we go simultaneous?' rather than 'Shall we be forced back onto consecutive?'.

8.1 The time factor and dynamics

Theoretically consecutive interpreting doubles the time required to transmit a particular message or chunk of information but in practice, given skilled interpreters and cooperative speakers, the time increase is probably more like 50 per cent where two languages are involved and around 90 per cent for three. This is due partly to the ability of good and experienced interpreters to establish and maintain a higher tempo than is usually found in single-language discussions, and partly to the tacit assumption made by the interpreters, with the tacit support of delegates, that some of the information will go across to all in the original speech and that successive interpretations can be increasingly summarised. Nevertheless we arrive immediately at one of the main limitations of the consecutive technique — it cannot reasonably handle more than three languages and is very much more effective with only two.

In fact even this 50 per cent figure is probably too high to be used in choosing between simultaneous and consecutive. If we assume that a particular chunk of lecture or discussion conducted in a single language would take 100 min, it is likely to require 110-120 with simultaneous interpreting. This increased time is taken up to a small extent with making good weaknesses in communication but mainly with overcoming the mechanics of the situation. It always seems, very understandably, to take delegates, interpreters and equipment alike a little time to settle down at the beginning of sessions and work up to a satisfactory rhythm. In a discussion the need to signal for a microphone and the subsequent switching takes a finite time which is significant if it is often repeated; and any failure of control from the chair, response from the interpreters or functioning of the equipment takes perhaps two or three minutes to sort out. On the other hand consecutive interpreting with principals and interpreters who are used to working together tends to set a rather high tempo and to lead to greater clarity and conciseness of expression than is usually the case where no language barrier is present.

For two languages one is thus looking at an effective difference in planning time between simultaneous and consecutive of no more than some 30 per cent. For sessions of any length a team of two interpreters per pair of languages will be required in either case, but unless the members of the meeting are exceptionally numerous and highly paid, the saving on equipment cost is likely to make the consecutive technique the most cost-effective for two languages. Simultaneous interpreting does however offer certain advantages in dynamics for detailed discussion within say a working group where the delegations and interpreters are well run-in as a team. This is perhaps particularly the case where a session is to be devoted to the drafting of an agreement, key plan or specification simultaneously in the two languages.

At meetings where any kind of negotiation or decision-making is involved, and this means most meetings held in a commercial or industrial setting, the dynamics of the meeting are a major factor in its successful outcome. It is extremely difficult for a linguist to comment on this, as for him consecutive interpreting is profoundly boring unless he needs thinking time, while most simultaneous equipment allows him to monitor one or sometimes two language channels through his headset while taking an additional language live, and thus to correct any deviations in interpreting by inconspicuous and timely feedback. But there is little doubt that despite an inevitably lower standard of communication, the presence of an electronic link, the isolation of the interpreters and other factors militating against *rapport,* many principals will prefer simultaneous interpreting in a negotiating situation because they can then control the tempo and the interpreter is bound to follow. With consecutive interpreting the interpreter has complete control both over the tempo itself and over the second-order dynamics affecting pressure and *rapport.* Cost apart, the choice between simultaneous and consecutive is a very evenly balanced one and probably depends on the quality of interpreter available. If interpreters of AIIC standard are not available, consecutive is likely to be the more cost-effective method; with conference interpreters of average skill and experience simultaneous should yield better results; but with a really outstanding interpreter who is prepared to involve himself on behalf of his client and contribute actively, it is the consecutive technique that will make the best use of his talents. This of course raises once more the problems mooted in Chapter 6 on the interpreter's code of professional ethics.

Generally speaking only interpreters with political or top official level experience seem able to read the temper of the meeting and the mood of the principals well enough to maintain the same psychological dynamics as would prevail if the discussions were being held in a single language while staying strictly within the bounds of interpreting procedure.

8.2 Consecutive interpreting on formal occasions

An interpreter may be able to interpret off the cuff as well or rather better than most people speak off the cuff — and that means not well enough to sustain a lecture, address or speech to a large audience. We mentioned in Chapter 5, and shall be stressing in Part 2, that copywriting in a foreign language was an act of re-writing rather than translating, and much the same applies to interpreting on formal occasions.

Where the content is mainly informative and objective, as in the typical scientific paper, it should be sufficient for the interpreter to be provided well in advance with a copy of the text. If a speaker is working from notes, the interpreter will need a copy of the notes and will probably need some time with the speaker to fill out some of the detail. It is particularly important that he should be warned in advance of any jokes or anecdotes and that his advice should be taken if he says that they are untranslatable.

Equally interpreters should be able to interpret off the cuff the kind of speech that most speakers can make without preparation. Broadly speaking then the interpreter will need about the same amount of support in the way of scripts or notes as the speaker has, should normally have some preliminary discussion with the speaker and will require a certain amount of preparation time between the completion of briefing and delivery of the speech.

The second prerequisite is that the interpreter should be given reasonable opportunity to present himself and what he says to the audience. All too often one sees a small interpreter being forced to hold forth over a large speaker's shoulder, or an interpreter perched on the edge of the dais and clinging for dear life to the lectern; or seated in the well of the room where few if any of the audience can see him. While the interpreter must never upstage the speaker, he cannot hope to get the speaker's message across unless he is given identical facilities in terms of comfort, visibility to the audience and above all access to any visual aids. One acceptable solution is a table on the dais with two chairs (three if there is a chairman) with the speaker and interpreter sitting side by side and rising alternately. Another layout, particularly suitable if one or more screens are in use, is to have two lecterns, one on either side of the screen, with the speaker at one and the interpreter at the other. But whatever the physical factors, the point is, so to speak, equality of opportunity.

Speakers who are not used to working with interpreters tend to sub-divide their material much too heavily. Clearly if someone who is not a professional interpreter is filling in a gap, ample time must be allowed and the speech must be broken down almost sentence by sentence. But this is not what consecutive interpreting is about. To maintain an acceptable flow and rhythm, chunks should last at least five minutes, and in a longish address ten or even fifteen. Most talks will fall in one way or another into about five sections, and it will be helpful both to the speaker and to the interpreter if it is taken a section at a time. If there is a script and if this is broken up by paragraphs representing a 'mindful' rather than sentence by sentence as many scripts are today, the paragaraphs should provide a reasonable guide. The breakdown is something that speaker and interpreter should arrive at by mutual agreement at the end of any briefing discussion or, if necessary, immediately before going on.

Very much greater problems arise — even more perhaps than they do in simultaneous interpreting — when the content of a lecture is both 'difficult' and highly subjective, involving perhaps the use both of true neologisms and of existing words in special senses. For instance the chapters of Jacques Monod's *Le Hasard et la Nécessité* were, it seems, originally given as lectures. Professor Monod happens to speak both French and English, but one only has to look at the problems of interpreting what he says into German or Russian to see the magnitude of the task. Normally matter of this kind is delivered in the originator's own language and audiences are such that they are expected to understand it; but if such material, or much of what is now written in the field of the soft sciences has to be interpreted, the interpreter must be given opportunity for extremely long and careful preparation and for discussion with the speaker. If what he says is to be intelligible, he must not only have grasped the essentials of the subject but also mastered — or if necessary made up — the terminology in advance. It may even be necessary for the speaker to use a full script and the interpreter to work from a secondary script he has prepared. Such problems lie perhaps in the academic rather than in the commercial field, but with the mounting emphasis on conservation and on the social responsibilities of industry, it may well become necessary to discuss difficult abstract concepts and value judgements in a commercial or industrial context — and thus to interpret them.

8.3   The small meeting

Not being directly associated with the use of more than one language, the ritual nature of most conferences and large meetings can perhaps better be discussed in Part 2. Suffice it to say here that most real exchange of views and negotiation goes on in small meetings convened in their own right or as working groups in association with some larger assembly, or of course over meals and in less formal circumstances. It is therefore in these small meetings rather than in imposing plenary sessions that the quality of interpreting really matters and that the interpreter will usually have scope to bring his full talents to bear. The number present at such a meeting, including one or possibly two interpreters, may vary from three to a maximum of perhaps ten, in which case each delegation is likely to consist of a hard core and of specialists who come and go depending on the matter under discussion. Certainly anything over twelve calls for more formal control via the chair and destroys the intimate atmosphere necessary for open discussion and sound negotiation.

8.3.1   The quality of interpreting

As has been indicated earlier, the interpreter's task in a situation of this kind goes way beyond the changing of one set of words into another. If consecutive interpreting is being used, as it is likely to be in the smallest and therefore potentially most fruitful meetings, he is quite literally the lynch-pin. In   any event he must first set out to gain the confidence of both parties, for until he has done this real communication is likely to be very limited. Generally a half-day initial session or even a separate preliminary meeting is necessary to run the two individuals or teams and the interpreter(s) in together, although dinner the evening before or lunch or arrival will often provide a sufficient ice-breaker. Once mutual confidence has been established and he feels uninhibited, the interpreter's task is to involve himself totally in conveying the whole message of each speaker down to the last nuance and — more difficult — in at the same time reflecting the moods of the principals and making a contribution of his own towards the relationships needed for free discussion and fruitful negotiations.

Personal acceptability on the one hand and treatment of the interpreter as an equal on the other are essential to cementing relationships. If there are two interpreters, they will need some time to confer together and they will also need a rest; but if they are cut off from the delegates outside the sessions themselves the necessary *rapport* will never be established and they will not be available to help out in serious discussions arising at a social function or a chance encounter.

Clearly an interpreter hired or detailed from some organisation's pool for the day, let alone one picked up on the spot at the last minute, is unlikely to fill this bill. If the client insists on regarding the interpreter as no more than a human computer, he is likely to get only an indifferent performance at that level and no contribution at any other. If on the other hand he allows the interpreter reasonable briefing and preliminary discussion time, involves him in the project and treats him — as he would any other professional expert — as an individual with a bunch of talents all capable of contributing to the occasion, he will quite quickly get in these more intimate situations a level of communication at least as good as would arise in single language working.

8.3.2 Consecutive or simultaneous?

The small meeting is in our eyes of such supreme importance that we have tended to veer in earlier discussions towards the choice of technique for it. Very frequently the setting or the circumstances will preclude the use of simultaneous because of the equipment needed. In any case simultaneous is not the most appropriate technique at the stage at which the two sides are sounding each other out and the *Gestalt* of the group as a whole is being established. If however the same conference interpreter is being used throughout, it may well be worth arranging meetings with simultaneous equipment when the stage of detailed discussion and drafting is reached. Horror of horrors to the uninitiated — one of us has even found it valuable, with the wholehearted agreement of the other delegation, to hand over the chair to the interpreters for work of this nature!

Likewise whisper interpreting may sometimes be suitable, but this needs two interpreters working at once and is thus precluded for sessions of any great length, as small groups are most unlikely to have more than two interpreters available in all. The ideal use of whisper (and this requires only one interpreter) arises when the head of one delegation speaks the other's language so that discussions can be conducted in that language. The interpreter's task is then by whisper to keep the non-linguist members of the team in the picture.

And so, despite some of the drawbacks discussed earlier in this chapter, matter.

8.3.3 *Interpreter or intermediary?*

In this discussion on consecutive interpreting the flexibility it offers has been stressed and the possibility of the interpreter, or shall we say the professional linguist, moving outside the limits of the interpreting convention has been at least hinted at. It is now time to bring this question into the open. We have seen that, apart from the sheer time consecutive interpreting may require, simultaneous and consecutive techniques are each subject to a peculiar major drawback which tends to lower the effectiveness of communication below the 100 per cent level represented by single-language working. With simultaneous working we have the slight lag between visual signals from the speaker and the audio follow-up from the interpreter that destroys the synchronisation of all signals put out by the speaker; and the interpreter, being at least away to one side if not boxed up in a booth, cannot provide any visual fill-in. In consecutive interpreting, not only is the quality of supreme importance, but adherence to the conventional interpreting formula can make it very difficult to maintain the dynamics required in a tough negotiating situation.

One of us having had considerable experience as a member and leader of delegations and user of interpreters before himself taking to the hot seat in the middle, found that he was tending more and more to do two things, and that this tendency was both accepted and actively welcomed by his clients and the other party. One was to assume chairing control of the meeting, in the sense of controlling who spoke when — this is to overcome the natural tendency of those not experienced in multilingual working to follow their normal practice of all talking at once; and the other was to worry away at a point and elucidate it in the one language until he understood exactly what he had to put across in the other. The first of these is really no more than an interim and educative measure in the absence of a chairman experienced in multilingual working; but the second opens up more interesting lines of thought.

Let us now come at this from the other end and consider the case of a non-linguist senior sales executive going to visit a foreign client accompanied by his agent in the market concerned, who will presumably speak both languages. The tendency at a meeting of this kind will be for the agent to lead and to conduct discussions in the client's language using his principal's language only to keep the latter in the picture and to discuss details and crunch-points with him to obtain additional information or guidance. Leaving aside any legal niceties over the commercial use of the words 'agent' and 'intermediary', the agent is now acting as an intermediary. Taking this argument one stage further, we see that there is no rational need for the sales executive to be present at all. The agent could just as well be acting as a representative with his principal at the end of a telephone or telex. (However one knows very well that this extension of the argument ignores a number of important psychological factors.)

Reverting now to the interpreter, the more he tends to draw together and thrash out points in one language before putting them across in the other, the more he begins to act as an intermediary and the closer the dynamics of the discussion come to resemble those of single-language working. Not only is a great deal of time saved, but a great many small misunderstandings are eliminated because they never arise. By a mixture of advance discussion and coded verbal signals, the interpreter — or intermediary — can be instructed just how hard to ride the opposition and when to give way — which one does in fact in these circumstances by saying that at this point it is necessary to brief or to consult one's client and then coming back with the concession.

Equally, if the head of his delegation is a linguist, the interpreter can be used simply to keep the rest of the team up to date by whisper or otherwise, or, if the linguist delegate is on his own, as a bilingual aide who can prepare any minutes required in both languages and a report in English for the rest of the delegation.

Once an interpreter has acquired the confidence of both parties in the role of intermediary and is well known to the opposition, he can perfectly well be sent as a representative on minor liaison or exploratory missions which do not themselves involve negotiation. This maintains the *rapport* that meetings will have established while saving both money and executive time. And if the interpreter is a person of suitable qualities and experience, he can finally step into a consultant's shoes and himself carry out negotiations within an agreed brief.

There is no doubt whatever that, given the right individual, this extension and liberation of the interpreter's role leads quickly to faster and more efficient working and, as relationships develop, to notable economies. There is, however, one other aspect of it that deserves mention. Imagine a working-level meeting between the specialists of two companies in a high-technology field aimed at an exchange of information and at putting the flesh on an outline collaborative agreement that their top managements have reached. Before any real discussion can start, this is going to involve one visit each way most of which will be given over to briefing. Since in the scenario envisaged some members of each team are likely to have a reasonable understanding of the other's language without necessarily speaking it, briefing by consecutive interpreting is not only time-wasting but extremely tedious. Given a script, or even once he is thoroughly in the picture on a mixture of written or spoken briefing, the interpreter can perfectly well put the briefing over direct in the other team's language, bringing his own team's members into play for questions and discussion. Again in this scenario, some of his own delegation will have sufficient knowledge of the other language to monitor him. This notion of the interpreter taking the place of the original speaker in certain circumstances has however even stronger application to demonstrations or works tours, considered in the next section, and to the instructional situation, touched on in Part 2.

We have so far considered situations in which the main purpose of the gathering was the spoken exchange and the venue and programme would presumably be designed to this end — in other words situations in which the interpreter is or should be operating under ideal circumstances. We now have to consider cases in which the verbal element of communication is subsidiary to the visual, and more particularly where this visual element has to be witnessed *in situ,* or at least out of doors or away from the conference and committee room. Here the interpreter's problems become those of the bear leader — hearing what is said to him, making himself heard, and simultaneously explaining the exhibits or situation and keeping control of a moving group. Unless the client is experienced or the interpreter is in a position to insist, the latter is likely to find himself wandering desperately through some roaring machine shop taking in inaudible explanations in one ear and shouting whatever comes into his head with no help but the voice God gave him at a group of people who are steadily dispersing and making for the machines operated by the sexiest-looking girls.

8.4.1   *Control of movement*

The first point that needs extremely careful attention is the control of movement. First it is essential to contain a group on the move physically by having one guide or such at the head and another (perhaps the interpreter) at the rear. Only in this way does the interpreter have a chance of keeping all concerned within earshot. On the other hand, while to make himself heard he will be need to be at the rear or in the middle of the group, he and not the host must be the one to determine the moment at which the group moves on. Otherwise he will be still explaining the complexities of a lathe while his party is walking through the milling section, and this will merely thicken the cloud of incomprehension that two-stage inaudibility has created. In fact, even considered in isolation, the problem of controlling movement makes it generally desirable and essential in difficult circumstances for the interpreter himself to conduct the tour having been suitably briefed and rehearsed, the host helping to shepherd the party and standing by to field questions.

8.4.2   *Factory and site tours*

The second factor that argues for handing the tour over to the interpreter is the difficulty of explaining things to him on the spot and the time taken to do so. Since he cannot count on being able to hear what is said, he must in any even have briefed himself meticulously and walked the course. And the periods in which explanations are being fed to the interpreter, which would represent acceptable lulls in the comfort of a lecture theatre or conference room, become intolerable and cause the party to lose interest and disperse. If the host as a matter of projecting his image wishes to seem to give the explanations to the interpreter, this can well happen provided the requisite motions are gone through as the party approaches each lot of exhibits so that the interpreter is ready to start as soon as they have grouped themselves round it.

In the case of assembly lines, transfer machines or indeed any large object all aspects of which cannot be seen from a single point and to which approach may be difficult, it is important to rehearse exactly where the interpreter will stand. If the host takes up his usual position for conducting parties in his own language, the interpreter may literally be left with nowhere to go. On one occasion, to point out the controls of a large machine from an area already occupied by the host and two operators, one of us inadvertently backed off onto a safety plate and thus brought to a halt the process whose control he was attempting to demonstrate.

But however much preparation can reduce the need for spoken communication between host and interpreter, the link between interpreter and visitors is indispensable. If the environment is at all noisy or if much movement in the open air or in large halls is involved, the interpreter must have a power loud-hailer. This enables hm to stand off a bit whilst keeping control and to forget about audibility and concentrate on what he is saying. Those models in which the main apparatus can be slung over a shoulder so that the horn faces backwards and the microphone can be detached are ideal, as the interpreter can then physically lead the party while remaining fully audible and, when appropriate, can turn and face them with the need only to swing the loud-hailer body round his hip.

Any demonstration or tour should as a rule be preceded by a briefing and followed up by a debriefing, both held under comfortable circumstances suitable for spoken communication and for the use of audiovisual aids. When working across a language barrier, the need for these sessions becomes even stronger, not least because the limited number of linguists available will probably mean that larger than normal groups have to be taken round. Again, if at least one of the interpreters is capable of conducting the tour itself, he should also be given the task of putting the briefing across direct and of in effect sharing out the questions that will be put at the debriefing. The ideal formula would be a speech of welcome by the host, of which the first sentence or two would be learned by heart in the visitors' language, and the rest consecutively interpreted; then the briefing and the tour itself, which the interpreter should do direct; and then the debriefing, which the interpreter can perhaps best coordinate but in which the hosts must play an increasing part, culminating in a farewell speech so that it is with their image in mind that the visitors depart.

8.4.3   Briefings, presentations, etc.

Short briefings such as might precede a works tour present no problem because they can be given in one chunk and in one voice without monotony setting in. But longer briefings of the kind mentioned in Section 8.3, or two to three hour presentations given in the foreign language, present special problems. The management of these will be discussed more fully in Part 2, but the language-technical aspects are formidable enough. There are two balances that have to be struck:

1   The balance between the need for the host team to present themselves and their image and the need to avoid tedium and loss of momentum by giving all the briefing in English and then interpreting it.
2   The balance between monotony from a single interpreter's voice, coupled with the problem of interpreter fatigue, and the cost and variation in quality that will result from using several interpreters.

When the briefing or presenting team is operating on its home ground or at an exhibition or some other neutral venue in its own country, neither of these should prove particularly difficult or expensive to achieve. But when Mohammed goes to the mountain, cost quite simply prohibits taking a full team of staff and two or three interpreters. The solution here lies in the use of audiovisual aids prepared in advance. Small 8-mm film projected onto a built-in editor-type screen can be synchronised with commentary tapes in a number of languages. Spoken items in the presentation can be pre-taped in the languages required and either played back direct with the interpreter pointing the visual aids or given by the specialist concerned, using a suitably cued tape as if it were a consecutive interpreter. These pre-recorded tapes will provide the necessary variety of voices, and if he has only to operate a tape recorder or cue and point visual aids for most of the time, one interpreter should be able to handle live the key sections of the presentation and subsequent discussion. The equipment needed for this — mini-projector, cassette recorder and portable overhead projector — will fit into one average-sized suitcase or round personal luggage in the boot of a car.

However, with this level of audiovisual support it will still be necessary to take at least three people, and the overall quality of presentation, although it may be more than acceptable, will inevitably be lower than it would be on home ground. It would clearly be uneconomic to make a 16-mm sound film, dubbed into each language required, of a complete presentation, because changes in product detail, state of the art and personalities would make it out of date before the first print was ready for use. But because it is reusable, requires no processing and can now be recorded within and played back onto a normal monitor from a suitcase-sized unit, videotape offers very interesting possibilities for any firm that wants to make presentations to its actual and potential export markets. Each presentation could then be tailor-made and recorded together with an equally tailor-made works tour by the same team of staff and interpreters that would give it at home. It can then be presented wherever required by one linguist executive or a senior executive accompanied by an interpreter with exactly the same standards of presentation as could be achieved at home. The only restriction would be the absence of specialists to field technical questions in the live discussion sessions at the end.

Stands at international exhibitions present a rather unusual combination of language problems. The display copy and any literature available for distribution must be beyond reproach in quality of language, even if for one good reason or another translation of some leaflets into some languages are made available only as inserts. The interpreting required is however less than might be supposed in quantity and very limited in scope. It would naturally be advisable to have a linguist executive, language consultant or fully qualified interpreter moving round with top management in case there is opportunity for any serious discussions either inside or outside the exhibition on sales or collaboration, but for manning the stand an average multilingual secretary backed by a team of students is more than adequate. This situation is acknowledged within the profession by the cut-rates recommended for exhibition work, but in fact their work is at once so tedious and so exhausting that fully fledged interpreters are unlikely to be prepared to do it even at full fees.

9
Telecommuni-
cations across a
language barrier

The progressive decline in importance and hence in efficiency in the national postal systems of even the most advanced countries, coupled with the general failure of third-world governments to shake their postal services out of the traditional rut, has made use of the post for international commerce a kind of nightmare game of roulette played on a crooked, ultra-slow-motion wheel. Similarly the telegraph and cable system is less and less used, and nothing has been done or is likely to be done to eliminate the great drawback of using it to cross a language barrier. If it is sent in the sender's language it will be garbled at the far end; if in the addressee's it will be distorted as it is typed into the system. Thus cables of any length or complexity represent a no-win situation.

The telephone, and more particularly telex, have become indispensable, and both can be used economically and effectively across a language barrier if certain ground rules are followed. From the language-technical point of view there are really no problems that have not been touched on in our discussions of written translation and interpreting, but some of these are compounded by the nature of the system.

Problems that frequently arise from the overloading of channels, time differences and technical shortcomings in radio links of the system are outside the concern of this book and, as far as telex is concerned, establishing communications is simply a matter of following the instructions in the international telex directory. The monitor/enquiries stations in London and other major centres are extremely helpful and will often pick up an incorrect coding and send back correcting instructions without even being asked. The only special need is to have a list of very simple introductory and sign-off courtesies in the required languages, literally just 'Good-morning' and 'Message received, thank you. Will deal with as soon as possible', on a millboard at the telex operator's hand. This gives an impression of international outlook, courtesy and efficiency at virtually no cost, and more practically a suitable sign-off will serve as a holding reply while the incoming message is being translated.

Establishing communication by telephone is rather more difficult and calls for an understanding of both the home country's links to the international network and the target country's internal system. In most developing countries knowledge under the latter head can be generalised as follows: Since no-one can ever find a directory less than 5 years old, it is impossible to obtain a number other than from a business card or a correspondent's letterhead; and even if you know the right number you are unlikely to reach the person you want within the scope of a working day. Both on links to the third world and on the more heavily overloaded channels in advanced countries, fixed-time personal calls booked the day before are by far the best means of getting through.

But while many telephone operators speak one or more foreign languages, relatively few telephonists on firm's switchboards have this facility. There is thus for the non-linguist a further hurdle between the number he wants and the person he actually wants to speak to, and there are two ways of overcoming this. One is to go through the operator and make the call a person-to-person one or, if this is not appropriate for some reason, simply to ask the operator's help in getting from the destination switchboard to the person you require. The second is either to give your own telephonist a list of suitable phrases, or, better, to enlist the help of a multilingual secretary in establishing the connection.

Quite often however the caller and his correspondent will not have a common language and, if the conversation is too complex for the in-house language resources at one end or the other to handle, an interpreter or language consultant will have to be used. This is the subject of the next section, but it is worth dealing with the purely communicatory aspect here.

It is quite unnecessary to go to the expense of calling the linguist in to the caller's offices. Either he can dial through or go through the operator on his own telephone, in the one case noting the number of units and in the other asking for 'AD&C' (Advise duration and cost) on the call; or his client's switchboard can itself book the call and accept the charge while arranging for the call to be put through to the interpreter's number. Conversely foreign callers can be asked to call the interpreter on his own number rather than his client.

9.2   Avoidance of direct interpreting

Even if the linguist is sitting in the caller's office — and this is just as true for an experienced conference interpreter as it is for a green multilingual secretary — direct consecutive interpreting should be avoided as far as possible. It is extremely difficult for the linguist, particularly if the line is a bad one, to stay tuned in to the correspondent and to talk face to face with the caller. The pauses are infuriating for the person at the far end and may easily lead to one of the switchboards or exchanges involved cutting the line; and it wastes a lot of money. The linguist here must act as an intermediary in the way touched on in Section 8.3.3, and only consult the caller when this is for some reason necessary. It is often better to take two bites at the cherry by making a call and arranging to call back later to allow time for consultation. This principle should be applied even in simple conversations over travel arrangements, meetings, etc. If the interpreter is to be asked to deal simultaneously with two communication situations, two completely different levels of volume and quality and two languages, the risk of error is extraordinarily high. The rather tense situation that is apt to develop on these occasions can be greatly eased by the use of the type of unit known as a conference telephone, as this keeps the caller quiet by giving him something to listen to and greatly reduces the difference in sound level, if not in quality, between telephone and direct voice.

Experience suggests that where the linguist is well known to and trusted by his client it is usually better for him to make the call from his own home or place of work and to brief his client at the next opportunity. Since he will then be able to make the call from home, the considerable constraint imposed by time differences leading to minimal overlap of working hours is eased if not avoided. Also he can ring correspondents at their homes in the evening.

Even when using expert linguists, however, clients should not ask too much of them over the telephone. International lines going through private switchboards often produce an extremely poor quality, and we are prepared to admit that one needs rather more information in the communications-technical sense to comprehend a foreign language than is the case with one's own. The effect that readers will have noticed in English of certain sounds being indistinguishable on a bad line is thus aggravated for, say, an Englishman talking in French. Another danger, against which there is absolutely no safeguard, is that the correspondent may fail to do or abide by what he has agreed, claim a misunderstanding and blame the linguist. It is therefore greatly preferable to use telex where any serious negotiations or decisions are involved.

The principal advantages of telex are related to the language barrier only to the extent that this barrier compounded with the limitations of postal and other telecommunication systems makes these other links less suitable for interlingual working. The main points are first that, if circumstances require, an almost telephone-like conversation is possible; and second that the sender's copy of the telex topped and tailed by the call-up and answer-back constitutes a legally valid proof of transmission and receipt — and, of course, of content.

The punched tape facility is gradually becoming more widely used. Although this may not be cost-effective for domestic working in the operator's own language where the bulk of messages are short and simple, it is indispensable for international and more especially for interlingual working. For those not familiar with it, this facility enables a message to be typed and punched onto a tape at leisure with the machine set to 'local' so that there is no transmission cost, and then sent compressed, that is at high speed, after communications have been established. Since the tape cutting process also provides a typed copy, the tape can be checked and corrected before being sent. By this means a message that would require at least 5 minutes direct transmission by a skilled operator working in her own language and almost any time one cares to name for a non-linguist working in a foreign language can be sent in 30 seconds or less.

However, cutting the tape from the manuscript in blocks or even a typescript can be a rather slow and painful process for an operator with no knowledge of the language. One should therefore either employ a telex operator with a smattering of the languages concerned or, better, train a multilingual secretary to operate the telex to the extent of cutting foreign-language tapes. Tempting as it might then be to use her as a combined interpreter-operator for a telex conversation, this would not be reasonable. Just as for telephone conversations, the rules here must be preliminary briefing and free play.

Telex messages used normally may often be of considerable length and complexity, and if they are to replace both letters and telephone conversations, this will be even more the case. It is therefore by no means certain, rather the contrary perhaps, that the smaller organisations will have a linguist on their staff capable of drafting or translating outgoing messages. Recourse must then be had to a professional linguist, but it is clearly impossible to call him in in person every time a telex is to be sent, and the delay of return of post may be too long. If both the linguist and a multilingual secretary at the client's firm have telephone-linked dictating machines (the Philips 84 and 99 and the Grundig Stenorette range among others are suitable for this) it becomes very quick and easy to dictate the draft or the brief over the telephone onto the linguist's tape and for him to dictate the reply onto the secretary's instrument. Theoretically she could then transcribe direct onto the telex, but it may often be better to knock out a rough typed draft first.

One point on which agreement between the linguist and his client is essential is the style to be adopted for telexes. Many organisations feel that, particularly if the tape facility is used to cut down transmission time and if the telex is being used to any significant extent in place of postal correspondence, telexes should be as nearly as possible in normal letter form as opposed to telegraphese. This is almost certainly true of person-to-person letters passing by telex between senior executives, but it does add considerably to the length of routine messages, and the linguist should if possible be given freedom to draft or, if not at least freedom to use telegraphic style in his translation. In other languages just as in English, this is an art that only comes with experience, and those who wish both their linguist staff and any outside linguists they may call in to produce good crisp telexes need to give them plenty of work on incoming telexes in the language concerned so that permissible abbreviations and omissions become instinctive.

Long experience of waiting for letters to foreign countries to reach their destination and produce a reaction and for the full replies to arrive, coupled with hours spent attempting to unscramble garbled cables and exhausting battles with inaudible and not always cooperative telephone and switchboard operators have convinced us that telex represents a real breakthrough in international and interlingual communication. The installation of one or at least the arrangement of access under a shared or club system is a must for any organisation that takes international dealings seriously.

Part 2
FOREIGN WORKING

10
In-house resources

One morning not many weeks before this chapter was written there appeared on the doorstep of one of us a junior executive from a nearby firm breathless with haste and excitedly waving a letter in Spanish. He was duly provided with an instant oral translation: 'In reply to your letter of... I am sending you under separate cover for your information a copy of the catalogue of last year's Madrid... show'. Quite apart from the minimum translation fee, this dramatic information had cost the firm 10 miles motoring and half an hour of executive time—but of course the letter could have contained something important and urgent.

Most small and many medium firms regard the setting up of even minimal in-house language resources as something quite beyond their scope and budget. The purpose of this chapter is to show that a quite useful facility can be established at a relatively small cost, which will almost certainly be offset in terms of direct cost by the saving of fees paid to extramural language resources and indirectly by speed of response. Any organisation that has three personal secretary or suitable junior executive posts can in fact cover two of the major languages in addition to English at the routine correspondence level. With experience and perhaps continuation training this same team should become able to tackle more specialised work within the firm's own field and probably simple *ad hoc* interpreting, the escorting of visitors and exhibition stand work.

However this rosy picture must be captioned with a serious word of warning. Both the employer and the linguists themselves must have a very clear understanding of the latter's limitations. Not only must there be a clear understanding in advance of the type of work that will and will not be done in-house. Relationships must be such that the linguists feel able without hesitation to say that they need expert help for such and such a piece of work, and the employer must accept this without demur. Otherwise very expensive disasters may result. For the smaller firm the ideal arrangement is probably a minimal in-house team of the kind described below combined with some kind of *contrat cadre* or retained arrangement with a language consultant. This will obviate the temptation to avoid the cost of seeking expert advice in marginal cases.

(The *contrat cadre,* or skeleton contract, is much more widely used on the Continent than in the UK. Essentially, like a retainer, it offers a guaranteed minimum payment over the period concerned in return for some advantage such as a guarantee of availability, reduced rates, etc.)

10.1   Definition of the requirement

The first step is a precise analysis and definition of the requirement, and if the firm does not have an executive who is also a high grade linguist outside advice may be of help here. The most important thing to get right from the start is the priority of languages to be covered. These will normally be French, German and/or Spanish, but if the client firm has an existing or foreseeable outlet in a minor language market, it may well be worth giving this language preference because of the difficulty of getting good translations in minor languages produced quickly from outside resources. A minor language requirement will usually involve finding a native-speaker; training in the language may be difficult to arrange and prohibitively costly.

It is then necessary to analyse the past foreign-language workload and extrapolate this forward to determine the level of language ability required. This analysis will also serve to support or revise subjective judgement on language priorities. It is sufficient to break the load down by languages under such broad heads as telexes and routine letters, telephone traffic and the handling of visitors, and specifications and quotations. Except in larger organisations with a language section of the kind discussed below and those well supplied with linguist or foreign executives and specialists, advanced work such as technical and legal documentation or promotional literature will have to be done out of house. This analysis will indicate the level and nature of qualifications required in each language, and of course in English for those of foreign mother-tongue.

The third need at this stage is to optimise the deployment of linguist staff so as to place them where they are needed. The production director will not be particularly pleased if the export sales staff are constantly dragging his secretary off to make telephone calls or do translations. However since the whole clue to the economic setting up of a language facility is that the linguists should be fully and constructively employed on other duties when their languages are not called for, and since the most obviously suitable posts may be filled by an excellent employee of long standing, some compromises over deployment will have to be made at least initially. Once the language needs and the nature and level of other duties with which language work is to be combined has been determined, a meaningful job specification can be prepared as a basis for recruitment.

10.2   The linguist executive and the time problem

An executive who is in the popular sense of the term 'bilingual' will be able to work in the foreign language as quickly and effectively as he does in his mother tongue, provided he does not at the same time have to keep an account of and report on what he is doing in English. But few people other than conference interpreters can really work as fast in another language as they can in their own, and the moment translation in either direction is required, translation being in any event a more laborious process than drafting, the executive acquires a specific language workload.

The extent of this load can perhaps best be illustrated by an example drawn from personal experience. One of us (RES) was at the time controlling three distinct but related fields of activity, of which one took up between 50 and 60 per cent of his time, the rest being equally divided between the other two. He agreed for particular reasons to take on the complete language work on a substantial project in the major field, and quickly found that this took up most of the other 40 per cent of his time so that he was forced to delegate almost entirely in the other fields, thus creating an overload one level down and a bottleneck in work moving upwards through him. Even after he recruited the best imaginable expert support, he was still left with a language load as such of some 10 to 15 per cent of capacity.

The moral is clear — senior executives and specialists should indeed be encouraged to make the fullest use of their languages, but it is quite uneconomic to impose a load of language work on them. They should be given as far as possible a free hand to work in the language without constantly coming back to English and linguist support in every way capable of carrying the entire language load as such with only minimal supervision. This executive time problem is one of the major factors that support the approach proposed in this chapter.

No matter whether her appointment goes by the name of office manageress, personal assistant or executive secretary, the multlingual secretary is without doubt the lynch-pin in the kind of in-house facility that a small or medium firm is likely to establish. There are three reasons for this. First her combination of skills enables her to take a document through all stages of its preparation, a letter for instance from the English in shorthand or on a tape to the foreign-language version ready for signature. Second, her position puts her in the swim so that she can sensibly read between the lines of the texts she is handling. Third, she can be fully employed on other duties when her language skills are not called for. On top of this a good senior secretary has the *savoir faire* to handle people and situations on her own initiative.

10.4   The staff linguist

By contrast staff linguist appointments as such have everything going against them. It must be said frankly that this is a rather unexciting dead-end appointment unlikely to attract people of calibre who are capable of doing the work well. A staff translator is likely to be set to work on his own in a dark corner so that he will probably be ill-informed on what is going on around him and consequently unable to appreciate nuances. The kind of work he may be given to occupy his spare time is scarcely calculated to improve his motivation. But above all he, like any other one person, will only be able to work from two or three languages into his mother tongue and therefore will not be in a position to cover the full span of basic needs adequately. Specialist language appointments only begin to pay off when the organisation and its language load is large enough to carry a team capable of dealing with all normal requirements.

10.5   Language panels and sections

It is fairly easy to calculate the annual level of extramural language costs at which payroll employment of a full time team to cover, say, English, French, German and Spanish or Russian both ways would begin to pay off. Using UK 1974 real-cost yardsticks and going rates one arrives at a figure of £20,000. This adds up to a formidable amount of language work; it could be seen as very roughly equivalent to the complete major language sales and technical documentation of three large and complex products or the language costs associated with export contracts to the tune of £3 million per year. Against the advantages of specialisation and speed of response must be offset the fact that minor language coverage will not be provided for and that at the salary levels envisaged the members of the team are unlikely to be capable of any but the simplest interpreting. In fact the largest international organisations find it more

economical to employ separate teams for interpreting and written
translation.

The fact that the largest engineering concerns do have substantial language sections indicates that there is a payoff if the requirement is substantial enough and the workload is reasonably steady. Once established such a section can undertake many tasks other than translation as such, for example the devilling of foreign scientific and engineering literature and of competitors' documentation and the maintenance of a technical library and information service. But outside the largest multinational firms and international organisations, the justification for a full-time language section would appear to lie in an extensive requirement for technical translation.

Where this does not exist the building up of a 'translation panel' is probably a more economical solution. Statistically a large organisation is likely to have on its payroll a fair number of middle-piece and junior employees with various combinations of language skills and subject knowledge. These individuals can be used on translation work either in office hours under their contract of employment or on a quasi-freelance basis. In either case the result will be a reasonable quality of translation with a good speed of response at a cost considerably lower than the use of extramural resources would incur. Because of the ease of consultation, this framework allows the use of people with a relatively low level of language skill for reasonably difficult work. Even the coordinator need not be full-time. Operation of the panel can be focussed either in the personnel department or in the functional department most concerned with foreign working. Where the conditions fit, the setting up of a language panel of this kind undoubtedly offers a highly favourable and economical solution for at least the bread-and-butter translation workload.

10.6   Structuring and development of an in-house language facility

The way in which internal language resources might be built up is probably best illustrated with the aid of a generalised case study.

Consider a small to medium conventionally structured engineering firm with a staff of some 25 and a labour force rather over the 100 mark producing a range of specialised trade products. Successful management has raised the export content of their turnover over two to three years from unit per cent to some figure in the upper twenties, and their exploration of export markets indicates that they are now at a point where they can push this up to 50 per cent or more of their existing production, probably combining this with an expansion of production capacity. Quite possibly their earlier export programme was largely confined to English-speaking markets and our entry into the EEC has made them think seriously for the first time about moving into foreign language markets and extending their supply base across the Channel.

Let us suppose that at this point they picked on a language

organisation that suited them and a consultancy relationship of some kind has now developed. Both the instincts of their top management and hopefully the advice of their language consultant now indicate that they should set up an in-house function to cover French and German, with the intention of extending this later to Spanish. Although they are well staffed, their new plans involve an expansion of the marketing department and the post of secretary to the marketing manager is currently vacant through normal wastage.

The first natural move would be to bring in an experienced multilingual secretary to fill that slot. Assuming that the previous occupant was a fully qualified personal secretary and paid accordingly, this is likely to involve a salary increase of around 12.5 per cent, amounting to a real cost increase of some 25 per cent — an expense which should be offset in the first year or so by saving in extramural language costs. The next step is rather more adventurous as it involves foreign recruitment. Although the priority language is French, the multilingual secretary's French is very much stronger than her German and it is decided to balance this by recruiting a German girl first.

Recruitment is discussed below, but there are many advantages in bringing over a girl newly out of training. Typically she would be aged about 22, having qualified for university entry and then opted to take a secretarial diploma. There is no suitable hole in the marketing side at the moment, but the company secretary, who has hitherto shared the managing director's secretary, has now been given the specific task of office management and requires an assistant for this task. This is a good position for a trainee as it will give her a knowledge of the working of a British firm. The salary level here will be about the same initially as that for an equivalent English person, although some help possibly including initial financial assistance may be required over housing.

Move three is to recruit a French girl. Unless someone already living locally can be found, and this is not improbable, it will again be wisest to bring in someone who has just completed training. By this time the marketing manager's secretary will have acquired considerable knowledge of the firm's workings, products and marketing plans and the workload on the marketing and sales side will have expanded. She is therefore ready for promotion to a junior executive appointment under the marketing manager, in fact to provide a firm base during his increasingly frequent absences. The French trainee can now be slotted into her former position to work under her supervision, again at a fairly modest initial salary level. These three steps have provided a language team capable of routine work in any direction between English, French and German, of handling visitors and of interpreting on exhibition stands (though almost certainly not of interpreting at formal meetings).

When the expansion programme allows, the team can be provided with a reserve and the language facility rounded off by the recruitment of a language graduate with a secretarial qualification as research assistant to the marketing and technical sides and in particular to set up and operate a technical library of the kind discussed in Chapter 17 below. If she leads in Spanish with French or German as her second language, this will extend facilities to cover all the major languages bar Russian. Although contrary to the code of the language profession, it is probably acceptable to use a fluent Spanish speaker of English mother tongue for routine work into Spanish, as it may prove extremely difficult to find a Spanish or South American girl who can make an all round contribution, even if the need should justify the effort of recruiting one and the cost of employing her.

This firm has now built up an in-house language team which will meet all its routine language needs and make a full contribution in other directions as well. No less important these people will be deeply involved in the firm's activities and will have a progressive career open to them in it. The only addition that might be worth considering as and when opportunity arose would be the employment of a French or German designer-draughtsman in the drawing office, one of whose functions would be to advise on the purely engineering aspects of translation and more particularly on the interpretation of foreign drawings and the production of drawings for foreign-language markets.

This fictitious but hopefully not unrealistic example serves to show the way in which a small firm with a very limited office staff can progressively build up the language facility it needs. There are really no principles here — it is simply a question of making a flexible plan and implementing it as opportunity arises.

10.7 Recruitment of multilingual secretaries

But 'first catch your hare'! The recruitment of good secretaries, let alone multilingual or foreign ones, is no easy problem.

To deal first with timings and cost, the time to recruit people fresh out of training is between Easter and Whitsun, i.e. just before the end of the academic year. Linguists who are at one remove from their training after two or three years abroad and therefore suitable for more senior posts are also likely to be on the move at about that time or a little later. For English people there is no particular reason why their language abilities should cause the cost of recruitment to deviate greatly from the norm for appointments at this level, namely 30-40 per cent of first year's salary. For French or German candidates, the cost can vary from near zero to 100 per cent of first year's salary depending on the method of recruitment, and if it tends towards the latter figure it will clearly be necessary to arrive at some understanding over minimum duration of employment.

The work will sometimes carry a high responsibility, and one is therefore looking for a rather special combination of qualities. The people who will flourish and develop in an appointment of this kind will require a high standard of general education and knowledge and familiarity with the countries to which they may be working. Since some element of technical translation is bound to be involved, ability to conceptualise and a rigorousness of approach, which indicates a readiness of research, are also important factors. Accuracy and a very high standard of presentation are more important than high typing speeds, but good shorthand in one language is valuable for minute-taking. In the case of English native-speakers the likely qualifications are:

London Lycée Bilingual Secretarial Diploma.

London Chamber of Commerce Private Secretary's Diploma, combined with at least Associate Membership of the Institute of Linguists (AIL) or preferably with a language degree perhaps backed by Membership of the Institute of Linguists (MIL).

RSA Bilingual Secretary's Diploma plus AIL or MIL.

A good A-level is the minimum useful qualification in a second or third foreign language.

It is sometimes said about recruitment that an employer who is forced to embark on a formal selection procedure has lost the first round. This is certainly the case here, for appointments of this kind fall between two stools. Relatively few employment agencies are fully geared to handle them, and they are rather small fry for the head hunters. A language consultant may be able to help, but here again the cost seen as a proportion of salary will be rather high if he has to go through the full cycle of advertising, interviewing and shortlisting. He is probably best seen in this context as an extension of the firm's own grapevine. The London Lycée and the Institute of Qualified Private Secretaries (based on the London Chamber of Commerce) maintain registers of alumnae, or in the latter case members, and the Institute of Linguists may occasionally be able to suggest somebody. Even though one is not seeking a person fresh from training, many Polytechnics and Colleges of Further Education do keep track of their products for a number of years and are also well in the local secretarial and language swim.

The qualifications to be expected from foreign candidates depend of course on the structure of their countries' educational and vocational training systems, but it is important not to be fobbed off through ignorance with qualifications which in fact indicate a relatively low standard of educational achievement. The following indications may be helpful:

AUSTRIA	'Europa Secretary' Diploma of European Secretarial Academy* (followed by 'Management Secretary Certificate' after post-experience course).
FRANCE	*Brevet de Technicien Supérieur de Secrétariat (BTS de Secrétariat).*
WEST GERMANY	BDS (*Bund Deutscher Sekretärinnen*). Letters after name when final exam has been passed.
HOLLAND	*Diploma Europees Secretaresse.**
SWEDEN	*Akademisk sekreterare* (graduate secretary, i.e. a first degree option). Certificates/diplomas of individual secretarial colleges.

*Also in Belgium, West Germany, France, Italy, Norway, Portugal, Sweden, Switzerland and Czechoslovakia.

Here it is even more important to proceed through personal contacts and recommendations, as the cost of interviewing will be high and a full assessment of personal qualities and motivation is particularly important. Foreign business contacts can be of great help here, as they are likely to know people who are keen to move to the UK or the States at least for a limited period. Except where considerations of confidentiality dictate otherwise, a middle- or long-term programme of exchanges between firms having a strong and ongoing link can provide a very happy solution indeed. A language consultant may well have a grape-vine that can be helpful and can also advise on where and how to advertise in the press. Recruitment of this kind is strictly speaking outside the scope of the Central Bureau for Educational Visits and Exchanges in London, but this organisation has exceptionally wide scope and might well be able to advise or even help actively in the recruitment of people coming fresh from graduation or training. Although it is again slightly outside their scope in some cases, the Central Clearing House of the University Appointments Board has international links and should certainly be able to help over graduate appointments. Similarly many polytechnics and colleges of further education have a link, often a very well established one, with sister institutions in the main European countries, and the possibility of working through a series of people who are personally acquainted makes this channel a particularly good one.

The problems of recruitment and the limited availability of suitable candidates combined with the need for gradual evolution of appropriate methods of working suggest that the building up within a small or small-medium company of the kind of language team with which this chapter has been mainly concerned should be planned well ahead and spread over two to three years. On the other hand the full team envisaged should be budgeted for as soon as the decision to form it is taken so that a good candidate who appears out of the blue can be quickly and smoothly absorbed.

10.8   The language aspects of recruitment

Apart from those that operate on the international scale, relatively few personnel departments and personnel selection consultancies have specialised language expertise in-house, with the result that the language aspects of an appointment may sometimes be brushed aside, and in particular a candidate's assurance of his skill in a language may be accepted. This is yet another point at which an experienced professional linguist who has managerial experience and knows the firm well can help.

Language skills do not fit very happily into the spectrum of qualifications and experience normally considered in the drafting of a job specification or a recruiting advertisement, particularly when they are not necessarily associated with knowledge of the target market. For example there is no particular reason why someone with good French should have knowledge of the French ex-colonies. Further, experience indicates that, even where the requirement for language and language-related ability and experience can be precisely defined, it is not particularly helpful to slot this into its logical place in the priority list of qualifications.

Typically one of more languages would fall into the category of 'strong advantages' or 'advantages', but for some reason which we have been unable to pinpoint candidates with the required language seldom seem to reach the shortlist stage when this approach is adopted. This appears to be an exclusively British or at least Anglo-Saxon phenomenon, perhaps associated to some extent with a historically insular and imperialistic outlook and undoubtedly with the low priority accorded to foreign languages in the British and North American educational systems and the lack of status of the language profession in these countries. Certainly many Britons and Americans of the generation now in power regard foreign languages as a dangerous mumbo-jumbo. One suspects that they may unconsciously see attainment in a foreign language and even more the readiness to use it as a sign of character weakness running counter to the concept of managerial virility.

Be all this at it may, it appears necessary in practice to take a clear-cut decision right at the start and put the language requirement either at the top of the list or at the bottom. In the former case foreign recruitment should be carefully considered and probably brought in right from the start rather than after an attempt to recruit within the employer's own country has failed. Here again extreme treatment is called for — one should either go to a personnel selection consultancy which genuinely operates at the international level or rely on contacts; working direct to a smaller, and therefore somewhat less expensive, personnel selection consultancy in the country of the language is unlikely to produce particularly good results because of the extreme difficulty of briefing the consultant adequately on the full spectrum of requirements and even more on the background.

A more expedient middle course is probably to seek advice from the London or central offices of the appropriate national Chamber of Commerce, and this is one factor that makes membership of these organisations well worth while for the serious exporter even if his primary interest lies in the third-world sectors of the given language market. Where language skill is an add-on, it is probably better, particularly in the case of younger candidates, to seek proven ability to learn languages rather than knowledge of the particular languages required. Fluency in any foreign language is probably the best *prima facie* indication of this.

We have found, together with our colleagues, that no reliance whatever can be placed on candidates' claims of fluency in a language, even when these are backed by qualifications and the standard required is a relatively low one. Language testing is therefore an essential part of the selection procedure, though for reasons of economy and ease of administration it could well be inserted at the short list stage.

Next to sex and driving, language ability is one of the most personally sensitive areas, and assessment of it must therefore be carefully planned and properly carried out if candidates are not to feel resentment. First, candidates must be warned in explicit terms right from the start that any language skill they claim will be tested and should be given some indication of the nature of the test.

Unless a particularly high and specialised standard of ability such as the drafting of contracts or patents is sought, in which case one is probably looking for a native-speaker or true bilingual anyway, assessments should be entirely oral. A valid test can then be dovetailed into the normal interviewing procedure and can indeed make an important contribution to other aspects such as the evaluation of personal qualities. It could be said that an oral language test introduces a high stress situation without the need to resort to the often rather fictitious techniques of stress interviewing. Written tests are of course valueless unless they are conducted under examination conditions, something that is neither easy to arrange nor psychologically sound in the case of mature candidates. The test panel should consist of one highly qualified native-speaker of each of the languages to be tested plus an experienced linguist of English mother tongue. Even where the standard sought is relatively low, testing by anyone other than a native speaker is neither fair nor seen to be fair. To keep the cost of this procedure within bounds, it is probably safe to confine assessment to one or at most two languages, preferably those which the candidate claims as his best. If he is really good in these, his claims to other language skills acquire a great deal more credibility.

With all due deference to common academic practice and that of the Institute of Linguists, we do not consider that the thirty minutes normally allotted to tests of this kind is sufficient to provide a valid assessment except at the lower levels. It is too long to serve as a preliminary filter if one is required, a simple conversational session of 10 to 15 minutes being fully adequate for this purpose. For shortlist testing on the other hand at least an hour and preferably one and a half hours should be allotted for this purpose, and it will thus be necessary in terms of economy to make the language test, as suggested above, also serve certain other purposes within the selection procedure as a whole. An experienced candidate who has been given the necessary indication of the nature of the test can easily pre-charge his batteries for a half hour run, and it is more satisfactory from every point of view to allow rather more time than to attempt to catch him out by springing a surprise on him.

An unstructured phase of 15 to 30 minutes should be included to give the candidate a chance to show his strengths and the panel one to probe his weaknesses, but for both practical and pscyhological reasons at least 50 per cent of the session should be fairly rigorously structured and situation-oriented. For reasons enlarged on below, the scenario should include brief social and everyday situations as well as professional ones such as selling or negotiating.

If there is a requirement to give talks or presentations in the language, the ability to do this must be assessed by means of a lecturette followed by a question-and-answer period. The institute of Linguist's technique of asking the candidate to prepare a number of topics and selecting one of them at the last moment is a particularly useful one for this purpose. Since at least occasional interpreting is almost certain to be required, this skill must also be tested, as fluent linguists are sometimes completely lacking in it.

Even where the selection procedure as a whole is highly formalised and quantified in an effort to attain objectivity, the language assessment panel should be left a relatively free hand. In the case of a language examination as such, syllabi and standards are laid down and both the general and specialised aspects of candidates' knowledge and ability are likely to lie within a reasonably predictable bracket. But in *ad hoc* language testing in the context of a managerial or specialist appointment, the candidates will bring the widest imaginable variation of level and breadth, and in any event the panel should be looking for potential as much as for actual attainment.

Under these circumstances it is difficult to do more than to reject the patently inadequate and to place the genuine starters in an order of merit. If the language test is also being used as it can and indeed should be to evaluate personal qualities, the panel might best be asked to produce two separate orders of merit (language and personal qualities) plus an overall order which need not necessarily be an 'average' of the two. If they can slot in some objective and well known standard at some point in the language list, so much the better. There are clearly strong arguments for the employer or consultant, even if he is not himself a linguist, to sit in on the language test as an observer. Oral language tests are however one of the most stressful assessment situations at the best of times, and big brother in the corner may produce a stress level which some otherwise good candidates may find intolerable.

10.8.3 *Acceptability to foreign clients*

Very often one of the most important factors in selection for an appointment requiring languages will be the candidate's likely acceptability to the foreign organisations with which he will deal. This is an added reason for including a suitable native-speaker in the language panel, as it is something on which no other national can possibly pass valid judgement. For the same reason no generalised comment can be offered on it. Oddly enough perhaps, this aspect becomes doubly important in the case of a foreign candidate and may well justify the inclusion of a language test in the assessment of him on the pretext of testing his English or his knowledge of a third language. As is emphasised elsewhere in this book, chauvinism is not an Anglo-Saxon prerogative, and an individual who has emigrated from his native country or chosen to become part of the brain or management drain is apt to be regarded with a certain coolness and suspicion when he returns to operate in his own country as the representative of a foreign organisation.

10.8.4   *The need for acclimatisation*

It was mentioned above that a language testing panel should look for potential as well as for current attainment. Unless a candidate is moving across from a similar appointment with another organisation operating in the same field, it is rather unlikely that his languages will be free of rust or that he will be equipped with the specialised vocabulary required. In this respect language skills can be seen as analogous to product knowledge — an analogy that is a useful one on many counts in considering the language aspects of an appointment. In planning the takeover or indoctrination period for someone coming into an appointment which calls for languages, time and possibly funds must be allowed for language refresher training. In fact the process is rather a broader one than this and might be described as acclimatisation, particularly as it can best be carried out in the target market or at least in a country of the language. As will be discussed more fully under the head of training, one foreign language tends to 'force others back', and it is not reasonable to expect anyone to become acclimatised in two languages at once or even in quick succession, any more than it would be to move a soldier from the UK to the Tropics and then on to the 'arctic region and expect to be able to send him back to the Tropics still acclimatised. However one cannot stretch this analogy too far because strangely enough it is easier to brush up two quite different languages, e.g. French and German, in quick succession than it is closely related ones such as French and Italian. It is therefore necessary to stagger the indoctrination process fairly widely in accordance with market priorities. Ideally, especially if the subject has not been using languages for some time, he should concentrate on his best language first to regain full confidence in his linguistic ability.

10.9   Training

Experience has made us less than sanguine about the value both of staff language-training programmes and of efforts to teach an individual executive or specialist a language which he is expected to require. In the isolated instances of success we have encountered — and these surprisingly enough have mainly been middle-aged men in top positions who have arranged for themselves ongoing individual tuition—it has usually come out that the person was fluent in the language, or at least had it to a good working level, at some earlier point in their life. It appears that only the very largest public and commercial organisations are in a position to take the measures needed to build up and sustain by training a high level of language resources within themselves, the most notable British example being perhaps the Armed Forces and the Diplomatic Service.

The first requirement is the ability to take key men off their normal work for periods equivalent to at least six weeks without disrupting the very work that gives rise to the language requirement. Second comes the ability to afford either the cost of establishing first rate training resources in-house or of buying them in. Third the ability to ensure by career planning both that an individual who has just learnt a language can be sent to the country of the language for a substantial period of reinforcement immediately he has finished his course, and that he can be deployed over the years where he can keep his language(s) refreshed and put them to good use. All this is quite simply a matter of scale, and any organisation large enough to mount and see through a useful language training programme will undoubtedly already have at its disposal the training expertise needed to plan it. Small and medium organisations, and in particular commercial ones that carry—or should carry—little fat, are likely simply to waste time and money to no good purpose if they attempt to undertake planned language training. They will amost certainly do better to limit their in-house resources to what they can obtain by recruitment, mainly at secretarial level, and to fall back on extramural help when these resources are inadequate.

Their only real alternative is to send individuals who need a certain language for a specific purpose to commercial language colleges. At present universities, polytechnics and colleges of further education are not geared to running the type of intensive language course commerce and industry requires, although they in fact almost certainly possess the expertise, the physical resources and the teaching material to do so.

It is no criticism of the commercial language colleges to stress therefore that intensive language training is expensive, and doubly so in direct and indirect terms because it is available only in major centres; and that, while these colleges provide a tailor-made and highly skilled service, the pyramid representing the level of instruction is a rather squat, if not a truncated one, so that they may have problems in providing advanced instruction related to specialised fields.

Some of these colleges are now offering three types of course—the saturation course conducted in the country of the language, the intensive course run in the UK (both full time and lasting four to six weeks) and what one has named the 'executive course' consisting of up to six one-week modules of intensive instruction which can be spread over say three months. This last and comparatively recent option overcomes many of the known drawbacks of uninterrupted intensive instruction such as continuous non-availability, exhaustion and difficulty in retaining the language. Expert preselection by their organisations of candidates for these courses would undoubtedly save much wasted time, money and sweat, and generally speaking this form of instruction is best suited to people of 35 or less. But the prerequisite to real success and retention of the language learnt is undoubtedly a period of weeks and preferably months spent in the country of the language and away from English-speaking colleagues and friends *immediately after the end of the course.*

10.10   Extramural resources and their use

Both professional linguists and users of them should perhaps realise that in nearly every case the familiar term 'translation agency' is a misnomer. For translation bureaux, as they should perhaps be known, do not represent the linguists on their books in the way that an author's or actor's agent looks after his interest, nor do they act towards the client in any capacity beyond that of informed intermediary.

While the better bureaux do in fact go to great lengths both to look after valued linguists and to be active in their clients' interests, the commissioning of a translation through a bureau essentially creates a triangular situation instead of a bilateral one. Thus even if it accepts a centralised responsibility for 'revision' of the translation or for certain categories of typing, or even carries the ultimate legal responsibility for accuracy of the translation, the bureau will be concerned to maximise profit from the mark-up it can apply by minimising its own effort.

Language bureaux really fall into three categories. There are the high-grade specialised bureaux working in such fields for instance as the medical and para-medical, which in the nature of things really merit the title of agencies, or perhaps better of consultancies, in that their clients and their linguists alike are few and therefore precious and satisfaction of linguist and client is essential to their continued working. Then there are bureaux run by fully qualified linguists. These will tend to use linguists with at least a middling qualification and will generally aim at a fairly high standard of work. They are likely to have the tacit or formal approval of the language profession's national organisation, and the advantage they can offer is contacts with translators covering a large range of unusual combinations of language and field. These first two categories should be covered by indemnity insurance against professional negligence and perhaps libel, and the client who asks whether they have such insurance will at once gain respect in their eyes, ensure that his interests are covered and check on their status.

Unfortunately neither the Institute of Linguists nor, as far as we know, their opposite number in any other country has at the moment an exclusive charter. In other words there is nothing to prevent any unqualified individual or group setting up shop as a translation or interpreting bureau. They may offer splendid-sounding gimmicks of improved service and remarkably low rates, but the user who turns to them is doubly at their mercy. He has no check whatever on the standard of the work they produce, and if a situation arises in which he can sue them for negligence, their own resources will probably prove negligible and there will be no insurance to back them. The manager who turns to such an organisation may fairly be said to deserve what he gets, but unfortunately there are also a number of 'grey' organisations which cover low standards with a veneer of respectability.

The reader will now perhaps understand why, despite the excellence of many bureaux, a considerable prejudice against them exists, being most marked in fact in West Germany. The advantages of the freelance from the client's point of view are clear enough to see. He knows or can easily get to know the person with whom he is working; the number of links in the chain of communication is reduced by at least one — and by two if the freelance has access to specialists within his client's organisation — and a higher standard of work at lower cost is likely to result.

On the other hand a freelance will have only a limited capacity and may be fully booked or on holiday when needed, he will cover only a limited number of combinations of language and subject and is unlikely to work both ways between more than two languages if at all; and there is no reason why he should accept any responsibility for arranging for someone else to do work he cannot himself accept. The organisation that sponsors a large number of translations or has frequent call on interpreters therefore needs to establish its own freelance panel, and this is inconvenient and expensive as some payroll employees then have to spend time coordinating this panel and assigning work. There is clearly scope for one organisation that would offer most of the advantages of bureaux and individual freelances without the drawbacks of either, and might achieve greater flexibility of working into the bargain.

The provision of high-grade language services by consultancies is nothing new. Law and accountancy firms, management consultancies and PR and advertising consultancies which work on an international level have done so since their inception. However the concept of a consultancy operation centring on foreign-language working is one that is only just beginning to take root, perhaps as a result of increased awareness of the problems which form the subject of this book. There is in fact little doubt that many language problems call for a consultancy rather than an agency or simple executive approach, but the justification for the concept of language consultancy is perhaps twofold. The service so created is adapted to the needs of industry and commerce as opposed to having grown out of the imposed structure of the language profession. The language consultant will see and examine language and language-related problems as a whole and respond to them with the advice or executive work and the method of working that in his view best meets the total situation.

Where a formally established language section exists, its head will be the language adviser to management and will thus be responsible for the arrangement of extramural support when this is required. But in other organisations too management will require a single individual to whom it can turn when faced with a task beyond the capacity of its in-house resources; and direct contact is important here. Where there is a substantial and reasonably steady load of translation, say to the tune of

£5000 a year or more, the best solution will probably be to work to a nominated individual in a carefully selected major translation and interpreting bureau. This arrangement is however only likely to work well where the bureau's profit from the actual assignments passed to it is such that time spent and costs incurred in giving advice will not make a significant dent in this.

The best balance between in-house resources and the use of extramural support has to be assessed on the merits of the case, and will in fact usually be established by a natural process of give and take as the in-house facility develops. But management should realize that no organisation or individual is going to feel particularly happy or committed to working with them if he or it is simply left to field the balls that beat the bat and to give free advice to the payroll linguists in the meanwhile. A small or medium firm intending to set up its own language facility will therefore probably do best to retain at an early stage either a language consultant as such or an experienced freelance translator and/or interpreter capable of acting as one. He can then advise on and assist with the build-up and in doing so establish a mutually acceptable relationship.

Checklists for defining the requirements for in-house language resources and for planning extramural support are given in Appendices 2 and 3.

11

The approach to foreign working

All too often a promising export project founders, or at least loses most of its profitability, because of hidden passive resistance within the exporting firm and/or of shaky personal relations between exporter and customer. Much of the content of this chapter is subjective and some perhaps tendentious, but we venture to makes these observations, first, because many of the problems arise from things of which someone who did not know the country and its language and people well would be unaware and, second, because weaknesses of these kinds are often more easily seen by someone standing on the touchline than by those involved in the heat of play. Moreover they may pass unconsidered because they are not easy to discuss within the hierarchical constraints of an organisation. Let us begin however, with two basic ground rules that are indisputable although frequently overlooked.

11.1   Ground rules

11.1.1   Security

However strong the evidence to the contrary may be, one must never assume that the opposition cannot understand English. It is surprising how often this self-evident principle is ignored in the commercial setting.

Asides within a delegation can, if deprecatory, wreck the entire relationship, and even if relevant and justified may expose internal weaknesses or disclose a complete negotiating hand.

One of us recalls a major contract in which negotiations had been particularly long drawn-out and difficult, not least because of the refusal of the entire opposition team to speak or even acknowledge one single word of English, even in non-negotiating settings such as booking into hotels. Throughout all this certain members of the exporter's team had been in the habit of discussing even prices or points of friction between sub-contractors quite openly in front of their customer. There were thus some very red faces when, over dinner one night, the leader of the customer's delegation, who had himself caused most of the problems, suddenly started holding forth in near-perfect English on the intricacies of some of the severe and very severe climbs in the Cairngorms.

Even if the opposition cannot hear or understand asides, they may gain a great deal of valuable information from the secondary signals, both audio and visual, discussed in earlier chapters. A facial expression of relief or dissatisfaction may give away the very weakness that one is most concerned to conceal. If negotiations in a commercial setting should seldom come to resemble a game of poker, they are perhaps not unlike bridge, where both etiquette and success call for a self-imposed discipline of discretion among players and kibitzers alike.

Another source of unintentional disclosure often overlooked lies in notes made by or passed between members of a delegation during a session and subsequently left even for a short time, such as during a coffee break, on the table. The same risk exists with documents for internal use only, such as negotiating briefs, and also with copies annotated with, say, the negotiating price range for a series of items even where unannotated copies have been passed to the customer. Unfortunately the need for security no longer ends with the observation of these simple but often neglected rules. The use of bugging, the creation of blackmail situations and other forms of intelligence gathering within the countries of the Soviet bloc has become a kind of world-wide black joke, but it is probably less widely realised that even the most reputable firms in the most respectable West European countries may also make discreet use of these techniques. And there is little reason to suppose that the third world is not equally adept in them.

Lest readers should regard this as a wild statement, one of us has direct experience of two such incidents. In one case, when he was invited to visit a certain organisation accompanied by his wife, they were able by a ploy to obtain virtually certain indication that their luxurious suite in the organisation's country club was bugged. The other was a rather clumsy and obvious night-club hostess situation.

Obviously any employee will out of normal loyalty to his firm pass on any information he gleans from a party with whom they are in negotiation, but the story does not end there. Guides, taxi-drivers (where the taxi is summoned by the firm) and even hotel staff may be earning something on the side as 'agents'. Where one is dealing with national or nationalised companies, as is of course the case in the Warsaw Pact countries and in much of the third world, governmental resources may be deployed for this purpose if the contract is a big one, and the risk is correspondingly higher.

Thus anyone going to represent a firm in export negotiations should be briefed on security drills. As well as the avoidance of asides and the leaving about of notes or papers, these should include the placing of all papers in a locked briefcase whenever they are left. It should also cover conduct at the negotiating table and the extremely careful choice of environment for sensitive internal discussions; a stroll in the open or a public room in a different hotel are the safest. There is always a high risk of indiscretion immediately after a meeting has broken up, when the visitors are leaving perhaps in a lift and then in a company car. However strongly one feels the need to let fly, one must postpone this satisfaction for a later and safer occasion.

All these things are second nature to an experienced negotiator, and this type of security is generally covered in the syllabus of some management and sales training courses. And they would probably appear as simple common sense to anyone operating in his own language in a familiar environment. But a senior executive of a small firm or a junior specialist in a large one sallying forth for the first time may easily overlook them unless he follows a set drill. Until one is used to it, the strain of being in an unfamiliar and exotic environment and of having to work across a language barrier is sufficient to produce a psychological reaction which on the one hand makes one overlook points which would otherwise come naturally and on the other leads one to act indiscreetly within the protective micro-environment of one's own delegation.

11.1.2 The avoidance of bluff

There is an element of bluff in every negotiating situation, but this is a weapon that executives and salesmen quickly learn to use with extreme restraint when operating within their own country because of the virtual certainty of the bluff being sooner or later called. It would seem however that these same people sometimes feel free to make quite outrageous offers and promises when operating in an export market, or to gloss over such matters as the lack of approval of the product, its suitability for the proposed conditions of use or the presence of foreign components which will create import difficulties at the delivery stage.

We shall discuss below both the importance of establishing mutual confidence and, in the case of Britain at least, the need to avoid overstretching a credibility which has worn dangerously thin. One must suppose therefore that the bluffs one hears used in efforts to close an export deal are made on the assumption that the customer will not find out or at least will not find until the contract has been fulfilled and payment made.

The damaging effects of a bluff that come home to roost are threefold: even if trivial it will destroy confidence and if more serious it will not only negate the possibility of further deals between the same firms but will indirectly damage the country's export programme as a whole. Perhaps bluffers feel that, if their bluff is called, they can duck by blaming it on the interpreter or brush it aside among the minor temporary misunderstandings that are inevitable in complex multilingual negotiations. This attitude implies the dangerous assumption that the opposition cannot understand English.

11.2 Motes and beams

Britons of the generation currently in power can recall the days when Great Britain was a leading, if not the leading power in the geopolitical and economic fields and still had a colonial empire. Attitudes change hard, and however well concealed the tendency to dislike and even despise all foreigners, let alone the peoples of British and other ex-colonies, still often shows through or at least governs an individual's actions. It is one that can bring disaster to potentially successful export contracts: on the one hand by hampering the establishment of a sound working relationship and by causing practical difficulties in execution; and on the other, less obviously, by causing procrastination and mishandling within the exporting firm itself.

Taking the external aspect first, its most immediately dangerous symptom is an obstinate determination to ignore, skate round or even ride roughshod over the importing country's statutory regulations. Reluctant as one might be to admit it to the Civil Service, the United Kingdom is in fact far less tightly bound in red tape than most other countries and her junior officials on the spot have much greater powers of discretion than their foreign counterparts. This is a fact we have begun to learn fast since our entry into the EEC. It is something we appear to take as read and accept in dealing with Communist countries, where only one official import channel exists in a given field and breaking the rules involves a real and known threat to personal liberty, but to resent elsewhere, whether it be Western Europe, North America or the third world. Oddly enough perhaps it is France and her former colonies that pose the most severe problem here, especially where the latter have combined French bureaucracy with a Marxist or indigenous brand of socialism. It is true that customs, exchange control and technical approval procedures can cause real and severe difficulties in maintaining the profitability of an export operation and indeed in executing it at all, but one only has to put oneself in the other man's shoes and consider an illegal or dubious import into this country to realise the binding necessity of meeting these requirements. This is why so much stress is placed in later chapters on the broad subject of market intelligence. Problems that are known in advance can be overcome and allowed for in timings and costings; it is ignorance of regulations as well as a chauvinistic outlook that often creates a difficult if not unresolvable situation.

The second external effect, and this makes itself evident particularly in dealings with the third world, is a failure to credit the customer himself or any government agencies that may be involved with normal intelligence and *savoir faire*.

One reason for the tendency to bluff discussed above is undoubtedly the assumption that the customer has not done or will not do his homework on the exporting firm. This may have been true in the past, but now his awareness of the need and his resources and channels for meeting it are as good as our own, if not better. Those experienced in dealing with the third world agree that its entrepreneurs and senior managers are at least as shrewd and competent as those of Western Europe and often turn out to be men of the highest intelligence, culture and all-round ability. Even the most superficial study of history will give no reason to suppose that Europe and the English speaking world have any monopoly of entrepreneurial talent. Third world technologists may be extremely thin on the ground, but they will often have been trained at leading European and United States institutions, and the very necessity of looking to the world market for their needs gives them a broader outlook and experience than some of their counterparts in major manufacturing countries possess.

Many developing countries show, and will continue for a generation or two to show a very marked falling off of ability from the middle management and junior specialist grades down to the shop floor and the individual operator. But this is a problem of which their governments and management, and even the individuals themselves, are acutely aware and to which exporters must react positively and helpfully if they are to develop a healthy and ongoing commercial relationship. Another factor which is easily forgotten here is that most foreigners are at heart at least as chauvinistic as we are. The need for a major effort to overcome this psychological barrier which is superimposed on all the practical ones is discussed more fully below.

But these motes in the other's eye are something that people in the front line of exporting and international dealing, backed up with good briefing and language resources, will quickly see and remove or come to terms with. No less serious and far more insidious is the beam that chauvinistic attitudes often create within the exporting firm. The perturbations and relative decline of the British economy over the last 25 years have placed and continue to place great psychological pressures on manufacturers to export regardless of the profitability of export operations, the suitability of the product for export markets or indeed the wish of boards and top management to enter these markets. Quite apart from direct fiscal and other financial incentives, it has become part of the national ethic to regard firms that achieve visible or invisible exports as 'goodies', while the rest are merely features in the unacceptable face of capitalism. And owing partly to a deliberately induced misunderstanding of the meaning of the Common Market in export terms, Britain's entry into the EEC has further stepped up this psychological pressure. Many well-intentioned small firms took wing or wheel to the Six under the impression that an easy export market was about to open its doors to them and came back with a more or less bloody nose. In fact of course, apart from tariff advantages that do not as yet and probably will not play a dominating part in the competitiveness of overall prices, the EEC represents a very tight market. If it eventually develops along the lines intended, the EEC will in all senses represent a manifold expansion of the home market. Meanwhile it offers little more to manufacturers than a broadening of the economic base.

The result of these pressures has been to lead many medium and small firms to plunge into the export market when they were ill-prepared to do so and when many members of their boards and executive and specialist cadres had no desire to do so, some even being deeply opposed to it. This passive resistance, conscious or otherwise, leads to procrastination and to the kind of departmentalism that the 'marketing approach' seeks to overcome. One comic but indicative symptom of this attitude is the tendency of incoming foreign-language correspondence, and more particularly of enquiries and formal requests for tender, to find their way to the bottom of the pending tray or even to some more secure hiding place.

One March our organisation was asked for an 'urgent' translation of a full request for tender from South America dated the previous October and marked as received in early November.

Very frequently enquiries with a closure date fail to reach the department which must act on them until that date is either past or too imminent to be met. More seriously perhaps, when for some reason a major project has to be referred back to the Board for successive decisions within a phased programme, there is a tendency for the Board to approve the earlier phases — presumably on the grounds that 'they can't do much harm anyway' — and then to negative or postpone decision on the crunch phase at which substantial funds and resources have to be committed. This not only puts the export side in an impossible position, because commitment to the later stages was implicit in the earlier, and prejudices the project in question, but also spoils any other prospects there may be in the same market.

It seems however to be on the engineering side that the strongest passive resistance, almost certainly unconscious, occurs. We often talk of a project as somebody's 'baby' without appreciating the extreme appropriateness of this expression. In small technical departments responsible for design, development, testing and preparation for production — and often for the product research that precedes these too — one team or even one individual may have carried the project not just for months but for years. There is a deep-seated natural reluctance to put their brainchild at the mercies of the production department or to expose it to the horny hands of home-market users, let alone to allow it to be subjected to the disrespectful gaze and strange imprecations of foreigners. The accounting and legal side too, who can deal with home-market problems with a flick of the calculator or a stroke of the pen, may be hesitant to launch forth into the unknown waters of faraway markets. In a conventionally structured organisation, even a fairly small one, this resistance can produce a cumulative inertia which will completely cripple the efforts of the export sales team.

Thus, quite apart from the obvious steps of making a thorough assessment of the market and ensuring that linguist executives and specialists and other in-house language resources are correctly deployed, preparation for a serious invasion of an export market calls for critical examination of organisation and personalities as well as of the existing order book and the capacity available to meet it. For firms that have not already formally or otherwise adopted the 'marketing approach', in the Harvard sense of that term, this preparation offers an excellent opportunity to apply it, at least to the extent of deliberately setting up a team of well qualified and motivated individuals both to support the export sales team proper and to participate in negotiations when their specialities are affected.

11.3 Mutual confidence and interest

The Coca-Cola steam-roller and many others of its kind have successfully imaged their way across the world. Since the marketing of a consumer product generally depends on the creation of a new demand rather than the meeting of an existing need, the basic promotional techniques can be applied to any market given only that the level of the target market's economy is high enough to make mass sales possible. To use the hackneyed example, one could sell refrigerators to Eskimos by demonstrating to them that keeping immediate supplies of seal meat and fish in the refrigerator rather than under the ice made these more palatable or quicker to cook. Since there would be no electricity, one could sell them bottled gas too and then open their eyes to the whole range of appliances that could be run from it. However, there are various reasons why the large scale promotion of consumer goods into foreign markets, while undoubtedly profitable to the company concerned, may not make any particular impression in terms of export/import balance. First the promotion operation must be launched and developed within the target country, and this will involve a massive outlay of funds and quite possibly the overheads of setting up a subsidiary (all equivalent to an invisible import). Then the need for a rapidly increasing and assured supply of the product at a competitive price, quite apart from political considerations that may arise in developing countries, will sooner rather than later dictate full or partial production in the target country. Consumer durables, which also call for massive promotions and the hard sell, are a very different story, but the fact remains that if an advanced country is to have a sustained and successful visible export programme, it is capital goods and specialised trade products that will be its backbone.

The penetration of new export markets with such products calls for a considerably less expensive but much more subtle approach. Although manufacturers of them do advertise, often fairly expensively, in the appropriate technical periodicals, we have yet to find one who believes that advertising of itself does much more than draw attention to the existence of their product and from time to time gain them an editorial mention or even a feature article, except of course in the case where a new product fills a glaring market gap.

True, the closing of a sale in these fields may be just as competitive an affair as it is on the consumer side, if not more so. However the coming into being of a sale situation occurs on the one hand because of the identification of a known and unsatisfied need and on the other of spreading the word, intentionally or otherwise, by satisfied customers. In other words sales come from the existence of a common interest and the establishment of mutual confidence, and sales effort as such consists mainly in ensuring excellent communications with actual and potential customers and seeing to it that they stay satisfied.

This creates enormous difficulties in entering new markets with capital goods and trade products, usually in the face of world wide competition and a language barrier. An exporter can easily be caught out by assuming that, once he shows his face, things will run as sweetly for him there as they do in his established markets. However, unless his firm or his product is one of genuinely worldwide repute this can scarcely be the case. This kind of penetration calls for forward planning and a preparatory phase lasting perhaps even two or three years. The first requirement is to produce good, clear up-to-date literature in the appropriate languages, with some form of supplementary documentation slanting it towards the immediate area of interest within each language market, e.g. slanting the German edition towards Czechoslovakia. This aspect is discussed in a later chapter. Good and appropriate literature serves not only as a means of communication but as an earnest of serious intent.

Armed with this and suitable hardware exhibits or models and visual aids, an exporter can still exhibit at suitable specialised or regional trade fairs at quite modest expense. He will be fortunate if this leads directly to sales on any substantial scale, but it will bring him into contact in the atmosphere of bonhomie that prevails on such occasions both with potential customers, giving him the feel of the market, and even more important with his native competitors, giving him an indication of possible ways into it.

Simultaneously, using either his own resources or possibly a consultant in the target country, he should carry out a programme of market and product research, not of the broad-ranging statistical kind familiar in the consumer field, but relating the individual product in a very specific manner with competing indigenous products and imports from other sources, and identifying and accurately assessing possible outlets and end users. His name will now be getting known in the new market, and it is at this stage that spin-off from his repute in his established markets will begin to come into play. Even if sales as such remain minimal, he may be able to achieve some return while gaining time and information by limited collaboration, based upon common interest, with an indigenous producer. In this way, before needing to enter into any really expensive or irrevocable commitments, he can arrive at an optimised penetration plan along one of the lines discussed in Chapter 16; or he can reach a well-founded and not unduly costly decision not to enter the market.

While it will serve many other useful purposes, the main aims of a preparatory phase of this kind are the identification of common interests and the establishment of the potential collaborator's or customer's confidence in the exporter. However this is only one side of the coin. He next needs to convince those with whom he has identified a common interest that this interest in fact exists and to develop truly mutual confidence with those with whom he hopes to deal. The techniques for achieving these ends must be suited to the case, but such things as limited cross-sales or even buying in to meet his own shortfalls, technical level discussions, exchange visits and the leakage now and then of interesting but not too dangerous titbits of information are all likely to further this Grooming phase. And it goes without saying that the fostering of really sound personal relationships is the best aid of all.

In sum the kind of preliminaries that can safely be taken as read by a sound manufacturer with a good product operating in a market in which he is established require conscious and intensive effort in penetrating a new one. Perhaps the most important thing here, particularly *vis-à-vis* the third world, is to avoid any suggestion of patronising or exploitation. Some countries with a colonial past are so sensitive that even an unasked for explanation of a product or process, offered with the friendliest of intentions, may be taken amiss.

11.4   First choose your image

A friend of one of us, who might be described in the nicest possible way as the model of an English gentleman, had exceptional and prolonged success in dealings with the States. In passing one might mention that, arriving at JFK Airport fresh from London and still in bowler hat, dark suit, stiff collar and umbrella, he was greeted by a cab driver with the remark: 'Gee, are you for real?' His technique for communicating with his American opposite numbers was to shout at them in an 'American' accent by Damon Runyon out of a thirties B film. Despite this, all he met from highest to lowest ate out of his hand. Consciously or otherwise he had selected for himself and built up a highly successful image.

Even for someone who speaks the language fluently and knows the country well, it is never easy to decide just how to present oneself in the context of an actual or potential negotiating situation. One mistake certainly to be avoided is to be more, shall we say, Roman than the Romans. In the USSR where the diversity of peoples, dialects and accents make it very difficult to tell at a glance whether or not someone is a Soviet national, they often prefer to deal as far as practicable with people who do not speak Russian. And for someone who is cut off by a language barrier, appearance and behaviour become doubly important because they indicate where he stands within the rather narrow spectrum of disrespect (of which Americans are so often accused), serious but detached respect, and flattery by imitation (to which the Germans are sometimes prone). Difficult as many find him to deal with, the established French professional or businessman, the *homme sérieux,* rigorously selected and expensively schooled for the purpose, perhaps presents a model in this respect. Since the best advice can only be to behave exactly as one would on more formal occasions in one's own business, professional and social environments, this discussion would be pointless but for one reason. This is that the psychological pressures on exporters, amplified within their own organisations, complete or partial ignorance of the language and customs and a strange environment combine to launch such an attack on one's self-confidence that one is apt to over-react in some direction or other. It requires a conscious effort just to be oneself.

Talking still in terms of the establishment of mutual confidence rather than of high-pressure selling, it is probably fair to say that, regardless of his standing and his qualifications in all other respects, a person should not lead in dealings with a foreign country unless his genuine feelings towards it are at least no more adverse than open-mindedness tinged with respect. For example a man embittered against one of our ex-enemies by some particularly cruel blow struck him in World War II should probably not be sent to do business with that country even if he happens to speak the language and superficially accepts the situation. He may react unpredictably, even if only for an instant or a syllable, in the heat of negotiations. It is also probably unacceptable to communicate entirely, even at the social level, through an interpreter, because one cannot then tell what image of oneself is being presented verbally. It is seldom practicable and not necessarily even desirable for an executive or specialist to make an enormous effort to learn a language to the level at which he can do business; unless he happens to be really fluent, and sometimes even then (see Chapter 8) it is better to work through an interpreter or intermediary. But knowledge of the language to a very basic conversational level, which is not particularly difficult or time-consuming even for older men to acquire, combined with a readiness to make a fool of oneself trying to use it, makes a splendid ice-breaker, which will often evoke a reciprocal effort from the other side. Similarly, if one is the host, just two sentences learnt by heart and reeled off as a welcome will always help to break the ice. (One thinks here of Charles Morgan's introduction to his 1936 lecture at the Sorbonne on creative imagination: '*Ne craignez pas que je vous inflige longtemps le tourment de m'entendre parler francais. Mais permettez-moi d'user, d'abuser peut-être, votre beau langage pour vous dire quelques mots en guise de préambule...*) And it is surprising how well two people can communicate at the social level each using his own language and having a limited understanding of the other.

In transactions between complex organisations, particularly where a language barrier is involved, it is most important that there should be created on each side a figurehead who symbolises one party for the other, and that these individuals should make a firm effort to cement their relationships to the point where they are recognised as what one might call biased arbitrators for the resolution of difficulties and misunderstandings.

11.5   Manners and customs

A German friend once said jokingly to one of us who had arrived at some function with British rather than German punctuality: 'You know you English do have incredibly bad manners. I suppose it is the Hanoverian influence. Certainly Hanover is the worst-mannered town in Germany; why if two friends are walking on opposite sides of the street and see each other they just wave their hands, but in any civilised place they both stop and the younger one crosses the street and removes his hat to pass the time of day with his senior.' While we might feel that good manners turned on rather different considerations, it is a fact that even when we think we are being formal we are far less so than our counterparts in other countries. This is true even of the States and the Scandinavian countries, as well of course as of the former Dominions, and there is no doubt that British people abroad, whether on business or on pleasure, frequently give deep and lasting offence by ignorance of a custom or lack of punctiliousness just when they think they are being most forthcoming. Once again, there is no need to overdo things in an attempt to flatter; unless one has lived long enough in a country for customs such as bowing and kissing hands to become natural, a vague gesture indicating one's knowledge of the custom is more than enough. Nor is it possible to set out here all the various come-ons, put-offs and mutual gestures practised in various parts of the world. Anyone going to a country for the first time and wishing to make a good impression can easily brief himself on the do's and don'ts. But it may be worth mentioning a few points as an illustration of the scope of the problem.

11.5.1 Social contacts

One custom that is a must in most parts of the world and is important because it goes with first and last impressions is handshakes. The custom is gradually catching on in business and professional circles in the UK, but elsewhere it is established and universal — 'NATO' and 'EEC' wrist are well-known conditions in many British circles. The handshake at the beginning and end of the working day is indispensale, as it is at the beginning and end of any social function; and whenever anyone shows any sign of shaking hands in between whiles, it is as well to follow his gesture up.

It is also, even more so than here, essential to remember people's names, something that is never easy, doubly difficult in a language one does not speak and trebly so in many parts of the third world. Once again this is worth a planned conscious effort. The English-speaking world, probably following a custom initiated in the British and American armed forces during the war, uses first names right from first acquaintance, so much so that the use of 'Mr. Smith' is more than a mild put-off and addressing someone by the bare surname is almost unknown. One aspect of the greater formality that prevails outside the English-speaking world is the much wider use of titles and surnames, and the survival of the use of bare surnames. Premature use of first names is apt to be regarded as a kind of insult, this being a recognised step on the road to real personal friendship.

English being one of the very few European languages which have not retained the intimate second person singular, the use of this presents an additional hazard for the Briton. It is quite widely used in most European countries and French and Spanish speaking third-world countries in the office or shop floor setting (and of course in the armed forces). But a foreigner, or indeed anyone outside the organisation, should never use it in this way as it carries here some connotation of inferiority. (In fact a secretary would address her boss as *Sie* or *Vous* while he would address her as *Du* or *Tu*, much in the same way as she might call her employer Mr Brown while he always called her by her first name.) Since by the time the social use of the second person singular could possibly arise the Englishman is likely to have acquired at least some smattering of the language, it may be helpful to him to know that change from *Sie* to *Du* or *Vous* to *Tu* normally follows from an invitation extended by the senior or older of the people in question.

11.5.2 Drinking customs

How to act in those countries which still regard the downing of a rapid succession of extremely strong drinks at one gulp as a touchstone of manliness and goodwill is a problem that must be left to the individual. But quite apart from this, both alcoholic and non-alcoholic drinks are fraught in many countries with a variety of hazards. Apart from the English-speaking world, it is mainly in Europe that alcoholic drinks are normally offered other than with a meal. Remember when you wish to oil the wheels by buying your hosts a drink that in most countries, except in the smallest pubs and cafés and in places that specifically proclaim themselves as cocktail bars or such on the Anglo-American pattern, it is a gross breach of etiquette (and also incidentally in many countries of the law) to order or collect drinks from the serving bar. This can easily undo the good impression you are seeking to make. People of the Latin countries are generally more concerned that you should appreciate and enjoy the drinks they offer you than with the number of times you lift your glass. But as one moves East ritual sets in, and since customs vary significantly from region to region (for example within West Germany), the only safe rule is to watch and follow your hosts. Generally speaking custom requires that not only the first sip when a toast is offered is taken together, but all subsequent sips too. Although a spoken toast is normally only given before the first sip, the glass is raised again after this and subsequently before and after each sip. If you are drinking a national or local speciality, such as Swedish punch, your host will normally indicate to you whether this is to be sipped slowly or downed in one gulp.

A very high proportion of export markets now lie in Mohammedan countries, and in most of these alcohol is not drunk on social occasions. If it is offered as a gesture to infidel visitors, it should be drunk in extreme moderation. Not all individuals in Muslim countries are practising Mohammedans, and if you know that someone normally drinks then it would be in order to offer him a glass of wine on a suitable occasion, though never to press it on him. Coffee drinking in coffee houses is surrounded with a certain amount of ritual, varying widely from place to place but in principle not unlike German customs over alcoholic drinks. One important point, though not entirely concerned with drinking, is the need to plan dealings with Mohammedan countries so that certainly visits to the country and preferably the acceptance of visits from it do not take place during the month of Ramadan or in the ten days following it. As they spend most of the night eating and drinking, those who are fasting are apt to be half if not fully asleep for most of the day, and it is extremely difficult to get any business done. Also since nothing may pass their lips between sunset and sunrise (or laid down equivalent times) the visitor is placed in an acutely embarrassing position, especially in a hot climate.

Moving further East, all that can be said in general terms is that the type of ritual that goes with the drinking of alcohol in Europe may attach to coffee, tea or other beverages. Again a breach of etiquette instantly conjures up the phrase 'white devils' in the Oriental mind.

11.5.3   Meals and functions

It is usually fairly easy to avoid committing a solecism at a formal meal, as there is plenty of opportunity to follow the hosts' example. Cocktail parties and receptions are very similar to our own, except that the rule about breaking off conversations in order to circulate are rather less free and easy in that either the person you are talking to will take you across and introduce you to somebody else before disappearing or you should park him or more particularly her with another group before abandoning them. However on the whole few people share the preparedness of the British and Americans to socialise standing up, and any party you give will be far more successful if you limit the numbers so that everyone can sit down. This does not prevent circulation at drinks parties and buffet suppers, but on more formal occasions such as balls the lady seated on your right becomes your 'partner' for the evening. You can of course dance with others at your table or elsewhere, but you should not leave her alone and should not go and sit at another table unless she invites someone else to sit for a time in your seat. If there is any risk of your being required to make a speech, make sure that you have one prepared and that you have either your own or another interpreter with you. This is a good occasion on which to deliver a sentence or two, learned by heart, in the language and then to go on in English. But keep your speech short, because consecutive interpreting doubles the time it takes, and make sure you have agreed any funny stories in advance with the interpreter if you hope for the point to go across. Many stories, dirty and otherwise, are quite untranslatable and having to interpret a round or two of jokes after dinner at the end of a hard day's work is an acid test even of the most experienced conference interpreter.

The long drawn-out and elaborate business lunch is rapidly becoming a thing of the past, drinking and entertaining starting only after the day's work is finished. In France and her ex-colonies and in other Latin countries the long lunch-hour tradition dies hard, but even here you may give an impression of idleness by taking a long midday break or inviting your customer to an expensive lunch. The pub lunch or its local equivalent is now almost universally preferred, and in Scandinavia and parts of Germany sandwiches with coffee or a soft drink in the office may be the order of the day. In these countries it would be quite normal to make a lunch-time date with someone in his office, bringing your own sandwiches!

The notes above can do little more than highlight some of the more common pitfalls and indicate the importance of finding out the local form. Your interpreter should be able to brief you either beforehand or on the way out, but if top-level meetings, particularly with government departments or agencies, are involved, it might be as well to seek advice from the Commercial Counsellor at the Embassy or High Commission.

1.6 Hospitality to foreign visitors

11.6.1 General

Visits by foreign customers or prospects to you are your real opportunity to put across the company image and to cement relationshps. Conventional business hospitality, lavish as it may be, is apt to leave a great many gaps and, at least in the case of communist and third-world socialist countries, to give a wrong impression. Cast your mind back to the last major business trip you made. You arrived on a wet night at a strange airport, and having struggled through the sheep pens to collect your luggage you found, if you were lucky, a driver with a card to meet you. You were dumped in your hotel to be collected at a rather ungodly hour the following morning and whisked into the rush-hour traffic. Having arrived rather jaded at your customer's or supplier's office, you were greeted by a charming secretary who told you that the person you had come to see had been called away and would not be available until the afternoon. After a disorganised day of waiting around and talking to people you did not particularly want to see, your main discussions went on well into the evening, when your host excused himself as he had a prior engagement. By the time you had got back to your hotel and had a shower, you had difficulty in finding a good dinner because the restaurants were either fully booked or closing. Or perhaps you went straight on with your host to a working dinner followed by the inevitable nightclub and staggered into bed exhausted in the early hours with an early start for a local airtrip and another similar day in front of you. You will have seen nothing of the country except a few wet pavements, and your last day's programme gets so badly behind schedule that you have to buy presents for your family at the airport. You return home exhausted, perhaps with a sense of achievement but certainly with a slender and indifferent impression of the places and people you have seen.

All this rush and struggle is not only wholly avoidable, it is also bad business and leads to misunderstandings and unsound decisions and commitments. If when you receive visitors you are prepared to 'do different' and do better by expending a good deal of preparatory effort and a relatively small amount of money, you can greatly strengthen your negotiating hand and build up the kind of personal relationships which count when the chips are down. It is true that the experienced West European or North American business traveller can largely look after himself and may impose restrictions on you by making himself available only for a few hours; but third-world visitors have a rather more human sense of time, are likely to be suffering from either time-zone disorientation or change of climate or both, and may find themselves truly at a loss in a European urban environment.

The first requirement is to meet them at the airport with a car and someone responsible who speaks the right language, so that any administrative problems they have can quickly be sorted out and they can then switch off completely. This is the first step in creating the impression of relaxed efficiency and professionalism that you wish to give. One sometimes finds in people visiting the country for the first time a genuine fear of the unknown, almost as if they were being taken off to the salt mines. It is thus worth spending a few minutes explaining to them with the aid of a map where they will be going and anything interesting they will see on the way. If the journey is a long one, it is better to break it with a good meal on the way; visitors will be tired and off their guard at this point and a relaxed discussion may yield very useful information. When they reach their hotel, they should not be left until all their needs and arrangements up to the next moment of contact have been dealt with, not forgetting that the English breakfast is a profound mystery to most foreigners and that menus for room service and breakfast are nearly always in English.

British government departments and many international or multinational organisations have an excellent rule that no decisive discussions should be embarked on in the first twenty-four hours after a major time-zone displacement or climatic change. Although you may be 'wasting a day' in some people's language, a relaxed first day's programme will pay off even if it means restricting the time given over to definitive discussion. Thus one might devote the first part of the morning to shopping and sightseeing so that they have some idea of the kind of place they are in and can get their shopping problems out of their minds; a shopping list prepared on the journey down is of great help here. The second part of the morning can be given over to a really slick company presentation (see Chapter 15) followed by a buffet lunch at which, if the language problem is not too insuperable, they can meet some of your key men at all levels. The afternoon is a good time for a tour of the works and any hardware demonstrations in the programme, preceding each with a short seated briefing (see Chapters 8 and 15). Entertainment is discussed below, but it is helpful to round off the first working day with a question and answer session and a review of the agenda for the main discussions, adapting this to cover any points which have come up during the day.

With the opportunities that will have arisen during this first day for clearing up any misunderstandings or points of doubt, it should be possible to clear the main discussions in a morning at a fairly formally organised meeting (Chapter 15), and to despatch the visitors after lunch, still escorted, to the airport or their next destination. If a long car journey is involved and time allows, some interesting diversion en route will send them off with a good impression.

11.6.2 *Entertainment*

Although it is difficult to believe that the impression of England that foreign visitors wish to take away is the mockery of luxury offered by lavish but indifferent restaurants and night clubs, it may be necessary to make some concession to the conventional pattern of business entertaining for guests from the Western world. Visitors from Communist countries and the third world, if they wish to hit the town at all, usually prefer to do so on their own as this is regarded as an unsocialist activity. Apart perhaps from a good musical, theatres are out because of the language problem, but good cabaret, if it can be found in conjunction with edible food, and speciality evenings such as the 'Elizabethan banquets' put on at various places in London and the provinces usually prove a much greater success, even with sophisticated visitors, than a long drawn-out meal at which discussion is inhibited by the language problem, followed by a night club. But one knows from one's own experience as well as from others' reaction that what really makes a lasting impression on visitors is to invite them home, taking them for an hour or two out of the dreary aircraft, hotel, office and high-life circuit; this is of course doubly valuable in handling visitors from the developing countries because it confirms the key impression of accepting them as equals. Even if a home dinner or buffet supper party is impossible, it is worth making a considerable effort to have visitors home for a drink before taking them out for the evening. Ideally the company should be represented on such an occasion only by the hosts and any necessary linguists, the party being made up of people in other fields who know their country or speak their language.

For visitors from the Western world and Eastern Europe, food presents few problems except that of finding restaurants that will give them food of the standard to which they are accustomed — and good food ranks very high in the impression that most of them will take away. Drink however does require a little thought. Even the allegedly alcoholic French drink less, and in particular less spirits, than is customary in many British and American business circles. They will often be happy, apart perhaps from a liqueur, to drink through an evening on wine, and they do not have the Anglo-American inhibition about quenching their thirst with soft drinks even at stag gatherings. For those from further North and East on the other hand, spirits are the thing and gin and whisky make a very acceptable substitute for their local tipple. Although they may feel in duty bound to knock back a ritual pint of bitter, very few foreigners like English beers, and if there is an occasion when beer is to be drunk, bottled or draught lager is a must.

With current trends in export markets, an increasing proportion of those who come to England on business will be Mohammedans, and looking after their needs does require rather careful planning. Although not all practise their religion and in any case dispensations are given to those travelling abroad, a serious effort to help them comply with their rules will always be very much appreciated. As far as food goes, the main point is to observe is that pork in any form, and even food cooked in pork fat, is forbidden to them, and even non-practising Moslems tend to observe this ban. The Islamic code also forbids alcohol; non-practising Moslems may like to drink vermouth and wines, but only the most widely travelled and sophisticated will accept spirits; thus a supply of good soft drinks becomes a must. The problem of Ramadan was mentioned earlier, and although there is dispensation from the fast for those travelling abroad, some who are out of their country only for a few days in the month may wish to continue observing it. There is nothing one can do during the day but let them suffer, but they will need an early and reasonably large dinner, and special arrangements for food to be available in their hotel rooms. They normally eat for a second time shortly before midnight and then sup very early in the morning before the hours of fasting. Most hotels can arrange something suitable if given sufficient warning, but because both of natural reticence and of the language problem, this calls for action on the part of the host.

11.6.3 Sightseeing, etc.

Unless time allows a major sightseeing expedition, over a weekend for example, sightseeing as such is probably best confined to a quick drive round with time to pause at anything which excites the visitors' particular interest. Even in centres of tourism, the tourist sightseeing circuit has too many characteristics in common with the less desirable aspects of business travel to make it an attractive diversion. In the case of European visitors, one will probably know from earlier contacts what their particular interests are and these can be catered for. Third world visitors tend to show rather little interest in Western architecture, particularly as so much of it is ecclesiastical. The developing countries are however faced with an enormous education problem, and a visit to an educational establishment such as a University, Polytechnic or modern school will be an almost sure-fire success. Even if the visitors appear to speak English reasonably well, their knowledge may be rather narrowly limited to the business sphere, and it is essential to give all explanations in the sightseeing context in their language.

Outside the object of immediate interest, visitors can gain only a superficial impression, but it is a truism well known by all concerned with inspection of establishments that superficial impressions generally reflect the whole. Receiving a visit gives you what may be a unique opportunity to impose the image of your company and its environment on the visitor, and provided that you have costed in an adequate entertainment budget, you can exploit this opportunity at no expense save in time.

11.7 Foreign views of Britain

Some of the direct problems to which a chauvinistic outlook can give rise were discussed above, but more important still is the need to realise that the foreigner's view of Britain is even gloomier and considerably more adverse than the assessments in which we seem so masochistically to rejoice. It has taken the USA a quarter of a century to learn that one cannot be top nation and loved, and that generosity is apt to be thrown back in one's teeth. But if there is one thing less popular than a top nation it is an ex-top nation, and particularly one which, while seeming to retain many of its imperialistic attitudes and prejudices, fails to back these up with solid economic performance. Psychological pressures or no, any would-be exporter who studied the utterances of the world's media and took them seriously would decide to stay at home. To the Marxist establishment we are dollar imperialist running dogs, to the Chinese, one hears, hyenas, to the non-aligned countries — even those that are not in fact fairly closely aligned with the Soviet bloc or China — we are a firmly capitalist country carrying a share of the opprobrium rained on the States. Even to the ex-colonies of other nations we carry the label of a colonial power, and to Western Europe we are a reluctant partner that is slowly destroying itself by self-inflicted wounds. Even to our friends, we are rather a quaint place epitomised by pageantry, medieval architecture and old thatched pubs. In a word we do not exactly have everything going for us in the export markets we seek.

Nevertheless it is not only the successive formal and floating devaluations of sterling and the need to support the British economy as a market for oil that is enabling this country to maintain and expand her export programme. Underlying the smoke-screen of political attitudes there is a surprising amount of goodwill for Britain, not least among those lands which she formerly dominated politically or economically. This is coupled with a persistent belief in British fair dealing and technical quality. Unfortunately, thanks to industrial relations problems of one kind or another, this commercial and technological credibility is wearing increasingly thin. There is a reluctance to offer the firm prices on long-lead items which most importers demand and which many importing countries statutorily require. Alternatively, if these prices are quoted, such heavy contingencies are costed in as to make them non-competitive. Delivery dates are not met, and not just by weeks but by months or even in some instances years; and imagining himself to be protected by provisions similar to those of his own country's law, the customer who has not had solid penalty and jurisdiction clauses written into the contract finds himself without redress. Deliveries are incomplete or not to specification, so that the material either fails to obtain official approval or is found unsuitable for the intended task. After-sales service, and in particular the execution of guarantee repairs, is slow of response and often reluctant.

Thus the exporter needs to go in with his eyes very wide open and his answers well-prepared and to redouble his efforts to build up confidence and credibility. And he needs to be backed by an organisation that will make almost ridiculous efforts, such as doubling or trebling up on material and component suppliers, to ensure that deadlines are met with fully satisfactory goods. A particular problem is the control of key sub-contractors, who are likely to be less motivated than the primary exporter.

Equally, both for practical reasons and as part of the process of building up confidence, negotiations with the customer should be meticulous and exhaustive on technical and financial aspects alike, so that once the contract is signed it becomes a truly definitive document to which both parties can adhere. Because of mutual suspicion it may often be extremely difficult to strike the right balance between punctilious adherence to the contract on the one hand and the goodwill and give and take inseparable from a complex project on the other. This is why so much stress has been laid both in this chapter and elsewhere in this book on the need for excellent and accurate communications and even more for really well-cemented personal relationships.

11.8   Inducements

This chapter has moved rather away from the main stream of the book in an effort to draw attention to and provoke thought on some of the broader aspects of successful international trading in which language plays only a secondary role, albeit an essential one. It would be wrong to close it without raising the delicate issue of what might politely be called inducements. Recent events both in the States and in the UK have shown that, where other standards may have slipped, disapproval and rejection of corruption remains such a solid plank in the White Anglo-Saxon Protestant working ethic that it is very difficult for us to realise, let alone to accept, that in most of the rest of the world it is not so much an endemic disease as a way of life. Yet it is probably only in North America, Australasia, Scandinavia and the established Communist bloc that covert as opposed to overt pressure by direct financial inducement on some scale and at some level is not a basic factor to be taken account of in competing for an export contract. It is very difficult to judge to what extent the puritanism of socialist or quasi-marxist doctrine, combined with the patriotism of new-found independence, has suppressed or eradicated what has always been an accepted and traditional practice in the cultures of many developing countries. Certainly it has made inept attempts at bribery very much more dangerous. The policy that an organisation adopts in this situation is very much its own decision, but it may be helpful to review briefly and in general terms the whole scale of practices from blandishments to major inducements.

British companies certainly lag behind their American and Continental opposite numbers in ensuring that no-one who visits them goes away without at least some small keepsake. It is of course tempting to use publicity gadgets for this purpose, but most companies of repute who distribute such gifts as a matter of course tend to preserve publicity gadgets for their suppliers and to give others either a souvenir in the narrower sense such as a medallion or plaque or a useful object or ornament which bears the donor's mark very discreetly if at all. There is no doubt whatever that quite apart from being expected by many foreign visitors because it is their own practice, these small keepsakes not only round off a visit agreeably but also serve to remind the recipient of the donor whenever he looks at or uses them.

The next and universally accepted stage is 'wining and dining' beyond what normal hospitality and convenience requires. It is a very open question, as has been suggested above, whether this actually benefits anyone except the purveyors of high life. On the other hand warm, well-planned and considerate hospitality will create firm friendship and goodwill, and it is along this line extrapolated to some rather ill-defined limit that an Anglo-Saxon exporter faced with a highly competitive situation may like to look. One might for example invite specific senior executives with their wives, paying all their expenses including travel as opposed to taking them over at the arrival airport; and having got them here one might extend their stay over a long weekend and take them around the country. This might excite people's sense of financial prudence but would scarcely arouse their moral indignation. It is when the guests have had a prolonged stopover in, say, Paris on the way back that eyebrows begin to be raised, and recent legal decisions have shown that all-expenses-paid holidays are seen as a corrupt practice by the British courts. The authors fully realise that these suggestions, so far from being original, are common practice in the PR-oriented fields of consumer goods and consumer durables, and in those specialised fields where wining and dining can be respectably dressed up as a learned or professional conference. However, such goodwill gestures often seem not to occur to, for instance, small and medium engineering companies, even when they are in a highly competitive situation and the value of the initial contract, let alone the follow-up prospects, is amply large enough both in absolute terms and as a percentage of their turnover to carry expenses of this order.

The only thing that can be said with any certainty about direct financial inducements to individuals is that an exporter must not let himself become involved in them. Identification of the right palm and the rules and etiquette of the game are so complex that no-one but a native of the country could possibly find his way through them. It is of course for this precise reason that an increasing number of developing countries have forbidden by law the use of intermediaries at least in connection with public contracts — and in such countries virtually every worthwhile contract is a public contract at least to the extent that it requires approval by one or more government departments.

Certain types of inducement which have so far been the prerogative of governments and the really large organisations can also be envisaged on a more modest scale so that their cost would lie well within the means of any company large enough to undertake a substantial export contract. They involve no irrevocable financial commitment until the contract has been signed and lend themselves to being scaled up if supplementary or follow-up contracts are subsequently struck. These inducements are educational and more particularly vocational training schemes. Within the framework of a long-lead engineering contract or a hopefully continuous marketing arrangement the exporting firm could agree to accept and carry the full costs of say a year's course for one or more of the customer's trainees. And if the requirement was for technical training and language presented a problem this could equally well be arranged in another country with the right language. Clearly a scheme of this kind would be most attractive to the developing countries with their desperate problem of middle-piece education, but there is no reason why, say, a year's attachment to the exporter's design department coupled with an advanced language course should not have strong appeal even to a French or German customer.

One might recall in this context Kwame Nkrumah's aphorism when dismissing his allegedly corrupt foreign minister: 'A golden bed is not socialism'. There may not be too much need to get worried if you see your leading competitor drive up to your prospect's office in a spit new you-know-which car obviously poised for handover. Inducements can also be devised at costs which are in scale with the project, and in ways which lie within the broad framework represented by the contract and are attuned to the spirit of goodwill and collaboration which must underlie it.

12

Multilingual conferences and meetings

Conferences and meetings of all shapes and sizes tend to be made or marred by details irrelevant to the main theme of discussion. Large conferences are almost as expensive to stage, and just as difficult to stage successfully as a theatrical production. In fact many of the problems of the conference manager are identical with those of the producer to the extent where we now have a new profession of 'conference producer.'

One common feature of all types of major conference appears to be that little real communication takes place or business is done in the formal sessions, any solid progress being achieved either in small working groups or more probably in quick chats over a drink or in the lobby. One could almost say that the plenary sessions do no more than provide a ritual focus for the gathering as a whole and publicity in some form or other for the main speakers. The only purposes therefore likely to justify a business enterprise, as opposed to a professional body, in setting up a symposium, conference or congress attended by people other than its own staff are the promotion of its image or its product, or the orientation and morale-boosting of, say, its agents. Nevertheless just because the occasion is essentially a ritual one intended to impress, the executive and administrative arrangements must be next to perfect if the aim is to be attained. However most of the techniques involved are the same for all meetings from the large congress through the single-customer sales presentation, symposia and courses right down to the small working meetings or *tête-à-tête* discussion where business is actually done.

12.1 Advance action

Any organisation needing to sponsor any kind of formal meeting should have a team consisting of a senior, a middle-piece and a junior executive earmarked for this purpose when required. This team will need to control the physical resources (projection equipment, such standard audiovisual aids such as 'company' film and standard material for hand-outs such as brooches, covers, glossy leaflets, etc.), standard operating procedures and checklists for the various types of function they may be required to stage and an information file of venues, sources of professional and administrative extramural support and programmes of past events that have proved successful. Unless some standing arrangement of this kind exists, it will be almost impossible to set up the function quickly enough when the need arises.

12.1.1 Budget

Any attempt to stage an impressive function on a tight budget invites certain disaster, so that at least the entire budget and probably more will be spent for very little real return. On the one hand the nature and scope may be predetermined, as in the case of a course for a customer's technicians or a sales-force briefing on a new product range. Here a sufficient figure should have been costed in either to the contract or to the product launch budget as the case may be. On the other it should be possible for corporate planners or marketing men to state, say, a promotional aim in broad and simple terms and put a figure on the value of achieving it. It is then for the 'presentation team' with such help as they may need to put forward for approval by top management or if necessary the board one or more costed and timed proposals of what could be done within this figure; if it then becomes clear that the budget envisaged will not suffice for the aim, management has a clear-cut choice between increasing the budget, modifying the aim or abandoning the project. Since large meetings and presentations are comparatively rare in medium and small firms, and since most accounting systems tend to lose the real cost of small, informal meetings under a number of sub-heads, managements often have very little idea of the level at which to budget for the larger functions. And the various possible scales and natures of meetings produce so many cost discontinuities as to make the use of general yardsticks very difficult. One might however venture as a rough point of reference the suggestion that, at 1974 UK going rates, a 24-hour gathering (for example, dinner, overnight stay, all-day meeting, disperse) for around 50 delegates with facilities in English, French, and German would need to be budgeted in four figures sterling rather than three; in fact, a snap answer would be £1750 ± 15 per cent. Within this figure the total real language costs would probably represent 40 ± 5 per cent. None of these figures include delegate travel, and the administrative element is at provincial rather than London rates.

We admit that these figures are open to attack but include them to give some idea of the order of costs involved in the kind of meeting that the management of a small-medium firm or the direction of a relatively small and poor trade association might very reasonably propose. As this chapter will attempt to indicate, there will often be very much cheaper and equally effective ways of putting the message across, but where an all-singing, all-dancing technicolor conference is necessary — and penny plain is worse than useless here — sponsors needed to start thinking in £500 units even at 1974 prices.

12.1.2 Timings

The second aspect which sponsors often fail to appreciate correctly and where once again language facilities are a critical factor is the planning lead-time. The authors have found that by the time they were brought in only the most hand-to-mouth of possibilities were still open, and it was sheer luck if the result could be described as improvised rather than botched-up. Most professional organisations which hold annual international congresses plan these over a year ahead, so that interpreters are actually booked from year to year and the venue (and hence any specialised equiment) will have been earmarked over a year ahead and firm-booked as soon as the conference has approved it.

The main conference seasons are the second and fourth quarters of the calendar year, perhaps with peaks from mid-April to mid-May and mid-September to mid-October, respectively. For exactly the same reasons these are the times at which most commercial organisations will want to run any major meetings. It may therefore be difficult to get any conference interpreters or the equipment they need at all, and six months' notice combined with some flexibility over dates will usually be necessary to get the best of either at these seasons. The spread of holiday periods in the various countries likely to be concerned effectively rules out the summer quarter for any sizeable gathering, but January to March is a period well worth looking at if weather is not a real factor, and is probably the only time at which a multilingual meeting of reasonable size can successfully be laid on at short notice.

Since not only the direct accommodation and administrative costs but also indirectly most of the other cost elements will be influenced by the venue, this should ideally be selected and provisionally booked even before the budgeting exercise is carried out, and confirmed at the same time as interpreters and simultaneous interpreting/audiovisual equipment are booked.

If guest speakers, i.e. speakers whose movements are not under the direct control of the sponsors, are required, they will also need to be booked six to nine months in advance, so that the minimum satisfactory lead-time from the initial decision to plan a large meeting to its taking place is, although not entirely for the same reasons, the same twelve-months period that, as mentioned above, some professional organisations adopt.

Once venue, visiting speakers, interpreters/equipment and dates are firm, planning can proceed on the rather more usual lead-times indicated in the checklists, although here too 'Languages lengthen lead-time' remains a useful slogan.

12.1.3   Choice of venue

The introduction of more than one language has two effects on the choice of venue. One, direct and comparatively minor, is that additional space will be needed for interpreters and secretariat, and for booths and other equipment if simultaneous interpreting is required. The second and more important is indirect and again applies mainly where simultaneous interpreting is used, whether the conference room chosen is permanently equipped for this purpose or specially hired equipment is brought in. Since the language costs will very markedly increase the total cost and form a substantial proportion of it, the cost of the venue will become proportionately less and therefore the cost difference between a really suitable venue and a second-best one will sink to second-order importance.

And lest the reader should regard this as a mere costing quibble, the considerable additional stress imposed on delegates, secretariat and administrators by having to work in several languages — and particularly by the need to use electronic equipment — will increase the practical and psychological adverse effects of any shortcomings in accommodation or administration. Relatively few organisers of functions of this kind, whether multilingual or not, seem to appreciate either the stress imposed on all concerned or the time lost by the absence of a second room to which the delegates or audience can withdraw in comfort and refresh themselves while leaving the arena free for the organisers, speakers and their assistants; and/or by the lack of cloakroom and reception facilities on a scale that will avoid queues, combined with a well-devised traffic-flow circuit and sensible gangway arrangements within the conference room itself.

For a meeting of any size and complexity *four* rooms are essential to smooth running:

> An anteroom.
> The conference hall.
> A refreshment room or area.
> A staff room.

Taking these in reverse order, the purpose of the staffroom is to provide the organisers and their executive and administrative staff with somewhere to which they can retire, where a secretariat can function, and where equipment, documents and personal effects can be safely kept. This need not connect directly with the conference suite but should in any event have toilet facilities either private or separate from those used by delegates.

Both the refreshment room or area and the facilities within it are of great importance, for it is here during the breaks that most of the real business will be done. It must therefore be large enough for groups to get together without the certainty of being overheard and provide enough comfortable seating for relaxed discussions to take place. These break-times which are so important both for informal discussion and for relaxation will be wasted if delegates have to spend their whole time queueing for coffee or drinks. Bars and other serving points — most of all of course buffets — must be large, well-staffed and well-arranged. Coffee can certainly be poured and put out round the room in a few minutes before a break, and it is worth doing the same with a small selection of suitable drinks, so that only those who want something special need go to the bar. To speed up service as well as for any other reasons that may be relevant it is always preferable to include an element for refreshments in the total fee (if delegates are paying) and in any event to avoid the need for cash payment on the spot.

Oddly enough it is outside the conference room rather than within it that lavishness will impress and thus bear fruit, but money spent there will of course be wasted if the conference facilities proper are inadequate. So often one sees rows of large men, perspiring gently in an overcrowded and unventilated room, packed to overlapping on linked nesting chairs and expected to direct their undivided attention towards a speaker they cannot hear and visual aids many of them cannot see. Figure 12.1 shows an idealised lay-out for a meeting involving both presentations and discussions with the use of simultaneous interpreting.

The anteroom is important in practical terms because it will create or avoid delays and in psychological terms because it gives a first and last impression. The area must be large enough to allow free movement even when most of the delegates are passing through it at the same time, and in particular deep enough to prevent the queues that will inevitably form at some point blocking or overflowing beyond the entrance. For initial reception and any other occasion on which papers are to be issued, badges and/or folders must be laid out in alphabetical order on tables facing the visitors. At these times there should be sufficient receptionists to allow the complete attendance to pass within the time allotted for assembly (usually 15 or 30 minutes) with each individual taking up on average one minute of a receptionist's time. The main reception desk should not be used for this purpose but be slightly to one side of this stream so that staff can refer individuals with administrative queries to it. This desk needs two telephones with outside lines, one of .them for delegates' use. The individual or team manning it must have all the languages concerned at reasonable level; for peak periods, i.e. before, between and after sessions, a staff of two will be needed, for the rest of the day it is advisable to keep it manned as a general reporting and administrative centre, and a multilingual secretary can do this excellently while also clearing any

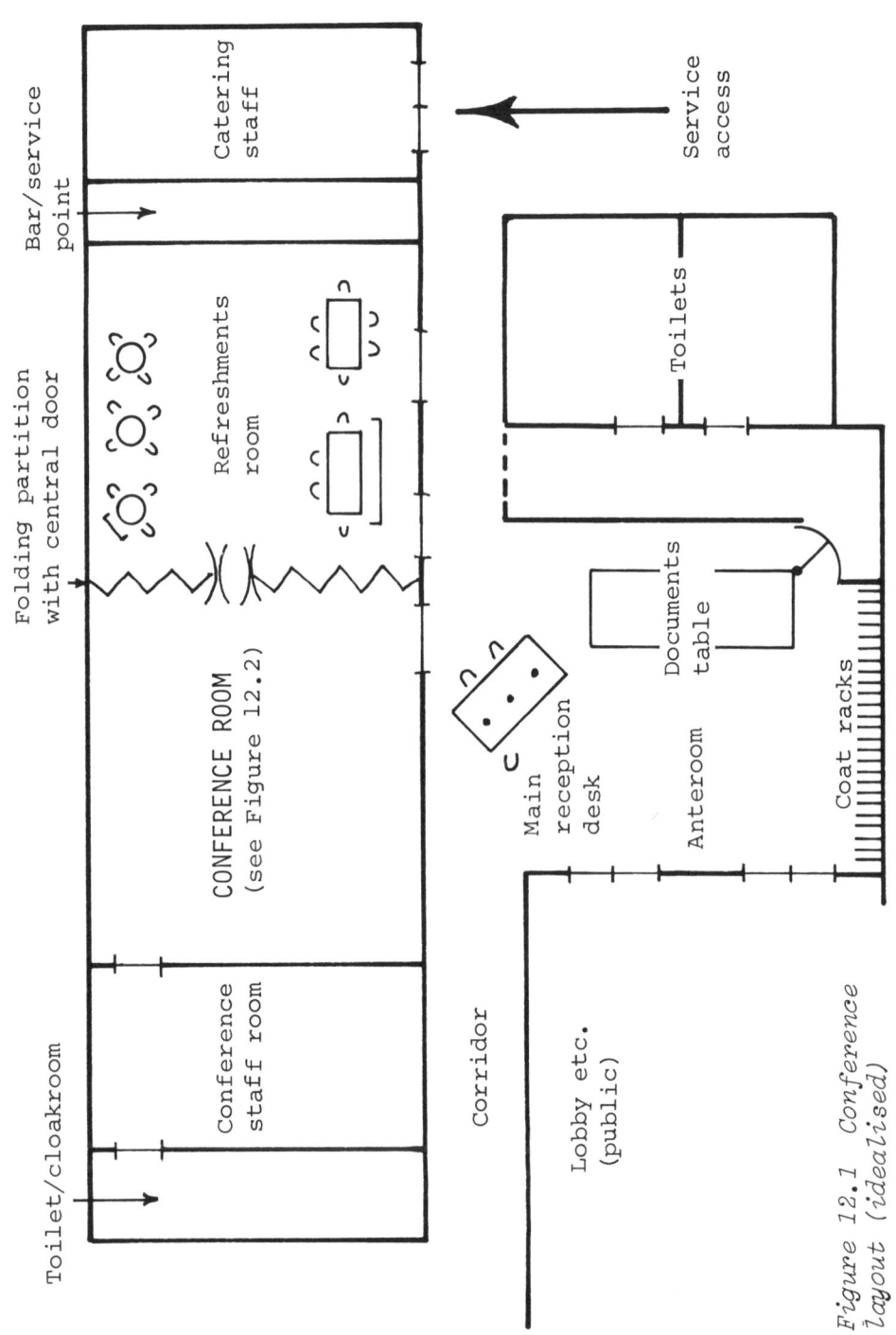

Figure 12.1 Conference layout (idealised)

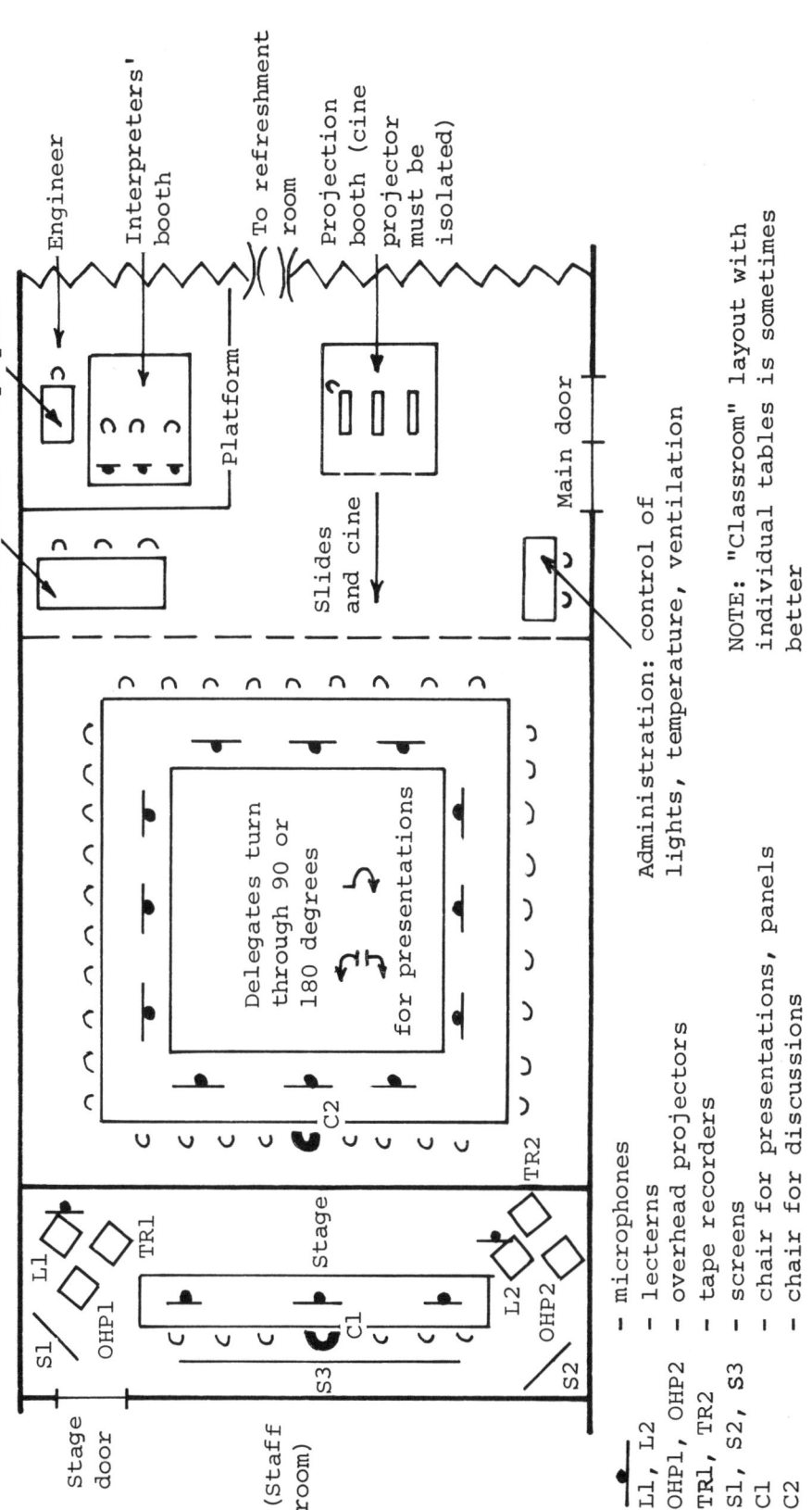

Figure 12.2 Conference room layout (for a mixture of presentations and discussions)

- microphones
- lecterns
- overhead projectors
- tape recorders
- screens
- chair for presentations, panels
- chair for discussions

L1, L2
OHP1, OHP2
TR1, TR2
S1, S2, S3
C1
C2

administrative typing. This main reception desk should be so placed as to control access at least to the presentation room and preferably to the rest of the conference area. For small meetings with a high proportion of hosts, e.g. a firm giving a sales presentation to a customer's staff and dealers, members of staff can take the place of the additional receptionists required to deal with assembly, combining the welcoming of guests with making sure that they get their papers and know where they are to sit.

A possible layout of the conference area is given in Figure 12.2. Clearly however these figures can be no more than a kind of visual checklist aimed at bringing out important and easily forgotten points.

One very easily forgotten point, especially if the venue is in a large city, is transport. Relatively few of the delegates are likely to have cars with them, and if they have these may not be conveniently parked; and the conference staff will be far too busy to drive delegates about except in cases of genuine personal emergency. In the ideal case of a self-contained venue deep in the country, no problem arises except at arrival and departure, but in city-centre or fringe locations the normal transport resources are likely to be totally inadequate, because the delegates are likely to have to move at peak hours. Whatever the circumstances it will almost certainly be worth hiring a coach for movement between airport or station and venue, a minibus with driver available full-time for all administrative purposes and if possible some special call on a taxi service. This point is mentioned here because it may be a critical one in the choice of a venue.

12.1.4 Language facilities

A major multilingual conference involves four distinct language functions:

Preparation of documentation.
Conference/working group interpreting.
Administrative *ad hoc* interpreting, etc.
Secretariat.

This does not mean however that four separate sets of linguists are required; the art is to appreciate the different functions and then to plan for the same people to perform two or more of them.

If the organisers have on their staff or have brought in a team of multilingual secretaries, this team, supported as necessary by translators, should carry out the preparatory documentation and the transcription/translation of the proceedings, and it will be economical to have enough people to man the reception desk as well as the secretaries' table during the conference and to carry out any necessary telex work. For a conference of reasonable size and duration a team of six, ideally two of each mother tongue and capable of working in at least one of the other languages, would not be excessive. Ideally, if they were sufficiently experienced and used to working together, they should work in three shifts of two, moving from reception desk to conference room to staff room for transcription and rest.

Unless some effort is made to push on with transcription during the
conference, the backlog of tapes is likely to become unmanageable; and in
any event experience suggests that an adequate secretarial team will be
worth its weight in gold both in achieving smooth running and in avoiding
contingent expenses.

The conference interpreters must not be used for any administrative
purpose or for written translations other than the drafting of agreements,
etc., in conference. They will almost certainly be required to — and should
be invited to — join with the delegates in social functions or visits, during
which they may well be called upon to interpret speeches; unless they are
exceptionally lucky or cunning, they will seldom be able to relax by
switching entirely into one language. Other most important duties which
they will usually perform if asked nicely are advising the chairman or his
immediate staff on the conduct of particularly tricky parts of the meeting,
liaising with speakers over terminology, the handling of any tricky passages
and the treatment of visual aids, and also giving speakers a little free
language instruction should they for good reasons or bad want to deliver a
small part of their speech in a language other than their own. On top of
all this they may be waylaid during breaks by groups of delegates who want
to caucus in more than one language, and they may find it difficult to
refuse. Most of these activities are strictly speaking outside their brief, but
are invaluable in oiling the wheels. Understandably enough, there is also a
marked difference in tone of voice between interpreters who are happy,
involved and not over-pressured and those who are dispirited and
exhausted — and this difference can have a critical effect on the spirit of the
meeting.

The wise conference manager will therefore give his personal attention
to the interpreters and make sure that the chairman too makes them feel
welcome, will handle them with even thicker velvet gloves than he does the
delegates and above all, particularly in a conference of several days'
duration, will make sure that they do not get dragged into other duties and
overtired.

At certain stages in most conferences, and occasionally throughout —
especially if delegates' wives have to be looked after — there is also a
requirement for what might best if rather chauvinistically be described as
'front and leg girls'. The sort of tasks involved are help with arrival and
dispersal, shepherding of individual groups on conducted tours, escorting
delegates in transport, helping with personal shopping and so on.
Language students, either undergraduates or those on diploma courses,
are ideal for this purpose; since it is excellent experience for them, their
college is usually only too happy to release them for a few days, and they
will come on an 'expenses plus' basis.

It will be obvious from the above that both in planning and during the
conference itself there is a requirement for a linguist in a consultative and
coordinating role. If one of the conference interpreters appointed is
suitably experienced and willing, we are convinced that he or she
is the best person to fill this need with payment either at the 'briefing' rate
or at the 'small team simultaneous rate' as agreed between him and the

organisers for each facet of the task. Unfortunately however the number of conference interpreters willing to act in this way is not great. The AIIC foci and other secretariats and bureaux in this and other countries offer a consultant interpreter service, but as far as we know this is confined to interpreting aspects such as the organisation and deployment of interpreters and the arrangement of suitable simultaneous interpreting equipment. Thus unless the organisers have a linguist executive experienced in conference administration whom they can spare virtually full time for a considerable period, there will be a need to call in a conference consultant who is also a linguist (or a language consultant with experience of conference planning) to plug this gap.

1 *Choice of interpreting methods* In an attempt to bring out all the points and complexities of running conferences, we are by implication considering a fairly large and formal trilingual meeting calling for simultaneous interpreting as the main technique. However, as the discussion in Chapters 6-8 brings out, it is not some kind of panacea for communicating across a language barrier; there are many occasions when consecutive interpreting will on balance give better results, and many situations in which simultaneous interpreting is quite simply impossible because the equipment it requires is not portable.

Completely portable equipment is of course technically feasible and we know of short-range VHF systems of the walkie-talkie type which could do the job as effectively and in fact in just the same way as induction loop systems do in an enclosed space. Delegates would require a certain amount of training and considerable discipline, but the excitement of using a walkie-talkie would probably make them put up with this. We believe in fact that at least one of the major UK firms specialising in conference equipment have, or shortly will have radio systems available for hire, and these would certainly be ideal in special circumstances. Another interesting possibility for any form of conducted tour, if time and cost allows, is the use of the miniature tape cassette playback instruments which a number of museums and other centres of tourist interest are now using to provide a multilingual commentary. However for combining crowd control with the requisite elements of audiovisual synchronisation and staggering of movement, direct explanations in the language or consecutive interpreting, both with the aid of a portable loud-hailer, take a lot of beating. And it would clearly be undesirable to introduce into social functions any form of electronics beyond the PA system that poor acoustics or poor speakers may require. The use of consecutive interpreting not only personalises the message but also has the great merit of keeping speeches short.

For the type of tour of facilities plus businesslike meeting that a group of firms contemplating collaboration or a small, specialised trade association might wish to arrange, an excellent formula is to pack all the round-the-table talking into one day when the group is at a suitable venue, and to lay on the full simultaneous set-up for this day. For the rest of the time a consecutive interpreter who can handle the languages concerned

going round with the group, combined with such mutual help as delegates
can give each other, will fill the bill nicely. And if this linguist can also act
as coordinating linguist and conference manager, this for once is a
solution — as we can assert from experience — that is as tidy and
cost-effective as it looks.

2 *Booking of interpreters* *Ad hoc* interpreters and often consecutive
interpreters of considerable experience and quality can be booked through
most translation bureaux and through some agencies which specialise in
interpreting; and a few specialised agencies do handle bookings for
conference interpreters. Moreover, if AIIC interpreters are required, the
organisers should either ask the Institute of Linguists (or its equivalent in
other countries) for details of an AIIC focus, or approach direct an AIIC
interpreter personally known to the organisers, who will usually be
prepared to this extent at least to act as a coordinator and consultant. The
choice between these will depend on how strongly the conference organiser
feels about getting one or more specific individuals, and this tends to be
something that most experienced organisers do feel rather strongly about.
On the other hand booking through a secretariat will ensure a suitable
and well-balanced team, and they will normally try to book an interpreter
asked for by name if he or she is available and in their view suitable.

The importance of booking early to get good interpreters was
emphasised in an earlier section, but there is another extremely trenchant
argument for early booking of conference interpreters. If you are trying to
book at short notice in the conference season, it may well be that no or
insufficient suitable interpreters are available from the UK pool and one or
more will have to be flown in from some other centre. The full travel cost,
subsistence allowances and supplementary fees involved are then borne by
the client. This could easily add 15-20 per cent to the total cost figure of the
example we considered in outline earlier in this chapter.

3 *Equipment* There are three categories of equipment that may be
required. The first is simply a PA system or portable loud-hailer for voice
amplification. The requirements are the same as those for single-language
working, except that rather more care must be taken to ensure clear
communication so that there is no risk of the (consecutive) interpreter
misunderstanding and also so that those with some knowledge of the
language being used can grasp as much as possible. A particular problem
that frequently arises here and must be checked is external noise; there
may be an unacceptable level of permanent background noise from a
ventilation or air-conditioning system, and in hotels one frequently finds
the proceedings rendered virtually inaudible by noises off in the shape of
vacuum-cleaning or washing-up.

The second group of equipment is that associated with audiovisual aids.
Organisers will sometimes have suitable equipment of their own; otherwise
they will have to hire it from specialist firms, and if feasible it is obviously
best to hire audiovisual and simultaneous interpreting equipment from the

same firm. The ideal requirements are:

A 35 mm slide projector with remote control (preferably plus one in reserve).

Two overhead projectors (VUGRAPHS), at least one of which should have a roll of foil for use as a projected blackboard.

Two 16 mm ciné projectors with sound plus sound equipment; at least one of these should be capable of accepting either magnetic or optical sound track at option.

Up to three screens.

At least one tape recorder for playbacks by speakers of recorded passages or effects (this is quite separate from the apparatus required for transcription of the proceedings).

The ciné-projector(s) must be in a portable soundproof booth if the hall does not have a projection room. The only possible exception to this is when simultaneous interpreting equipment with a full headset is in use and the signal from the sound-track is wired into one channel of it. Depending on control methods, lenses, throw, etc., it may be best to put the slide projector into this booth. Exceptionally there may be a need to use the 'epi' system of an epidiascope to show, say, a plate or diagram from a book; but this equipment tends to be awkward to position and circumstantial to use and should be avoided if possible.

Simultaneous interpreting equipment must be hired from a specialist firm. At the time of writing there are five AIIC-approved UK firms and the AIIC foci in other countries have similar lists. The International Conference Secretariat has itself developed an excellent boothless equipment for small meetings in two or three languages known as 'Archie' and the use of this spares the organisers the need to go out for quotes to the other firms. Equipment varies widely in detail, but from the user point of view there are probably three important differences:

Wired versus induction loop — the more old-fashioned wired equipment is usually associated with a traditional head-set or a stethoscope; the induction loop frequently appears in conjunction with the monaural hand-held receivers of the type found in theatres. As was mentioned above short-range radio equipment is also becoming available when circumstances demand it.

Booth versus boothless — for small meetings (maximum 3 groups, 25 delegates) boothless equipment is in many ways preferable, not least because it gives a better *rapport* between interpreters and delegates; it also avoids the physical and aesthetic problems of putting a large booth in a comparatively small room. However for a meeting of any size boothless equipment should not be used without the agreement of the individual interpreters concerned.

Supplementary functions — where the requirement exists or the facility would be advantageous, a check must be made to ensure that supplementary equipment such as one or more tape decks for

recording of proceedings and/or appropriate elements of the audiovisual system can be wired in.

It is of course very much simpler to use an established conference centre such as the London Conference Centre in Charles Street, where not only fully equipped rooms and suites but also a whole range of specialised services on the audiovisual side are available. This would not necessarily be more expensive than a solution using portable equipment, and it is for the organisers to decide whether the location and administrative facilities are in harmony with the impression they want to create. Where hotels and leisure centres offer 'fully-equipped conference suites' a very careful check must be made by an expert to ensure that the equipment meets the need. Nothing could be more disastrous than for delegates and interpreters to assemble only to find that the equipment is unsuitable. A number of hotels and other centres, whether or not they have permanently equipped conference facilities, offer a conference service which includes the arrangement of audiovisual and simultaneous interpreting equipment. In specific cases this service may provide an excellent solution, but in general it would seem unwise to entrust this vital aspect of a very expensive undertaking to a non-specialist when it is perfectly feasible to work direct to specialist firms.

12.1.5   Documentation and visual aids

The production of conference documentation and visual aids, together with the handling and possible translation of papers submitted by speakers, can represent a massive task and can easily get out of control in terms of time and cost. It is usually better not to send out to delegates in advance more paperwork than is essential to get them to the right place at the right time with the right brief and in the right frame of mind, and to issue them with a conference folder (with attached to it an identification brooch) as soon as they arrive at the conference venue or, if it is not the same place, at their hotel. Typically this folder would contain:

> The conference programme including instructions on the use of simultaneous interpreting equipment.
> An administrative instruction.
> Local background information.
> Information on shopping facilities, etc.
> *Either* sponsor's literature (in the case of a promotional gathering).
> *or* information on speakers, up-date on professional topics, etc.

The production of this folder in all the languages required presents no problem — and since it should be as brief as possible, no great cost — provided that both the data to go into it have been established and the drafting, translation and reproduction planned as far as possible ahead. It may be advisable to delay running the programme and administrative instructions until the last possible moment in case of amendments, but there is no reason why it should not be drafted, translated and prepared for reproduction well in advance. The rest of the contents of the folder are likely to consist of standard documentation already available in the languages required, such as for instance the leaflet on a city issued by the local tourist organisation.

The preparation of audiovisual aids is a more formidable task, the most difficult single aspect being film sound tracks. Even the most skilled simultaneous interpreters will be able to deliver a synchronised commentary only if the sound is fed into their booth and they receive a copy of the script *in advance*. Both the other possible methods call for advance action. One is for two interpreters to work as a pair, one reading from a script and the other watching the film and cueing the first. This can easily go wrong if done live, and once synchronisation is lost the commentary becomes meaningless; but it is also the basis of the second method which involves tape-recording a commentary and playing this back into the appropriate language channel in synchronism with the picture. This procedure calls not only for suitable equipment but also for a fair amount of know-how. Since both the sound engineer's reaction time and the small but finite run-up time of the tape deck have to be considered, it is usually best to put visual cues both on the film lead and on the tapes to give a precise start position.

Slides of colour photographs or of captioned illustrations from a book must be dealt with by the speaker and the interpreters, but diagram slides and vufoils should either carry a legend in all the languages concerned or have simply a letter or number code, the key to which can be shown simultaneously on a second screen. There will always be an element of confusion arising from non-simultaneity of pointing and explanation, and it is essential that this is not compounded by the use of different words on the screen and in the interpretation. Ideally then this particular piece of translation should be done well in advance by the interpreters themselves, but since this will very often be impossible and time must be allowed for the production of high-grade slides or foils, photocopies of visual aids must be included in the interpreters' briefing material and they must be asked to accept the terminology already established.

Organisers should always insist that the main speakers submit scripts well in advance. The ostensible purpose of this — and a very important one — is for briefing of the interpreters. Broadly speaking, to remain accurate and simultaneous an interpreter will need a copy of whatever written material the speaker is using. But an even more important advantage is that it gives the organisers an opportunity to check scripts for length and to take action either to shorten the script or to extend the time when there is a howling discrepancy.

This is perhaps a good point at which to discuss the length of scripts and timings. Speakers, particularly in English and the other 'shorter' languages, must not talk faster than about 100 words per minute if they hope to be accurately and simultaneously interpreted. This is not a matter of the interpreters' skill, but quite simply of their and the audience's physical limitations. But this does not mean that, say, 3000 words can effectively be packed into 30 minutes of programme time, especially if visual aids are being used. In our experience the best planning figure is 75 words per minute of programmed speaking time. This allows a small amount of slip time (late starts, etc.) and time for the operation and proper pointing of visual aids — and also a small cushion to allow for the fact that scripts always exceed their allotted length and one does not want to cut down to size a speaker who has made a real effort in this direction. These factors are not peculiar to multilingual working, but as in so many things the added complexity of working in several languages calls for more careful planning if disasters are to be avoided.

12.1.6 Secretariat and transcription facilities

If not carefully planned and rigorously controlled, the secretarial aspects of a substantial conference can get completely out of control. Suppose first that — as is the case with many professional bodies — a complete transcript of the proceedings will consist of papers, and scripts of these already exist and have simply to be reproduced. In a multilingual conference they may, however, also have to be translated. The cost and time required to do this are prohibitive. The only possibility is to record all language channels and to use a competent multilingual secretary to transcribe and edit what the interpreters have said. Clearly however this will not be a completely satisfactory solution, and under these circumstances organisers often ask speakers to submit their scripts in all the conference languages. Unfortunately speakers frequently do not comply with this request and there is then little that the sponsors can do.

As was mentioned earlier in another context, it is desirable to organise the secretariat in shifts so that a particular team can sit in on a session of the conference and form a general impression and take notes (while the proceedings are also of course being tape-recorded) and can then go away and transcribe while the next session is in progress. This technique will not keep them completely up-to-date, but at least it will keep the lag within bounds, will involve the secretariat sufficiently to make them really interested and will allow the proceedings to be issued before delegates have forgotten the conference ever took place. An important technical point here is to ensure that tape decks compatible in speeds, number of tracks, etc., with those used in the sound equipment are available for transcribing both during and after the conference.

For a business meeting on the other hand it will almost certainly be enough to have a secretary trained in minute-taking. She should preferably be a multilingual so that she can be certain of not missing the gist of any remarks which for one reason or another do not get interpreted. The minutes will then have to be translated in the normal way. Clearly it is not feasible for minute-takers to operate simultaneously in all three languages, as they will not necessarily arrive at anything like the same wording.

It may be over-cynical to say that conferences are judged on their administration rather than on their content but it is certainly true that a cup of cold or weak coffee or a delay over the arrival of transport can virtually destroy the impression that thousands of pounds and months of work have gone to create. Nor is this so absurd as it may sound, for success or failure will turn largely on the spirit engendered in delegates and staff alike, and well-administered comfort picked out with a touch of elegance provides a suitable ambience for the informal chat at which most if not all of the importance business will be done.

This is not the place at which to go into the full problems and techniques of administrative planning, and many of the special administrative points affecting foreigners were covered in the preceding chapter. But there are certain facets of administration that apply specifically to multilingual conferences.

12.2.1 *Planning of free and leisure time*

The extent to which and the way in which leisure time should be filled by a formal programme will depend very much on the type of delegate but certainly the presence of foreign delegates will call for some action to be taken in this direction. Experience over a very wide variety of circumstances suggests, oddly enough, that what most delegates are most interested in is going shopping, and for this all will require advice on shopping centres and shops and some will require language assistance which, particularly in the provinces, the shops may be unable to provide. One would go so far as to say that, if the planning effort, budget and time available for entertainment are all limited, it would suffice to put the whole of this effort into assistance with shopping.

While it is always worth giving visitors the chance to see something of the town they are in, serious sightseeing should probably be avoided unless there is something unique, spectacular and easily accessible or sightseeing can be combined with some other unusual activity such as a trip in a *bateau mouche* or a waterbus, which could easily form part of the main social function of the gathering. For a quick relaxed glance, linguist student guides can provide adequate language cover, but serious sightseeing such as the detail of a cathedral interior or a museum calls for a very high level of interpreting and it is asking rather a lot of the conference interpreters to do this. If the need does arise, they must be given full opportunity for preparation.

12.2.2 *Entertainment*

Many conference organisers plan a crescendo of expensive eating and night-life — from salami to Salome one might say — to fill every mealtime,

but even when wining and dining is the main though latent object of the
gathering the wisdom of doing this seems very doubtful. It is probably
better to focus money and effort on one major function and to plan lunches
and other evenings on lines of quiet and restrained excellence — if indeed
they are to be planned at all.

It is a nice point whether this major function should come at the
beginning, presumably on the evening of assembly, to break the ice before
the proceedings start, or be held at the end to give a good final impression.
The exact plans must depend on timings of assembly and dispersal and on
the characteristics of the delegates, but the need can generally be covered
by two occasions attended by all concerned and sufficiently formal for
speeches to be made. One of these could be a lunch and the other, and
principal one, a dinner. If speeches are to be made, interpreters should be
warned in advance. An experienced interpreter will of course be able to
cope on the spot with a standard speech of welcome or thanks, but if longer
speeches containing points of substance, allusions and most of all
anecdotes are the order to the day, the speaker and the interpreter(s)
should if possible go over it together in advance. Quite apart from briefing
the interpreter, this will give an opportunity for a pun or other
untranslatable story to be replaced by a translatable one.

12.2.3   Information and travel services

It was said above that the main leisure interest of most foreign conference
delegates is shopping, and it is probably also true that the second thing on
the mind of even the most hardened conference goer or world-girdling
executive is communicating with his office and family and getting home.
He may also want a host of other pieces of information such as the
telephone numbers of friends in other parts of the country, details of a
particular type of holiday, medical treatment and so on; the one thing one
can say about all these is that they are unpredictable and some are bound
to be totally unexpected. There is thus a need for a highly efficient
information service, armed in particular with shopping and travel
information but capable of getting the answer, say between the beginning
of a session and the end of it, to anything it may be asked. As was suggested
above, it is probably best to centre this service on the main reception desk
and to use a shift of multilingual secretaries who are neither sitting in nor
transcribing to man this desk. This activity may seem irrelevant to their
main task, but despite hectic moments it will give them an amusing and
welcome break from what is otherwise a very heavy slog.

12.2.4   Use of interpreting resources

It is probably worth stressing again here that conference interpreters
should not be used for administrative work, even if they can be persuaded
out of the goodness of their hearts to undertake it. The only exceptions to

this are speeches at functions and, should it be appropriate, a detailed and specialised piece of sightseeing. The multilingual secretaries' team backed up as necessary by linguist students should be able to cope with all the normal administrative detail. But if the conference manager is not himself a good linguist, it is important to have a responsible and experienced linguist — perhaps the language consultant who has helped him in preparation of the conference — around to deal with complaints and any serious crises. Delegates can sometimes be very difficult; not only is it more satisfactory for them to be able to hold forth in their own language to someone responsible for the situation or able to cope with the problem, but it would be quite unreasonable to expect a conference interpreter who had just been involved in a stupid row to go in and handle a long and complicated session.

12.3   Presentations and demonstrations

We can now turn from conferences, at which at least the purported object is the exchange of information, negotiation and decision-making to gatherings at which most of the communication is one-way. It may be useful here to establish some working definitions for use in the rest of this chapter.

A presentation is a briefing on a company or its products (or both) which can be carried out entirely within one room at any convenient location by the use of portable exhibitions and audiovisual aids.

A demonstration involves the use of equipment whose nature determines probably the geographical location and certainly the setting, but which can be shown to an audience seated at one stand or a succession of stands.

A visit is the detailed study of objects *in situ,* e.g. an exhibition hall, a shop floor or a museum, requiring the participants to be conducted, usually in small groups, from one exhibit to the next, with explanations given at each exhibit and sometimes on the way between them.

A tour is taken to be similar to a visit but encompassing a much larger geographical area, for example a tour made up of visits of all factories in the UK manufacturing a particular product, or a tour of the old churches of a region.

A course is a planned block of instruction aimed at imparting information and/or skills to the students on it.

A seminar is a short course for a small group at which instruction is carried out by discussion with a high degree of student participation, and which may also have as its object the exchange of information.

We apologise to the reader if these distinctions seem pedantic and somewhat artificial, but it is useful to have them — or something like them — as distinct concepts in one's mind because, whether they involve several languages or no, each of them presents a different set of planning, executive and administrative problems.

At the beginning of this chapter we compared a conference to a stage production, and this analogy holds more strongly still for presentations and demonstrations. It is not enough for execution and administration to be perfect. The producer must show a flair that will excite the audience, and the speakers or commentators must seek to establish a real 'across the footlights' *rapport*. It follows that a rehearsal programme culminating in the equivalent of a dress rehearsal is essential, and the problem of getting the all-star cast of the organisation's key executives together may require this programme to be spread over a considerable time. Equally once a presentation or demonstration has been worked up and given a few times, it can be repeated, even with minor variations, at short notice and with comparatively little effort. In planning and checklisting one therefore needs to consider quite separately the programme needed to work up a new production and the routine actions and checks necessary for the repetition of an established one.

If several languages are to be used on the same occasion, the planning and technical factors, and in particular the extended planning schedule, are very much those already discussed at length in Section 12.1. For a presentation in two languages there is a real choice between simultaneous and consecutive interpreting, but for three languages simultaneous interpreting — or at least a simulation of it — is essential. In demonstrations the type of interpreting required is governed entirely by the nature and tempo of the action. Very often, particularly if heavy equipment is being moved or operating, there will be ample time for a consecutive commentary in three or even more languages without delaying or disrupting the action; if there are several different stands, it may be possible to handle a single-language group at any one stand at any one time and simply give the commentary in that language, not forgetting the need in this event to cue the action by some other means. Again a simultaneous commentary could be given in several languages using radio links working to an induction loop system — although this would be far from cheap if it had to be established at several different stands.

Simulated simultaneous interpreting is worth discussing in a little more detail, as it leads into the technique best used for the preparation of portable presentation packages. The underlying assumption is that the speakers are working from scripts and can be counted on to stick with reasonable accuracy both to the content of these and to their timing. Where still visual aids are used, these must be provided with a multilingual legend (or a glossary on a separate screen) as synchronisation will never be precise enough to match pointing. The technique involved is the pre-recording of the interpretation and its playback either over simultaneous interpreting equipment or by means of the mini-cassette playback instruments mentioned earlier. Questions and discussions are then handled by consecutive interpreting.

In opening up a new overseas market or in introducing a new product range to an established one there is clearly great advantage in taking a presentation on the company and its products to the customer, a need that has already been touched on in Chapter 8. Similarly if mobile equipment is toured, there will be a need for a commentary to support demonstrations of it. Here one is concerned with one language only, but unfortunately it does not happen to be English. Other problems are the cost and undesirability *per se* of the whole presentation team, which probably includes most of the top management, being away at once, the cost of moving them and the cost and awkwardness of moving audiovisual equipment. An 8-mm sound film with an editing-type projector and a sound track for each language required is undoubtedly part of the answer, but it is not the whole because one change of personalities or product may put it out of date and it costs too much and takes too long to revise. The complete answer would at first sight seem to be the portable video-tape recorder, which can be connected up to an existing monitor in countries with a compatible system or to a portable colour monitor carried around with it. This is indeed a solution of great promise but it has three drawbacks. First it is rather expensive for the relatively low rate of utilisation it would find in a small company. Secondly, a fair amount of skill is needed to produce presentations for CCTV and to get sound and vision effectively recorded. Thirdly, and most important, is that putting the whole presentation in the can destroys the personal touch.

In the present state of the art a reasonable compromise would seem to be the use of a small team consisting of, say, the managing or marketing director, the technical director or chief designer and a language consultant capable of giving part of the presentation live in the language concerned and of interpreting — in fact chairing — the question and answer session. The problem then is to introduce sufficient different voices to prevent boredom, and this can be done by pre-recording some sections of the presentation on tape, using two or three different linguists, the visual aids being pointed by the principal linguist during playback. With just three people and equipment small enough to go with their luggage into a car boot one can then put on the following highly acceptable mix:

1   Introduction (managing or marketing director — a sentence or two in the language, followed by consecutive interpreting).
2   Company film (premises, image, notable achievements — material in this must not date quickly).
3 . . . sections on design, product range, marketing/sales policy, after-sales service, etc. — the most important of these given direct in the language by the principal linguist, the rest played back off tapes in a variety of voices).
6   Conclusion (managing/marketing director with consecutive interpreting, or linguist direct).
7   Discussion (conducted by consecutive interpreting).

The great merits of this formula are that it is the next best thing to a presentation by the full team. It minimises time-wasting by consecutive interpreting, only a small amount of equipment need be carried around and any one section can be revised simply by recording a new tape cassette.

Since the principles of timing presentations and demonstrations seldom seem to be observed, and since the use of more than one language will in some way or other impair communications and increase the risk of boredom as well as influencing the timings themselves, it may be helpful to discuss these principles. The first of them is that producer and speakers must impose on themselves a discipline that will allow the timetable to be held. For not very apparent reason, once timings start sliding it is not only impossible to pull them back, but the presentation usually loses coherence and drags on into a shambles overrunning its set time by anything between 50 and 100 per cent.

Theory has it that the first half of the morning is the best time to get a message across, but since those who attend presentations and demonstrations either travel the same morning or probably have a hangover from a function the night before, the first period after morning coffee would seem to be a more practical prime time. The second point is that receptiveness and learning ability are at their highest 15 to 20 minutes after a break, this will mean either slotting the key section in as the second or third item of the programme, or timetabling to create a break a suitable time ahead of it. What is more important and generally accepted from experience is that chalk and talk — and even more so elegant films or videotapes — are useless in the hour or so after lunch. In fact it would be fair to say that unless something involving physical activity or at least a high level of audience participation can be planned for the period after lunch, it is better to break for lunch late and wind up the formal proceedings first.

For presentations this effectively sandwiches them between morning coffee and lunch, except perhaps for a discussion period after lunch if the sponsors are confident that discussion will be lively. This gives a period of 2-2½ hours, which is in any event enough — perhaps more than enough — for a presentation; and within it no one section, i.e. no one speaker, should be given more than 20 minutes at the outside. If the afternoon is to be devoted to a demonstration, a visit followed by a final discussion period, or simply to a discussion period, time should be allowed in the morning session for the audience to clear any burning questions that may be worrying them, so that the rest of the day can be conducted on a basis of common understanding.

Some demonstrations may last only a few minutes, but for substantial ones the maximum effective duration is probably also 2-2½ hours, and the latter only if a fair amount of time is spent in moving between stands. Here, since the main activity is an exciting one, usually out of doors and usually involving physical movement at some stage, the ideal is to assemble about noon, follow a quick welcome and briefing session with lunch, then the demonstration proper, followed by tea or coffee and a formal final discussion if there is to be one.

Various points in connection with the questions and discussion period have already been touched on, but since this is both critical for the success of the presentation and extremely difficult to handle in a foreign language, it may be worth exploring the possibilities a little further. If simultaneous interpreting is available, there is no problem, but generally speaking it will not be worth laying on a team of conference interpreters and the equipment for an event lasting only a couple of hours or so, only part of which will call for interpretation. Otherwise, unless the managing or marketing director himself speaks the language well enough to take effective charge, there is a conflict between getting his image across as the man who counts and keeping the discussion under control. If he effectively chairs it, neither the dynamics nor control will be maintained because the interpreter (as he would then be) would have to advise him over such matters as the grouping of questions and giving preference to rival speakers. If the linguist chairs it, answering some questions himself and referring others to the managing/marketing director or technical director, he will tend to become the central figure and the person who is remembered. Unless the management concerned has a taste for using an outside chairman for its presentations, as some do, or special circumstances prevail, this tendency may well be unacceptable. This is very much a matter of personalities, and one can do no more than draw attention to the problem.

The second hazard of these discussions is misunderstanding. Suppose that one of the audience wants to ask a technical question about the detail of a design feature of the product. He may not have understood this feature perfectly, and in posing his question he is likely to use his own firm's terminology — which, as we have said elsewhere, may be little more than a family code. If the linguist then misunderstands the question because of the unfamiliar terminology, there are all the makings of really deep confusion. Since a slide, foil or model of the design in question will probably be available on the spot, it should be an automatic drill to get this onto the screen or into view as soon as possible after the question is posed. This will effectively close the loop and produce a convergent rather than a divergent situation.

The ultra-politeness that both the sponsors and audience are likely to observe on international occasions of this kind often makes it very difficult to bring the discussion period to an end. If the usual 'one more question' or 'five minutes more' is considered insuffienctly tactful, one solution is to invite the senior member of the audience (perhaps the customer's managing director) to wind up the discussion and to arrange for him to do this on a pre-arranged signal from the chair. As usual it is best to get up from the table feeling you would like a little more, and anyone who has a burning question will have an opportunity to put it to one of the hosts over the final cup of coffee.

The need for high administrative standards is the same as for a conference and many of the same factors apply and problems arise. Since a presentation or demonstration will be much briefer than a conference and therefore conducted at a rather brisker tempo, the need for good reception arrangements and control of movement between anteroom, conference room and refreshment area is even greater. This question of control of movement is one that we shall come back to in various contexts in the later sections of this chapter, but one important aspect of it arises in connection with demonstrations. If distances between base and stand, or between stands, are large enough to require the use of vehicles, spectators must be divorced on arrival from their cars and moved in buses clearly identified by a letter or number. Even if all movement is on foot, spectators should be divided into smallish groups—say 10 or 12—each group being identified by a letter and bear-led by a guide with a placard. Obviously it is desirable, though not essential, for the guide to speak the language(s) of members of the group. Even if buses are also being used, it is advisable to pre-marshall spectators in these smaller and handier groups, and then assign three of them to a particular bus, e.g. bus ABC would carry spectator groups A, B and C. Movement is difficult and time-wasting enough in a single-language event, and when two or three languages are involved any attempt to marshall or accelerate people by loud-hailer becomes protracted and gives a too sergeant-major like impression. Even if great attention is paid to control of movement, it is still advisable to be what to the planner sitting at his desk seems absurdly generous over timings for spectator movement.

12.4 Visits and tours

12.4.1 Planning

All those with experience of arranging visits and tours for significant numbers of people even without the added complication of a foreign language will know how quickly the occasion can degenerate into shouting desperately through a loud-hailer at the backs of small groups scattering round corners or plunging into the maw of some dangerous area. As was stressed just above these problems are redoubled when control has to be exercised in several languages. In the same way the normal difficulties of giving detailed explanations to a group standing around a running machine are compounded by the need to interpret. In fact this type of factory visit is one of the occasions that really calls for the linguist to be briefed in advance and then to give the explanations direct with the staff standing by to field questions, but this only brings the problem back to the single-language state.

Whether or not it is the organisation's practice for visits conducted in their own language, for visits involving one or more foreign languages a thorough advanced briefing with the visitors seated in a room where they are comfortable and can hear and see is indispensable. After a welcoming word from, say, the managing director, which will have to be consecutively interpreted, the visitors should be divided into language groups and briefed direct in their own language by suitably prepared linguists. The briefing should be in three parts:

1   General administrative instructions (refreshments, toilets, dispersal, etc.)
2   The detail and sequence of what they are going to see.
3   The exact route and method of conduct of the visit.

The visitors should then be divided into small groups — ideally no more than 5 or 6 if running machinery is to be looked at — and each group physically placed with and introduced to its guide.

There are two distinct methods of conducting the tour, and the choice between them depends partly on the circumstances but mainly on the number and quality of available linguists. One is to use the guides quite simply as guides and station interpreters at points where explanations are to be given. The other is that the guides act also as interpreters, halting their group at each station and giving the appropriate explanation before moving on. In either case an expert member of staff must be on each station to deal with questions. The second method is preferable for the visitors and makes control easier, but if there is a large number of groups it is rather unlikely that enough interpreters capable of taking them round the whole visit can be found.

If the number of visitors is large and more than one shop — say a foundry, a machine shop and a test and inspection laboratory — are to be visited, it would be normal to split visitors arbitrarily into three main groups before dividing these up in turn into the smaller groups which can move together. With visitors speaking several mother-tongues control will be much easier if each main group is made up of one language-group. Even if exhaustive control arrangements have been made and visitors have been fully briefed, it will be essential to have one linguist equipped with a power loud-hailer with each major (language) group, to marshall them in moving between main areas. As has been mentioned elsewhere, if the background noise level is high and/or the sub-groups are comparatively large — say in double figures — it will be advisable to equip every linguist with a power loud-hailer.

It will be clear from all this that one of the purposes of planning exercises of this kind must be to contain the language cost within reasonable limits, and this is definitely a case where it will pay to bring in an experienced language consultant at the very early stages to help plan the arrangements as a whole and the most cost-effective use of language resources in particular.

Nothing is more destructive of interest and evocative of aversion in visitors who have a long journey home than a programme that starts late, shows signs of overrunning in its early stages and ends up in a sprint for the bus and a dash to catch the last train. The need to put in adequate slip time where the movement of large numbers is concerned has been stressed in earlier sections, but in the multistand demonstration or more particularly a tour of factories or laboratories timings will have to be worked out in a way that will avoid groups meeting head-on in narrow doorways and passages or colliding in a restricted area. It is advisable to put a one-way system into force wherever possible and to establish buffer areas, preferably with seating, where groups can wait until another has cleared. The worst confusion is apt to occur where the visit is taking place in a number of separate rooms on several storeys of a building so that the guides cannot see where other groups are. In a large factory or in the open movement becomes to some extent self-adjusting.

Extravagant as it may sound, it is also advisable to have a whipper-in bringing up the rear of each group. This is essential if visitors are moving through areas made dangerous by machinery or by contamination. It is also desirable to plan movement and to exercise control in ways that will prevent the groups approaching one another so that visitors can switch groups. Otherwise the group with either the best-informed guide or the most attractive interpreter will grow as the visit progresses, or the stand of special interest or attraction will become surrounded by more and more people.

One of us recalls a recent laboratory tour which started in five groups and finished up in two — one sampling do-it-yourself wines and the other home-made beers. Quite apart from the chaos that results and the fact that the visitors do not all see what they are supposed to see, it is acutely demoralising for stand staff, interpreters and guides to find themselves progressively deserted. If the whole event takes place on one site and there are no particular risks to visitors, a balance needs to be struck between rigidity of control and creating an agreeable atmosphere, but if the programme involves long moves by vehicle, between plants for instance, a very firm effort must be made to stick to the timings and to keep everyone together and under observation. Otherwise either someone will be left behind or the programme will be held up while the lost sheep are found. Again the language problem can complicate matters. Once a foreigner speaking no English gets separated from his interpreter or guide, the chances of his getting back to his proper group or indeed rejoining the party at all are fairly remote.

12.4.3   *Administration*

Moving about in groups, particularly in confined spaces, is a tiring and stressful activity of itself, and when such factors as background noise and the need for interpreting are thrown in, two hours is probably as much as most people can stand, at least without a substantial and comfortable break. As the end of the programme approaches visitors will not only lose interest but tend to become hostile towards the message that is being put across to them. If they are to leave with a good impression not only must the part of the programme involving movement be restricted in scope and duration, but the administrative arrangements must be designed to cope with fatigue and any tendency towards aversion. It is worth introducing as a 'stand' a comfortable room with tea and coffee and/or drinks where the visitors can spend the allotted time resting, refreshing themselves and looking at some rather undemanding form of visual display. Whatever is done in this direction during the programme, visitors must be given tea or coffee and/or a drink in spacious, quiet and comfortable surroundings before they leave.

Some factory visits where movement is difficult or the noise level is high may easily stress visitors, guides and interpreters to the point where they feel faint or even collapse. Many processes involve contamination of the atmosphere and/or combinations of humidity and temperature and these may easily affect visitors with allergies or a bronchial condition. All staff involved must know the nearest place to any point on the route at which drinking water can be obtained, and there is a need for first-aid back-up which will allow anyone who is feeling unwell to be segregated and treated without disrupting the programme of a whole group.

12.5   Courses and seminars

Manufacturing and service firms are frequently called upon to arrange some kind of course of instruction for their customers, and the quality and acceptability of instruction given can be vital to the success of the project as a whole. Seminars may range from a short, informal course of instruction given to a small group of relatively senior executives or specialists to a sort of mini-conference of organisations with a common interest.

12.5.1   *Choice of method*

The duration and circumstances of most of the larger courses of instruction are such that simultaneous interpreting must be ruled out either on cost or for practical reasons. Consecutive interpreting, with the double opportunity it gives to hoist in the message, can work very well in a presentation lasting an hour or two, but becomes insufferably tedious and time-consuming when used as the primary method in a course of several days or weeks. For theoretical instruction in the classroom there is really no effective alternative to finding someone capable, after suitable briefing, of giving the instruction direct in the language.

This in turn dictates the use of the lecture, however informal, as the basic method, but each talk must of course be followed by a period of questions and discussion. Here the answers must be supplied by the experts and consecutive interpreting becomes necessary. This in turn means that the time normally allotted for this must be doubled either by lengthening the period or by curtailing the direct instruction.

With practical instruction as with shop-floor interpreting, demonstrations and communication by signs are the fastest and most effective method. Where verbal explanations are unavoidable there must of course be a linguist present to give them either direct or by consecutive interpreting. Particularly where there is an element of risk — and this applies to most industrial processes — the procedure or skill being taught must be fully explained and demonstrated before the students start to practise it, and it as well to provide each student with a précis in the language of safety precautions, the procedure itself and any dangerous errors together with the means of rectifying them.

For the kind of medium-sized group discussion which is generally known as a seminar — or sometimes as a syndicate discussion — regardless of whether it is concerned with instruction or with the exchange of information, only two techniques are possible. One is simultaneous interpreting, and this will need to be of the highest order; the other is to conduct the entire discussion in one language. We have attempted this method of instruction using consecutive interpreting, but it is dreary for the students and exhausting for the interpreter; in the case in question it quickly changed into a discussion held in the language with the English-speaking expert making explanatory sketches, filling in detail and handling any particularly fast balls. Where the aim is exchange of information, say between a group of professionals of the same discipline or a working group of members of a trade association or such, and it is essential to include someone who cannot work in the chosen language because of his expertise, whisper interpreting (see Section 6.3) can be extremely effective, and these are the kind of circumstances under which interpreters of sufficient skill and experience may be prepared to use this technique.

12.5.2 Planning factors

Given that any course of the kind being considered here is likely to be specialised in content, the need to work in a foreign language turns the task of planning even a short, straightforward course of instruction into something very like that of organising a small multilingual conference — unless of course the sponsor happens to have a suitable specialist who can give the instruction in the required language. In particular, and for much the same reasons, the lead times involved go from days to weeks and more realistically perhaps to months. The first problem is to find somebody capable of giving the more straightforward parts of the instruction in the language and of dealing with the rest by consecutive interpreting. This calls for someone who is a good linguist, a trained instructor and has at least some background knowledge of the subject. The people most likely to possess this particular combination of skills are retired members of the Armed Forces or retired engineers who have spent part of their career in a country of the language.

The language problem may also affect the choice of location for courses, the planning aim in this case being to arrange things so that under normal usages the customer will bear as much of the cost as possible or, if the supplier is committed contractually to carry out a training programme at his expense, the cost of doing so will be containable.

The linguist will need a very considerable amount of time to brief himself, to prepare his instruction and to write and get reproduced any précis or other documentation that may be needed to support it. It would clearly be unreasonable to expect him to do this in his own time and at his own expense, and even if the situation is one in which reduced rates would normally apply to time spent on briefing, it is fairly unlikely that a linguist capable of carrying out the task will agree to this. The fairest and best basis from every point of view is probably an agreed all-in fee, acceptance by the client of all travel and subsistence expenses and payment at an agreed time rate for any instructional or administrative tasks arising during the course beyond those planned and timetabled.

Many organisations faced with a long course or a series of short courses to be given in a foreign language attempt to plug the gap by recruiting someone temporarily onto the payroll. Anyone with sufficient experience to give the instruction direct is however rather unlikely to be prepared to participate on this basis. Students or the newly graduated should be able to handle this situation by interpreting, but they are unlikely to succeed in giving the instruction direct.

Courses run in the customer's country should produce no problems of student administration, although the problems and cost of administering the instructional team and of getting adequate facilities may be immense. Experience suggests however that third-world students of limited education coming to Europe for any length of time tend to become extremely unhappy. The linguist instructor may well have to act as a sort of mentor, which again suggests that an older person is more suitable. Further any gesture of acceptance, goodwill and personal interest is of such importance to student morale that it fairly comes under the head of course planning rather than of administration. If numbers are sufficient a football match against a works team is a splendid ice-breaker, a modest programme of sightseeing or excursions will reap a rich dividend in goodwill (and this is after all customer goodwill) and, whatever the language difficulties, any invitation to a home will be deeply valued by the visitors.

Experience with third-world technicians on courses of this kind suggests that their manual skills tend to be of a far higher order than is usually found in Europe today, and they can very easily be motivated to develop these skills or apply them to a new technique. But because their general education is limited and the language used for instruction is, after all, unlikely to be their true mother-tongue, a very high order of teaching ability is required to impart any theoretical matter, especially where generalised concepts are concerned as is so often the case in electrical engineering and electronics. In planning a course for this type of student, generalised theoretical instruction should be cut to a minimum and expressed in the simplest acceptable terms. Special attention should be paid to confidence-building and motivation both in and out of school. Extensive use should be made of visual aids — wherever possible of simplified working models of the kind used to teach elementary physics. But most important of all the time allotted to instruction of this type to third world students of technician level should generally speaking be three times greater than would be considered necessary for their European counterparts.

Finally even in the shorter courses some form of continuous and final assessment is essential. A reluctance to admit that they do not understand is a racial and cultural characteristic of students from many parts of the third world and — again especially where theoretical or generalised matter is concerned — some simple and informal form of test, perhaps no more than interrogation, is indispensable.

In sum the planning and execution of a training programme in a foreign language, and particularly one for third-world students, may call for a seemingly disproportionate expenditure of time, effort and money. Since such programmes often have to be costed in, at least in outline, at the quotation stage, advice should be sought from someone with suitable experience in order to arrive at a realistic costing.

12.6   Small meetings

The discussion above on seminars aimed at the exchange of information began to take us into what is, in our view, by far the most important aspect of oral communication across a language barrier. In the business world as opposed to the learned professions, small meetings, whether their purported objective is negotiation, the exchange of information, forward planning of collaboration or even some apparently social purpose such as the control of pollution, are — and indeed should be — underlain by the profit motive. Therefore unless the agenda is openly concerned with negotiations over terms or other financial matters, nothing that is said or done will ever mean quite what it seems. Negotiation is very much an individual art, and experienced and skilled negotiators vary enormously both in the way they like to stack the cards and in how far from their chest they hold them.

Thus interpreting at small meetings calls for a very high level of language skill and even more for a feel for both parties' reactions and an understanding of their ulterior motives. Whatever interpreting technique is used, and whether the interpreter acts in the conventional sense as an interpreter or is given freedom to play a part nearer to that of intermediary, this is where it pays to hire not only a conference interpreter but a hand-picked one.

For up to three language-groups of not more than two each, the presence of interpreting equipment merely serves to destroy the atmosphere of intimacy and consequently the *rapport*. Here the choice lies between consecutive and whisper; if only two languages are involved consecutive will probably be better, and with only three or four people present a skilled interpreter can in fact speed things us by using a mixture of consecutive technique and simultaneous whisper.

The largest gathering that could reasonably be considered a 'small meeting', and one typical of many specialist working groups, might involve up to four languages and twelve people. With four languages there is of course no alternative to simultaneous interpreting. With three, depending on the level of the delegates and hence the cost of their time, it will probably pay to use simultaneous for any formal speeches or presentations, going over to consecutive — using of course the same interpreters — for discussion unless the group and their interpreters already form a well-knit entity with a high degree of mutual confidence and/or the problem is one of drafting. With only two languages consecutive is generally more cost-effective and may well be preferable *per se.* If however a great deal of detailed work and in particular drafting has to be got through, it may be worth going simultaneous unless the key members of the two delegations have sufficient knowledge of each other's language to use a kind of 'each speak your own language' method with the interpreter, preferably assisted by a secretary, doing the drafting and when necessary blowing the whistle.

12.6.2 *Documentation*

For many small meetings, particularly higher-level negotiating meetings, the requirements for documentation may well be nil. But it is certainly not true that documentation varies proportionately with the size of the meeting, and the papers needed for example by specialised working groups are likely to be both massive and of great importance. In fact a working group holding a series of meetings aimed at, say, drafting a controversial standard, specification or statement of requirement may often find that the whole tempo of their project is governed by the time taken to get the preparatory documentation for each meeting drawn up in the languages concerned, forwarded to the other party(ies) and approved by them from the viewpoint of language and content. Once comments and counter-comments on the paperwork start flying about, the whole programme can easily become bogged down.

It is therefore important to have a standing colocated element of the secretariat responsible for preparing the documentation in all languages concerned. Between meetings, one of the interpreting team should ideally work full time with the group and himself do the translations. But if cost and/or availability preclude this, the interpreter must be on call to advise on terminology and to edit all translations. This approach may cause some rumblings from other delegations to begin with, but if this team has the skill and integrity to gain the confidence of all concerned the whole business both of preparatory documentation and of the drafting of texts during meetings will become as straightforward — though rather more time-consuming and considerably more expensive — than it would be in single-language working.

12.6.3   Control and chairing

If the meeting is large enough and so constituted as to require a chairman, the problem will be quite different depending on whether simultaneous or consecutive interpreting is being used. Briefly in the one case he only needs to control switchings of the microphones and to ensure that two people are not allowed to talk at once whether or not both their microphones are live. The meeting should then proceed exactly as a single-language meeting would.

With consecutive interpreting it is a great help if the chairman has sufficient knowledge of the other language(s) involved to be able to follow what is being said and to call delegates to order. If interpreters have to be used to maintain control, the response time will allow what may have started as a perfectly innocent simultaneous utterance by two delegates to develop into a nasty little fracas. It is also often very difficult to stop delegations splitting into groups; this effectively removes control of the meeting from the chair and puts the interpreter in an impossible position. In the type of meeting where real work is being done, it is clearly necessary for delegations to discuss points among themselves. But when they need to do so they should ask permission of the chair, and the chairman should then in the formal sense adjourn the meeting for not more than five or 10 minutes — though physically it is not necessary for anyone to leave the table. The chairman must also make sure, unless there is an understanding to the contrary, that the interpreters are given the opportunity to translate everything that is said. There will nearly always be members of one delegation who can understand another's language, and as the discussion warms up temptation to cut in becomes almost irresistible. But failure to interpret a statement at least in summary may lead not only to a serious misunderstanding but, what is much worse, to a loss of mutual confidence.

If the leader of one of the delegations is a good and experienced chairman and a linguist, he will generally be accepted by all as the standing chairman, although he may wish to hand the chair over to another for specific purposes on particular occasions. In small and informal meetings such as might typically take place when two firms in the same field are examining the possibilities of collaboration, there is a strong case for using as an interpreter someone of sufficient experience and standing to be acceptable also as an intermediary. In this case — with a rather liberalised form of interpreting — the tendency will be for the intermediary to assume the role of chairman in that he will effectively control the switching of discussion between one party and another and frequently between one individual and another.

Generally speaking it is very much more difficult to jolly people along in a multilingual meeting in the way that a good chairman normally would, and next to impossible to achieve the requisite variations of the dynamics with conventional consecutive interpreting. Only with excellent simultaneous interpreting within a well-knit team can the more positive aspects of the chairman's role be exercised.

12.6.4   Tactics of linguist delegates

Where more than two languages are involved the meeting is going to have to proceed by one of the conventional interpreting techniques and the scope for linguist delegates is thus fairly limited. About the only way in which they they can make active use of their languages is in using one of them to make a direct personal appeal to a delegate in his own language. A move of this kind clearly has a positive value but this can best be exploited outside the meeting proper. Speaking in the 'wrong' language can however be a valuable disruptive tactic for stalling, gaining thinking time or breaking up the development of a discussion; it achieves this because it takes the chairman by surprise, thus weakening at least temporarily his control, and breaks the rhythm of whichever system of interpreting is being used.

In bilingual meetings however the linguist has a number of more positive options open to him, particularly if he is a team leader. One is not to disclose his knowledge of the other language at all, hoping that the opposition will break the ground rule mentioned in Chapter 11 and give their hand away by caucusing in his hearing. The second is to use the language for social and business conversations outside the meeting, but to insist on the meeting being conducted by consecutive interpreting. If the opposition does not speak English this gives him invaluable thinking time while the next interpreter is holding forth. He can plan his next move carefully and come in hard and fast on the heels of the interpreter, thus applying pressure to the other side — he can in fact turn the problems of dynamics caused by the use of consecutive interpreting to his advantage. If the leader or key members of the opposition speak English, this advantage is neutralised and simultaneous interpreting or working in one language may be prefereable.

If agreement is reached on working in one of the languages concerned, there will be a need for back-up interpretation, preferably simultaneous, to the non-linguist members of the team whose language is not chosen and of course for interpreting if they intervene. One clearly places oneself at a disadvantage in powers of expression by agreeing to work in the other language, but very often the combined psychological advantages of courtesy and oneupmanship more than offset this. Conversely one should never insist on working in English even if one is in a position to do so, abilities.

Once knowledge of the language has been revealed, tactics can of course be varied or mixed to suit the occasion. Where only two languages are in use a sudden switch into the opposition's language is a far more valuable and constructive tactic than it is in a multilingual meeting.

12.6.5 Minute-taking and drafting

The ideal solution if full minutes are required is to have two multilingual secretaries working in shifts to prevent transcription getting behindhand; this will produce the minutes in one language only and they will subsequently have to translated and approved by all delegations before they can be formally agreed. If short minutes are required and it is important to get them out by the end of the meeting — as it often may be in a fairly fast-moving project — the ideal is to have two shifts of two multlingual secretaries each, one member of each pair taking in each language. The combination of short minutes and shift working allows the two members of the team to compare notes and produce texts that match to an acceptable degree.

A more important problem is perhaps the drafting of communiqués, agreements, specifications, etc., in matching texts for approval and, if appropriate, issue at the end of the meeting. In high-level meetings this is of course done by the secretariats who will present drafts to their respective masters for approval and then jointly to both sides for final agreement. In working-level meetings, however, drafting has got to be done in the meeting and this is an extremely difficult task. If it is carried out in full session it is undoubtedly best if somewhat unconventional to pass effective control of the meeting to one of the interpreters who can then offer proposals clause by clause in each language in turn. The agreed draft can then be recorded simultaneously in the two languages either by a nominated member of each delegation or by secretaries. In very small meetings where there is only one interpreter, and particularly if he is in effect acting as an intermediary, it may be best to let the interpreter do the drafting in both languages during a break or overnight and then offer these drafts for discussion and ultimate approval.

12.6.6 Disputes over spoken agreements

In single-language working, disputes over spoken agreements are comparatively rare partly because misunderstandings seldom arise between reasonably experienced negotiators and partly because challenging a spoken agreement amounts to a direct accusation of bad faith. However, if one of the parties is working in a foreign language he may often attempt to wriggle by claiming that he did not entirely understand what he was agreeing to; and if an interpreter is being used he of course provides an ideal scapegoat. Attempts are sometimes made to make scapegoats of translators in the same way, but in that case the evidence exists in writing should the matter be brought to a head, and the ploy of blaming the translator is really no more than a diplomatic way out of an impasse (sometimes used with the agreement of the translator concerned!). Similarly if two interpreters are present the risk is reduced. But an interpreter working alone in a small high-level meeting could easily find himself in a position that would be highly damaging to his reputation to say the least. It is therefore essential in everyone's interest, not least the interpreter's, to make on-the-spot notes, preferably in both languages, on what has been agreed and to get these initialled before the meeting breaks up. This is one reason why some emphasis was placed above on the problems of minute-taking and drafting and the frequent need to get agreed documents out at the end of the meeting.

Checklists for advance planning, one-time procedures, routine procedures and final and daily checks are given in Appendices 4-7.

13
The export contract

This chapter is written round the export of capital goods or other major specialised equipment to a market other than Western Europe—a situation, that is, where a broad approach to the market as a whole is unlikely to bear fruit and where the exporter will be competing with leading firms or consortia from many parts of the world. At the time of writing many of the factors discussed apply also to Western Europe, but this will become less and less so as the EEC and its associated free trade area develop. Opportunities would probably come from requests for tender advertised in the press, from personal contact with the customer or his associates or by recommendation from other specialised firms in the context of some broad project. However it may have come into being, the start situation facing the exporter will probably be a requirement to submit either a preliminary proposal or a full quotation against a very tight deadline, perhaps in a market that is new to him. This will call for crash action, and the main thing is to get some kind of submission in to keep the ball rolling while trying to avoid firm commitments on costs or specifications which may prove extremely embarrassing later.

The ability to snatch these opportunities therefore depends on the existence of adequate technical sales and language resources and of a senior coordinator with very clear ideas on priorities. More generally, the sheer management effort required to see a complex export contract through to a successful conclusion is far greater than those accustomed to working to the home market or established Western export markets suppose. The role played by the marketing or sales department is a comparatively small one here, and the bulk of the work tends to fall on line management and specialist departments. Thus to deal with a major third-world export contract successfully without severe disruption of other commitments, a firm will need an organisation with sufficient resources and flexibility to allow a senior manager backed up by a full team of specialists to be switched virtually full time onto the project. Even where an organisation is large enough to have a separate 'overseas' or export division or company, this function will need full support from specialists with the main organisation.

13.1 Market intelligence

Although the acquisition of market intelligence is a matter that often attracts more lip-service than actual effort, a good deal of market intelligence is likely to be available in the case of a planned entry into a new market on a broad front. But in the more specialised fields an excellent opportunity may suddenly appear in a market on which the exporter has done no homework at all, and he will be forced to set about acquiring knowledge of it at the same time as he is drawing up his initial proposals. To make good this deficiency he will need to assign effort to an intensive intelligence programme, and this is likely to fall under three heads.

13.1.1 Background and broad-field intelligence

The kind of background information that would have been built up in advance in a planned marketing operation will have to be gained by experience as the project progresses. But some research must be done into the main trends of the target country's economy, the current operations and short-term intentions of the industry concerned, the physical operating conditions and the standard of training and education of personnel at various working levels. Otherwise the initial proposals may be quite inappropriate or even completely out of scale, and this is doubly true of newly fledged third-world industries, where those who have prepared the inquiry documentation may have very little idea either of the technical requirements or even of the kind of commercial conditions they should set.

Useful scene-setting information can easily be obtained from the British Overseas Trade Board, the London Chamber of Commerce and perhaps from the UK trade association concerned. But this is unlikely to be specific enough or, in the nature of things, fully up-to-date. If contact has been made through a really reliable and trusted agent, he can of course be called back to give a briefing. Otherwise a reconnaissance visit by a senior member of the project team, accompanied if possible by the linguist who will be handling the project, is indispensable. This should take in as a first priority the British Embassy (or High Commission) in the country and allow time for a general look round the region or locality concerned; even if it is undesirable on tactical grounds to make direct contact with the potential customer at this stage, it should be possible to visit the relevant government technical agencies and banks to obtain precise information on the regulations that will apply. Another useful short-cut if circumstances permit is a discussion with contacts either in the former master of an ex-colony or in a known neighbouring market, e.g. Holland *or* Singapore for Indonesia.

13.1.2   Target intelligence

The same means can be used to acquire information on the customer. Perhaps the most important single point at this stage is to obtain an idea of his organisation and to pinpoint the individual who will be making the actual decisions, and of course in socialised countries to glean similar information on the sponsor ministry. Another important aspect is the similar or related equipment he already possesses, as compatibility with this may be a decisive point in closing the deal.

The Communist countries present the most severe problems under this head, as it is often next to impossible to penetrate either physically or by direct communication beyond the national import-export organisation, or in the case of the USSR itself the triangle of central, regional and field-technical agencies. On the other hand the amount and quality of intelligence available from British government sources (and possibly from the GB-USSR Association) are likely to be considerably higher than is the case with third-world markets.

13.1.3   Product intelligence

The question of compatibility with existing equipment and facilities was mentioned above. To optimise both the design to be offered and the way in which it is presented, it will also be necessary to have a reasonably firm idea of the intensity and conditions of use, the customer's maintenance and spares organisation (particularly in the case of mobile equipment operating over a wide area), the detailed operating conditions, e.g. dust or humidity, and the standard of operator and maintenance staff. The vital aspect of regulations and standards is discussed separately below.

More important still perhaps is to determine the precise purpose for which the product is intended, which may be very different from that indicated by the enquiry.

The other side of this coin is gleaning as much information as possible on the competition. In an advanced country this may come mainly from indigenous industry, but in the third world the problem is likely to lie with contenders from the exporter's own and other advanced countries, and the importance of trying to find out where the serious competition lies needs no stressing. Not only will such knowledge radically affect both the detail of what is offered and the way it is presented, but, for a really large and wide-ranging contract, it may offer the opportunity of joining forces on favourable terms with an exporter in another West European or North American country and so greatly increasing the chances of success.

13.2   Regulations, standards and approving authorities

The deadline for an initial submission (and here one is usually talking of unit weeks and sometimes even of days) may make it impossible to acquire full knowledge of the regulations, standards and approval procedures in the target country or even to make direct contact with the authorities concerned. Even an established agent may not be familiar with the requirements for a particular specialised field, and in this case it may be necessary to buy in expertise in the shape of a consultant who is familiar with this market. This is an expensive expedient particularly if he will not be required in the later stages of the project, but it is less costly than having to change a design after a commitment to costed proposals has been entered into or even having to modify a complete production run.

For third-world countries it is reasonably safe to assume in the early stages that their requirements will follow those of their former imperial masters or economic sponsors, and a quick visit to the official agencies in those countries will often produce much faster and sounder results than an attempt to contact the organisation in the target country direct. Experience suggests that civil servants at this technical level are likely to be far more helpful in such circumstances than one might suppose, provided that they are asked simply to advise and not to commit themselves in a matter that lies outside their true scope. For example one of us recalls a one-day visit to Paris on the day before the Christmas holidays began which, for the price of a good lunch, produced advice and information leading directly to a saving of many thousands of pounds.

The Communist bloc presents special problems in this respect. Not only is it impossible to get at the approving authority concerned or indeed at anyone expert in the approval requirements, but there is no give and take whatever and, as will be mentioned in a later chapter, enquiries from this source are apt to contain references to national or COMECON specifications which are not easy to obtain quickly and may or may not correspond with their Western equivalents. However this market is far less likely than the third world to produce unexpected short-term opportunities, and there should have been time to obtain and analyse all the necessary documentation. Again the British Standards Institution or ASLIB may well have the requisite documents ready-translated.

While some risks of this kind may have to be taken in the early stages, it is essential, however difficult it may prove, to obtain full, valid and up-to-date information on regulations, standards and approval procedures before the contract is signed and the offer price and delivery date thus become firm. If for example the vendor is faced with an inspection or calibration programme which he has not costed in, the dent in his profit margin is likely to be a deep one. Nor is it always safe to accept guidance from the customer. He himself may not be fully au fait with recent amendments to regulations, and since the contract is likely to require conformity with regulations in force at the date of signature, the onus then falls on the exporter. The only solution is a fairly protracted visit to the country aimed at contacting all approval organisations concerned, obtaining the most up-to-date version of the regulations together with a forecast of any changes likely to be introduced in the near future and agreeing the procedures for inspection and approval to the point if possible of establishing a costed programme. In addition to dealing with the approvals specific to the product, it is also worth probing broader areas of ancillary approvals for specific items, e.g. electrical equipment, and more general matters such as customs and exchange control regulations. The acquisition of all this information, its collation in usable form and where necessary translation into internal instructions requires a significant expenditure of time and money, but the consequences of failure to do so may be so serious as to turn a useful profit into a substantial loss combined with lasting damage to the exporter's repute.

It is perhaps in this area most of all that Anglo-Saxon exporters are apt to attempt to ride roughshod over the importing country's requirements. As was stressed in Chapter 11, this temptation must be avoided; even if the customer himself is flexible, foreign officials are not going to accept breaches of their regulations any more than our own Home Office or Customs and Excise would. The establishment of good relations with approving authorities and a patent effort to comply will often lead to relaxations which may represent a considerable saving. But once they feel they are being flouted they have little choice but to throw the book at the offender — and it can be quite a book.

13.3 Preliminary negotiations

It is the preliminary negotiations that set the tone of any transaction, and in the kind of contract under discussion here they call for quite exceptional skill. For one is trying at one and the same time to make a highly positive impression, to sound out the opposition and glean information, and to back-pedal as hard as possible until one has acquired the hard data needed to finalise and cost the proposal. The first and most difficult decision is whether to submit the initial proposal 'cold' and go into action only when some form of favourable response to it is received, or try to improve the chances of success by arranging discussions or at least asking intelligent questions before the written submission is made. This will depend very much on the overall situation and in the way in which the opportunity to quote has arisen, but generally speaking, even if it is not specifically ruled out of court, the kind of early selling initiatives that are customary and perhaps indispensable in the West are likely to hit a brick wall where the Communist Bloc is concerned and to arouse active suspicion and disfavour in the third world. Unless a personal relationship exists which can be used without infringing any restrictions on the employment of intermediaries that may apply, it is probably best to put all available effort into optimising the written submission and let it stand on its merits.

It is in these tentative but critical stages that the language barrier stands at its most formidable. Quite apart from the intangible problems discussed in Chapter 11, the needs for speed and certainty of response and for an intensive and well-coordinated but multipronged effort make the delays and imperfections of working across two languages really hurt. In-house language resources of the kind considered at the beginning of Part 2 really pay off here, but they may not be adequate in quality for the task and/or the load on the linguist executives concerned may become intolerable. Further, a lot of simultaneous but diffuse activities are called for, and no one person can take on more than one of them. In particular there is a need both for a trusted representative who speaks the language at the target end to obtain information and generally act as a link, and for language and market expertise at the exporting end to steer the documentation and keep everyone in the picture. Even if intermediaries are barred, an experienced and trusted agent can be re-hired in a consultant capacity for the purposes of the contract, and either a professional linguist who is able and prepared to act in a consultant role or a management or engineering consultant who has the requisite language and market knowledge can be brought in to cover the 'home' end. This is an ideal solution, and so far from being extravagant is likely to save money in the long run, because it will on the one hand greatly reduce the need for formal translation and on the other eliminate the cost of moving a linguist for every visit. It is, however, important that the two linguists should 'change ends' from time to time to maintain continuity and ensure consistent terminology. But individuals who can in every sense be trusted to handle work of this scale and importance are not easy to find in third-world countries, and the next best solution — in the absence of a suitable linguist executive — is to retain a consultant who is capable of conducting exploratory and technical-level visits on his own. This will not only ensure continuity but by reducing travel costs and saving executive time will eliminate the temptation to hold back from a liaison visit when one is highly desirable but not indispensable.

Reconnaissance and any preliminary negotiations are however too important to be delegated either internally or to a consultant or agent. The team leader, who may perhaps be the export sales director or manager or even in a small firm the managing director, must somehow find time to make the initial visit himself. Quite apart from the need for him to form a personal impression of the total situation, it is only in this way that access at the level required can be gained to government

agencies and to the customer himself. Equally it is not only extravagant
but misguided to crowd the stage at this juncture with a massive team.
This merely causes confusion in the customer's and others' minds and
gives the impression that the exporting organisation lacks any one person
of real authority and competence. The right people to field in the early
stages are the project leader and the language or other consultant.

13.4 Tendering

Even where some kind of preliminary discussion with the customer
himself is possible, the tender documentation is all-important. Often it
may be the sole means of putting the exporter's image across at the
crucial stage. Even if the only delays in receiving the enquiry are postal
ones, the tenderer is unlikely to have more than three weeks to get his
proposals off, and if avoidable internal delays or a holiday period have
intervened, the effective time may be as little as a week. Unless advanced
contacts are exceptionally strong, to the point where the whole tendering
process is something of a formality, a request for an extension beyond the
closure date will amost certainly lead to loss of the order. If only because
of the time and language factors, normal internal procedures for
tendering are likely to prove quite inadequate and the firm that takes
opportunities of this kind seriously will therefore need to establish and run
in a special standard operating procedure.

13.4.1 Enquiry documents

Unless there is an agent on the spot, a good deal of time is likely to be lost
in obtaining the full enquiry documentation as opposed to the notice of
request for tender itself. A telex to the Commercial Counsellor at the
British Embassy will often be the quickest solution. These documents
may vary widely in form, but are likely to be fairly massive and to contain
four elements:

1 Either the notice of request for tender itself or a cover-sheet which
   will give the reference of the enquiry, the contents of the
   documentation and detailed instructions on the time, place and
   method of submission.
2 The technical specifications, which may well contain ambiguities
   and present terminological problems, and will almost certainly be
   either so brief as to provide little guidance or so full as to lay down
   a possibly unrealistic solution in detail. Also they are likely to
   contain references to specifications, regulations, etc., which the
   tenderer may not have immediately at his disposal.
3 The special conditions, which in addition to their obvious content
   may include a good deal of background information on the project.
4 The general conditions, which will be framed in semi-legal language
   and which we have known to run to over 100 pages of typescript.

These have to be analysed with great care before any response is made. They frequently contain clauses which pre-empt the vendor to an intolerable degree, and submission of a quotation without appropriate riders is often taken as acceptance of them.

13.4.2 *Processing*

Since no-one can move a muscle until the contents of this document-ation are in his hands, and formal translation of them is likely to take up to a working week, this is a case where the tenderer must put his complete trust in a linguist executive if he has one or in a language consultant. The only effective solution is to give the linguist 24 hours or so to study the document and then hold a meeting of all concerned. This meeting will take most of a day, and to save executive time it can be programmed so that financial, legal and technical specialists need attend only an introductory briefing and then the particular part that concerns them. Once the linguist has given the general outline of the enquiry, the meeting can assign responsibilities and work out timings backwards from the submission date. Then the linguist briefs and comments on the documentation point by point and detailed decisions are taken and actions initiated. A full record of this meeting will need to be taken by a secretariat taking down and transcribing in shifts so that the transcript is ready the following morning.

Having thus got the design, costing, financial and legal work under way, the project leader and the linguist must next work out a programme for translating and producing the tender documents. The first task here is to draw up the covering sheet or letter of the tender which will give a list of its contents. This provides at least something on which translation can start straight away. In consultation with the department concerned, a steady flow of material for translation must then be arranged. The onus of planning translation and typing really rests on the linguist, because only he knows how long he must have to produce the various elements. But there is clearly a real crunch between him and the functional departments and the programme will not hold unless he has good personal relations with these and the support of top management.

As examples of what can be achieved by this unorthodox method of working, we have on three occasions been able to get complex tenders ready for signature and despatch in less than a fortnight from the receipt of the documents by the client. In one instance the documentation contained 40 separate specifications, and in another summaries of the individual quotations within the tender were prepared and sent by telex in addition to the production of the tender proper. With normal procedures these operations would each have taken about 6 weeks; and as it was they only just beat the closure date.

However pernickety the enquirer's instructions for submission of the tender may be, they must be followed to the letter if the submission is to stand a chance. This calls for unusually careful checking and close supervision, going right down to the final collation and despatch of the documents. Since various functional and technical departments often use slightly different layouts and the pressure may be such that the linguist is translating from manuscript drafts or tapes, or even drafting direct from his own or others' rough notes, responsibility for the final layout and its conformity with the instructions must be left to the linguist and his secretariat. This will also ensure that a reasonable and consistent compromise is struck between the exporter's normal practices and those acceptable in the country of the language concerned. Because of the need for a very high standard of presentation to project a good image, special efforts must be made to avoid changing texts once they have been cleared and passed for translation.

It is worth giving considerable thought to breaking down the documentation in such a way that each section of it will cover a particular aspect and thus be read by a particular specialist in the customer's team which examines the tenders. Likewise, even if this is not called for, it is worth providing several additional sets of technical specifications and drawings, as these will have to be studied in detail by a number of engineers. Another factor here is that the customer may require certain sections to be submitted separately, e.g. some sealed within an inner envelope. As a guide, a typical breakdown might be:

Cover sheet with index.
Covering letter.
Annexes to covering letter on, e.g. conditions, credit arrangements.
Quotation proper, i.e. summary of prices.
Introduction to/observations on specifications.
Specifications.
Drawings.
List of references (if appropriate).
Any declarations, etc. required by customer.

A special problem is often posed by conflicts between the exporter's practices and wishes and the enquirer's conditions. If the enquirer does not insist upon formal agreement to his conditions being included with the submission, it may be best simply to enclose the vendor's conditions and leave the details to be sorted out later, rather in the manner of a traditional naval exchange of broadsides. If however such a agreement is called for, it will have to be given subject to a number of riders. It is difficult enought to get long and complicated general conditions devilled and suitable riders drafted in a very short time, to say nothing of the tactical element here. The first problem is to decide how much one can accept in the hope of ducking the issue if necessary later, so as to avoid presenting such an array of objections that the tender will almost certainly be rejected. More difficult still is to pitch comments right and to choose between simple rejection and the putting forward of an alternative solution; for here one is trying at the same time to create the strongest possible negotiating position and to keep the prospect sweet. Some likely issues are covered in more detail in the next section.

13.4.4 Forward estimation of fixed prices

Pitching the price right might be described as the art of tendering, but with complex long-lead export contracts in an inflationary environment it acquires overtones of surrealism—so much so that a firm may sometimes prefer to opt out rather than run the risks associated with an immensely difficult and necessarily rushed decision. Communist bloc and third-world importers are apt to insist on a fixed CIF price even with a lead time of two to three years from the date of initial quotation, and although there may be some scope for renegotiation at the contract stage, the tenderer is faced with the choice of putting in such heavy contingencies as to make his price non-competitive or incurring the risk of a serious loss, the more so when the contract as a whole involves transactions in several different currencies.

This insistence on a fixed price is due less to any hard-line attitude than to the simple fact that authority for the expenditure has to be obtained from the sponsor ministry and then from the treasury, and the use of foreign currency must be authorised by the national bank or other exchange control authority. It is in fact something that anyone who has ever worked with a government department will understand perfectly. However, this bureaucratic involvement introduces the further hazard of delay. Typically six months or more may elapse between submission of the tender and the signature of a contract, and then—more serious—a further delay of several months before the signed contract is returned fully authorised and represents a firm order. Quite apart from their effect on production programmes, delays of this order completely throw any nicely calculated forward costing.

An attempt to eliminate risk completely will probably result in loss of the order, and it is a question of reducing the entrepreneurial risk to reasonable proportions. One solution, which has the advantage of bringing some pressure on the customer and his authorities to get the order through quickly, is to go in with two prices—an indexated price with the date of the quotation as its base-date, and a fixed price based on a stated set of assumptions. Typically these assumptions might be:

1 A fairly short limit on the validity of the quotation, to be interpreted as the period up to final authorisation and transmittal of the contract.
2 The actual receipt of all payments by the date due under the contract.
3 The right to re-quote if the customer requests any modification of

4   Tying of the main shipment, normally made against presentation of shipping documents, to a date of readiness for despatch, should the customer request the postponement of delivery.

The last three of these points will of course also be covered in the contract, but experience suggests that it is as well to introduce them explicitly at the tender stage.

13.5   Terms of business and payment

Countries with a socialised or centralised economy are apt to be remarkably inflexible over terms of business. Almost any contract will be in effect a 'public' one and will thus be subject to a code of public contracts not dissimilar from that ruling government contracts in liberal economies. This means that the customer's conditions must be taken very seriously, and some of the problems likely to arise are mooted below.

13.5.1   Date of entry into force of the contract

The probable delay mentioned above between signature of the contract and its final authorisation faces the exporter with a dilemma. If he follows normal practice and accepts the date of signature as the date of entry into force, he runs the risk of his costings being upset and his production programme disrupted; on the other hand he is left with some means of bringing pressure since any advance payment will then become due at the stated period (say 30 days) after signature. On the other hand if he uses the known likelihood of delay to insist on the effective date being that of receipt by him of the fully authorised contract, he may be faced with a hold-up of several months about which he can do nothing. There is clearly a span of options between these two extremes all of which would be more favourable to the exporter, but for obvious reasons he may have great difficulty in negotiating these.

13.5.2   Methods of payment and credit arrangements

Credit arrangements and special cases apart, methods of payment have become pretty well standardised over most markets. There is likely to be an advance payment ('cash with order') of between 10 and 20 per cent payable within a short period (typically 30 days) of placing of the firm order. The main payment is normally effected against presentation of shipping documents on the basis of confirmed irrevocable credit established in advance by the customer at a bank nominated by the vendor. A balance of, say, 20 per cent becomes payable against the same letter of credit either on receipt of the goods or on provisional or final acceptance (see below).

This is all simple enough, but in some markets actually getting the money is a very different problem. A publisher once remarked bitterly to one of us: '.....'s no good as a market. They ignore copyright and buy just one book and photocopy it; and then they don't even get round to paying for the one copy they've ordered.' *Mutatis mutandis* this statement unfortunately appears to hold good across the board, and an exporter to such markets will probably be well advised to try and get some provision against delays in payment written into the contract. The notion of a penalty as such, though attractive, is improbable, but it may well be worth aiming for a clause to the effect that any payment not made by the due date will attract interest at the going rate in the vendor's country at the time. Similarly it is necessary to make very sure that the letter of credit does get established, and to this end some contractual provision for it to be established at the time of the advanced payment or at least 6 months before the due date of delivery is highly desirable.

Credit arrangements are comparatively straightforward, because the vendor will be dealing with his own authorities or merchant banks, and we have experience of only two problems here. One is that the response time of the Export Credit Guarantee Department (ECGD), usually at least three weeks, is not compatible with the kind of deadlines often encountered at the tendering stage. Unless there has been time for advance action, it may therefore be necessary to submit a provisional set of credit proposals with the tender and follow this up with a firm document. The second is that if a really major delay, say of a year or more, occurs before the main payment — and hence the start of the credit arrangement — becomes due, the interest rates of the initial credit proposal may have been overtaken by events. The vendor would thus be wise either to ensure that this contingency is covered in the credit agreement or that a clause giving the right to revise the credit arrangement in the event of major delay is written into the contract. If the credit insurance premium is payable by the customer as a separate item and not costed in to the credit rate as a whole, the customer must of course be contractually bound to pay this premium with the advance payment on the contract.

13.5.3 *Jurisdiction and arbitration*

Certainly in public contracts and very often in others the customer will insist that the contract should be exclusively subject to the law of his own country and the jurisdiction of its courts. In theory this may have very serious implications, and an exporter will certainly need to take legal advice *ad hoc* if his own contracts department is not familiar with the law in question. In practice however the risks generally appear to be rather slight and, since he has little choice but to accept the situation or opt out, the vendor will do better to look with very great care at the arrangements for arbitration.

He can normally expect this clause of the contract to include a statement of intent to settle any differences on interpretation or execution amicably, and failing this to submit them to an appointed arbitration authority whose findings shall be final. Since the vendor should not accept the appropriate authority of the customer's country — and conversely the customer is unlikely to accept that of the vendor's country, the best and most usual solution is to appoint the International Chamber of Commerce (at Zurich or Paris) as the arbitration authority, usually with the rider that the arbitrator(s) appointed must not be nationals of either of the countries concerned in the contract.

13.5.4 Penalties and bonuses

As in any other contract, the penalty clauses need most careful study and are worth hard negotiation, the more so since in a public contract the initial proposals are likely to be unduly favourable to the customer. For example we have seen draft contracts from which the maximum limits of penalties had conveniently been omitted in the final draft. Some care is needed in defining contractually the value on which the penalty becomes payable when a deficiency of one or two small items renders a complete section of the equipment inoperable. And the problem of penalties is one of the main reasons for the inclusion of the next sub-section on delivery.

A special hazard that is likely to arise in contracts with Communist bloc countries is the treatment of technical documentation as part of the matériel for penalty purposes. This means that, if the complete documentation is not delivered with the equipment, the customer may not only withhold payment but also impose a penalty on the value of the whole contract or that part of it which he claims to be affected by the lack of documentation. In view of the rather relaxed attitude prevalent in many parts of the world over the punctual provision of documentation, this becomes an important planning point particularly where manuals have to be written for new or modified machines and then translated, reproduced and delivered in time.

Few third-world countries seem prepared to accept the idea, not uncommon in the West, of bonuses for delivery ahead of the contract date, and the most that an exporter can hope to do in this direction is probably to safeguard himself in the contract against delays and increased costs imposed on him by the action — or more probably the inaction — of the customer. There are two points at which problems of this kind are likely to arise. One is a request by the customer to postpone delivery or failure by him to take the matériel over on arrival, so that it is left on the quayside. Here it must be clearly laid down that the cost of storage before shipment and/or of demurrage at the far end*, and also

* The latter problem is becoming acute because of shipping delays entering third-world ports. Provision must be made for the customer to bear demurrage on board as well as on the quayside.

any consequential expense such as the repainting of steel surfaces delivered with a '6 months primer' will be borne by the customer. The second confirms the supervision by the vendor of installation and/or testing and commissioning, together with any associated training programme. It is of course normal to write into the quotation and/or contract agreed fees and expenses for extension of such supervision or instruction beyond the stipulated period, together with details of how such payments are to be made. But against the possibility of substantial extension or postponement, the vendor should also try to have written in the customer's responsibility for secondary costs so incurred, such as the disruption of similar programmes for other customers.

13.5.5   Definition of the term 'delivery'

We have found that many 'general conditions' emanating from the third world and elsewhere have the effect of defining delivery, and hence execution of the contract, as the commissioning or introduction into service of the matériel. Since many of the factors affecting this date are completely outside the control both of the vendor and his shipping agents, and since delays will not only involve withholding of payment but may also incur liability to penalties, this is clearly unacceptable. Usually the definition is made only by implication, so that a particularly searching scrutiny of the customer's conditions is called for. In the case of CIF, insurance may of course also be affected.

These delays are likely to arise either simply from the customer's unreadiness to accept the equipment, or from laggardliness on the part of customs and approving authorities. For example a delay of four or five months between the arrival of a vehicle on the dockside and its handover to the customer cleared for use would not be unusual. It is of course the exporter's responsibility to make sure that the import and approval documentation is completely in order (see Chapter 15), and he will probably need to allow for putting someone on the ground to supervise clearance and handover. But he should also seek to get written into the contract a definition of delivery and execution in terms of the arrival of the matériel on the dockside, and/or to impose a maximum period from the date of despatch at the end of which delivery will be deemed to have been completed.

But where the matériel is subject to multiple approvals, as for example in the case of specialised vehicles or chemical plant, defensive action of this kind is not enough to ensure satisfactory execution of the contract. There is a need to draw up, in consultation with the shipping agent, the customer, his Customs and all approving authorities concerned, a detailed programme covering the handling of each consignment or batch from completion of manufacture to introduction into service. This programme should include:

The manufacturer's own out-inspection and documentation.

Any inspection to be carried out by the customer, his approving
authorities or an international inspection authority at the works.
Packing and despatch.
Shipment (with suitable flexibility).
Customs clearance.
Final approval.
Provisional acceptance (see below).
Installation (if applicable).
Commissioning.

The drawing up of this schedule is tedious and expensive — sufficiently so to make it worth costing in — but experience suggests that there is no other way to ensure customer satisfaction and to avoid open-ended contingency costs. It has its positive aspects too, in imposing on both vendor and customer a healthy planning discipline and in giving opportunity for extensive contact with approving authorities. If possible the programme should be drawn up at the contract negotiation stage and annexed to the contract under cover of the delivery clause. Failing this it should be referred to in the contract so that it becomes a contract document when completed.

13.5.6   Definitions of force majeure

Although the definitions of force majeure commonly used in most countries appear very similar at first glance it is worth checking these carefully in a draft contract emanating from a socialised or Communist country. The most likely problems are, first, that since these countries do not have strikes they do not include 'strikes, lock-outs, etc.' in their definition. Second, the 'force majeure' clause may also contain rather extravagant provisions making the customer liable for secondary and consequential damages. This latter point applies particularly when the contract concerns the provision of know-how, data or training and advice as opposed to hardware.

13.5.7   Acceptance

Common usage in many countries calls for a rather complicated sequence of provisional and final acceptance. Quantitative acceptance occurs of course at the time and place of physical handover but, even if the matériel has been inspected by them or on their behalf at the factory, customers will often seek to delay provisional qualitative acceptance until testing and commissioning has been completed. This is one reason why the definition of 'delivery' is so important. Final acceptance may often be withheld until the end of the guarantee period, and this becomes significant where final payment or the release of banker's guarantees is tied to final acceptance. These provisions in fact present little problem where the vendor is committed to supervising assembly, testing and commissioning of the matériel, but need careful watching where it is simply handed over to the customer still packaged. Here the vendor will probably be wise to get written into the contract a stipulation that provisional acceptance will be deemed to have taken place at a certain time after delivery unless the customer gives formal notification to the contrary.

There is a language point here of such importance that management should be aware of it. In French (and sometimes in other Romance languages) the word *réception* is used to mean both 'receipt' and 'acceptance'. Where some contractual commitment, such as a payment, is linked to the physical receipt of the matériel as opposed to its technical approval, it is therefore essential that a form of words other than *recevoir, réception* is used in the French text of the contract. For obvious reasons draft contracts prepared by the customer, including some standard forms of public contract, contain this important ambiguity. A similar problem may arise in German from a fairly common commercial usage by which the word *Abnahme* represents the physical receipt of goods, but here the distinction can be simply made by the use of *Erhalt* (receipt) and *Abnahme*(acceptance). This example will serve to underline the need for management both to choose linguists carefully and to trust them and work closely with them.

13.5.8   Guarantees

The only special problem over warranty on goods supplied is that the start date may be laid down as the date of completion of provisional acceptance. This is an added reason for the vendor to seek some means of controlling this date.

Exporters will usually be asked to provide two banker's guarantees. The first of these is in effect a guarantee of execution; the contract will probably require it to be established at the same date and in the same amount as the advance payment (less of course any credit insurance premium or other special element in this). Release usually occurs on completion of delivery. The second, which is in effect a guarantee of performance and is likely to be in the sum of 5 per cent of the contract value, will usually be called for at the same time as the main payment is made, i.e. on presentation of shipping documents, and will be held until the end of the warranty period, which will often coincide with final acceptance.

Here again an important language pitfall arises in French (and sometimes in Italian) through the use of the word *caution* which means a 'deposit' but is also used to describe a banker's guarantee in the contexts described above. It is thus essential to find out which is intended (normally a banker's guarantee) and if possible to get this ambiguity eliminated. The distinction becomes particularly important in contracts

which for some reason involve both actual deposits and banker's
guarantees.

13.5.9   Arrangements for revision of contract

The standard forms of public contract in many countries contain
provisions for revision, cancellation and transfer of rights which are
unduly favourable to the customer. All that can be said in general is that
these clauses require careful scrutiny and may have to be renegotiated.

13.6   Contract negotiations

Much of what has been said above will serve to emphasise the care and
effort that the negotiation even of simple and relatively small contracts
requires, and also that, however rushed the preparation of the quotation
may have been, there is likely to be ample time to prepare for this. If the
customer will agree, it is far better to accept the expense and disruption
of fielding a fully representative team for a protracted meeting aimed at
getting the contract agreed and prepared in final form and signed on the
spot than to conduct negotiations by correspondence and repeated
exchanges of drafts. The combination of the customer's usual response
time, postal delays and translation time tends to make the latter method
so slow as to destoy the impetus of the project. And above all it is
essential to arrive at a really workable and mutually acceptable contract
in dealings with Communist or socialised countries.

Even if the customer does not request it, it is advisable to follow up the
receipt of a letter of intent or other positive response to the quotation
with a visit. This will serve both to clear up queries and
misunderstandings and to arrive at a plan for negotiating the contract
proper. This same journey can also be used to reinforce earlier contacts
with the approving authorities, and it is in fact highly desirable to iron
out some of the technical problems at triangular meetings between
vendor, customer and approving authority. Experience suggests that the
burden of coordination will in fact fall mainly on the vendor, and he will
do well to accept this from the start and so gain the initiative. It should be
possible to return from this visit with notes from which the contract
specifications can be written and either with notes on the main points for
negotiations within the contract (or preferably either with a draft
contract prepared by the customer to his standard form or an agreement
for the vendor to draw up the draft contract taking account of the
statutory and other standard requirements).

When some work has been done on the contract specifications and any
credit or other commercial proposals involved, a second visit — mainly on
the technical level and aimed at the approving authorities — will be
required to iron out any problems arising from incompatibility with
regulations and standards and to seek relaxations if necessary. If this visit

can also be used to draw up the first draft of the delivery programme described in Section 13.5.5 above, a lot of argument during the contract negotiations may be saved.

The two parties should thus enter the contract negotiations after all technical problems have been cleared both with the customer and with the approving authorities and armed with a working draft contract and a draft plan for the delivery phase. If he can find some justification for doing so, the vendor may also wish to table revised costings. The vendor's team should consist effectively of the main project team, and they must within reason be prepared to stay for as long as is needed. A certain extravagance with executive time here will save a great deal of time and direct cost later on. Any legal or engineering consultant involved, and representatives of any main sub-contractors, should also be present. Even if the vendor's team leader is himself prepared to work in the customer's language, it is almost essential to take two other linguists unless the customer can provide one. This relieves the team leader of having to lose impetus and wear himself out by back-interpreting to his colleagues during negotiations, allows working groups on specialised topics to be formed and makes it possible to release a linguist to sit down with one of the customer's staff and get on with drafting.

The real costs of a negotiating session of this kind are hideous, but they can at least be predicted and costed in. And if the outcome is a sound contract signed up on the spot, full coordination and resolution of all detail problems and misunderstandings, the unpredictable costs of things going awry later will largely have been avoided.

13.7   Installation, commissioning and training

Not long ago the installation engineer of a certain leading British firm arrived at the appointed place on the recently confirmed date to find a pile of packing cases standing in the middle of an expanse of virgin sand. But apart from such minor third-world hazards as this, there is no reason why installation and commissioning should not follow its normal course. Clearly it is advisable to check in advance, if possible by physical inspection, that the site is in fact ready and that the requisite plant, tools and expense stores are available on site, but the main special problem is that of interpreting. If the vendor has to supply an interpreter — as he almost certainly will — he must take account not only of the fee but also of subsistence and travel costs equivalent to those of the engineer in arriving at his installation charge. It may not in fact be particularly easy to find a suitable interpreter, particularly as this is a temporary job of rather uncertain dates and duration. A qualified interpreter is not only unnecessary and unduly expensive but is unlikely to accept the nature of work and the conditions involved. On the other hand, a man with a low standard of language and general education may be unable either to grasp what is going on or to express himself with the force and accuracy necessary in an emergency. Experience suggests that the actual assembly

and adjustment of machines is better and quicker done by demonstration
and signs than by the interposition of an interpreter, but this is no
solution where work has to be planned, instructions issued and reports
written up. Provided that the need is foreseen well in advance, there are
two satisfactory solutions. One is to contact a nearby University,
Polytechnic or College of Further Education and arrange for the
temporary release of a suitable advanced student or the temporary
recruitment of someone just completing their training. In either case the
experience will be invaluable to them. The other is to recruit to one's own
staff a young person with, say, A-level in the language concerned as well
as the primary qualifications, have this person trained up to an
acceptable start standard and then released from other duties as
required. Again such an assignment would provide invaluable experience
of every kind to any potential non-graduate engineer working their way
up via the drawing board.

Training is a more complex matter and one more severely aggravated
by the language problem. There are likely to be three elements:
on-the-job conversion training of operators and maintenance staff, which
can usually go on during installation and commissioning; intensive
instruction for junior engineers and shop-floor and maintenance
supervisors, which is best conducted at the exporter's own works; and
possibly broader operational and/or technical training of middle-piece
executives and specialists, which can be achieved by means of a single
course held either at the exporter's plant or training centre or at a
suitable central point in the customer's area of operations. On-the-job
training can and must be given by the installation engineer working
through his interpreter; but formal instruction given by consecutive
interpreting is wasteful of time and very boring for the students, and it is
worth looking for a linguist with sufficient subject knowledge and
instructional experience to get himself briefed and then teach direct in
the language using consecutive interpreting only for question-and-answer
and discussion periods and for certain demonstrations. Promising sources
for such instructors are retired warrant officers or non-commissioned
officers of the Services, and for higher-level instruction retired
professional men.

All-in-all the direct and indirect costs of the training programme
can be considerable. It is important not only to cost them in but also to
lay down quite specifically in the contract the precise extent of the
commitment and the costs to be borne by each party. The general
conditions received with the request for tender may often contain
stipulations on training couched in committal but rather vague terms,
and these pose a real difficulty in costing out the quotation, particularly
if the enquirer insists on their being blocked into the unit price of the
items of equipment. Since there will be no time to acquire fuller
information on the training need or to work out a training programme in
detail and since the unit cost element will depend on the final scale of the
order, it is probably best to comply with the instructions but also to show
separately a bracket figure for training costs with some indication of the

programme envisaged. It must also be made quite clear that this will have to be detailed at the contract stage and the cost revised and firmed up as necessary.

13.8   Follow-up and after-sales services

The provision of follow-up and after-sales services, both during the warranty period and afterwards, is another point that is likely to be written into the enquiry conditions, once again in a way that is at once committal and vague. These services are even more difficult to cost into the quotation than the training requirement, since the effort required to see the equipment from the docks through approval into the customer's hands will not at that stage be clear, it may be difficult to make reasonable assumptions about the distribution of the equipment over what may be a very large geographical area rather poorly served with communications, and in any event the cost attributable to the order under consideration will depend on the existence or otherwise of other service commitments in the same area at and after the time of delivery. It is worth considering contracting the service commitment out to a suitable technical concern in the customer's country but in a developing country it may be very difficult to find a reliable agency and in any event (for good reasons!) the customer may not accept this solution. In the absence of evidence suggesting some cheaper expedient, it is probably best to include in the quotation the cost of keeping one service engineer with his own transport continuously and permanently available at least throughout the warranty period; since this will in fact mean providing for two men and two vehicles, it will make reasonable provision for the work being spread over a wide area. An interesting possibility is that of sharing the service commitment with another British or other Western firm working in the same general field and exporting to the same country. Again if a figure for after-sales service has to be included in the quotation, it is advisable to show this separately and to cover it with a rider leaving it open to renegotiation at the contract stage.

These service engineers will have to hold a reasonable range of spares at their base, as penalties for delay in executing guarantee repairs may be severe and, delay apart, the real cost of air-freighting large individual spares is considerable. An experienced customer will usually ask for a slice of fast-moving and essential back-up spares to be quoted for and included with the main contract supplies. If he fails to do this initially, he should be given every encouragement to remedy his omission. It is probably worth including as a supplement to the quotation the provision of spares for one, two and five years of operation, and in any event a firm effort should be made to negotiate an appropriate spares slice into the contract. This will not only do much to eliminate customer dissatisfaction but will also tend to tie the customer to the supplier and so discourage him from going out for tender later for standard spares which he could obtain elsewhere.

At the time of writing the United Kingdom's reputation for after-sales service on export contracts is very poor, and it is therefore worth a special effort to provide reassurance backed up by firm proposals on this aspect from the quotation stage onwards.

Finally under this head either the general conditions or the contract itself is almost certain to contain a guarantee by the vendor to make spares available for, say 10 years from delivery. This should present no special difficulty if the contract goes through reasonably quickly, but the real possibility of major delays calls for vetting of the spares list to make sure that there are not items for which a 10-year limit would have a critical effect on availability or cost.

13.9   Language and language-related costs

If anything goes wrong with an export contract, irrecoverable costs are likely to escalate very rapidly, and this applies in particular to language costs. Since language and language-related costs represent a small—and sometimes a very small—proportion of the total, it is worth making reasonably lavish provision both to ensure that nothing will go wrong through lack of quality or capacity of language resources and to make realistic allowance for the costs likely to be involved. The policy should therefore be to plan for, cost in and contain language costs rather than skimp on them.

13.9.1   The need to plan forward and cost in

The influence of a language barrier on the costs of a major export contract may be relatively small, though not insignificant. However, its influence on timings is critical. Unless the exporter is certain that his in-house language resources are adequate in scope and capacity to cope with all phases of a contract of this nature, he would probably be wise to bring in at the beginning either a language consultant or a consultant in some other appropriate field who speaks the language fluently, knowledge of the target country being of course a key asset in both cases. In fact for any firm likely to become involved in such a contract it may well be worth retaining a suitable linguist on *contrat cadre,* that is at a low level of effort with the possibility of temporary expansion. Quite apart from the actual execution of the language work depicted above and in Chapter 15, there will be a need for constantly available advice on timings and on the best way of getting particular language tasks completed.

It is equally important to plan the language aspect of the operation in such a way as to minimise expenses as opposed to fees, or at least to predict and contain these. Experience suggests that if it is necessary to move an interpreter from the UK to somewhere outside Europe every time a visit is made by any member of the project team, the expenses involved will be approximately double the fees and the whole will be roughly equivalent to the real cost of moving an additional executive. Thus the plan suggested above of having a trusted linguist at each end is a highly attractive one.

The leading linguist, whether on the payroll or bought in, should be given the task of coordinating all the language work required so that the project team has one responsible person to work to on the language side. He will of course almost certainly, in agreement with management, have to bring in additional interpreting, translating and secretarial resources; but these will be more efficient and less costly if they are organised by an expert in the context of a coherent plan. In sum, the linguist wherever he comes from must in effect be an integral member of the project team.

13.9.2 *Language-cost yardsticks*

Both to decide whether the opportunity is an attractive one at all and to cost the language aspect into the quotation, it is essential to have some idea right from the start of the order of language and language-related costs. Experience suggests that for the type of contract envisaged in this chapter, which is likely to have a total sterling value running into at least five, probably six and possibly eight figures, the total language costs will come out at somewhere between 0.5 and 1.5 per cent of the total contract value and that this proportion will diminish as total value increases in a pattern that might be represented by a generic equation such as

$$y = 1 - ae^{-kx}$$

A shot estimate of this kind is likely to be at least as good as any attempt at forward analysis, although it should be possible to make a rather more accurate assessment before the contract stage. For initial assessment and quotation purposes it is probably safe to go in at 1 per cent for a contract value high in the five-figure range, 0.75 per cent in the six figure range and 0.5 per cent if the total passes the £1,000,000 mark. These figures make reasonable allowance for the travel and subsistence expenses of interpreters, but would not hold if things went wrong and frequent or protracted unforeseen visits became necessary; it is therefore probably prudent to include a rather higher proportion for language costs, say up to five per cent of the total contingency or, typically, 0.5 per cent of the contract value, in the contingency element of the costing.

It is difficult to validate these yardsticks from a truly representative sample, not only because firms are naturally reticent about their costing methods but also because relatively few cost the language element in at the beginning or analyse it out afterwards. However if they are of the right order — as we believe them to be — two conclusions can be drawn. First, the language costs are large enough to make an uncomfortable dent in the profit margin and must therefore be both costed in and contained by good planning. Secondly, since the difference in cost between making reasonable provision for high-grade language support and skimping on language resources will be of the order of tenths of a per

cent of contract value, it is worth bringing in a good linguist from the
start and making full use of him.

13.10 The creation of goodwill

This chapter has set out to expose in some detail the special problems and the pitfalls associated with exporting capital and other specialised equipment across a language barrier to a strange market. There are doubtless many other snags of the same kind which have so far escaped our notice and experience. At first glance the resulting picture may be a depressing one, especially for the smaller firm which feels a little chary of moving into these markets anyway. But careful study of the points discussed will show that with foreknowledge, sound planning and good teamwork the risks and the rough going inherent in a project of this kind can be reduced to manageable proportions. Even if the first venture of this kind throws up some unpleasant surprises, its successful execution is almost certain to lead to follow-up contracts with the same customer or in the same market which will run far more smoothly and very profitably. On the other hand the number of customers for a particular type of specialised equipment within a developing country is small, and failure to satisfy one may push the exporter right out of that market for a considerable period.

Both for these reasons and because the power and scope of the approving authorities tends to create a three-way pull between exporter, importer and authority, the creation and maintenance of mutual confidence and goodwill is a talisman for success. While the contract must be a realistic one which is genuinely acceptable to both parties and with which they can fully comply, it is quite impossible to cater for every contingency which may arise in the course of a project lasting two or three years. If the two parties trust each other and in particular the exporter demonstrates that he is really out to serve both the customer and the importing country's economy, most of the difficulties will resolve themselves.

No less important are the relations between the exporter and the customer's financial and approval agencies. Tiresome and even impractical as they may be, the various sets of regulations are the lifeblood of the officials in these agencies. They are just not going to budge to suit some importer's convenience and thicken the lining of his pocket. Once their backs are up, they can make life impossible for the exporter. On the other hand, if he is clearly going to great lengths to comply with the regulations and shows readiness to seek their advice as experts, they can and usually will do a great deal to cut corners for him by probing into the depths of their dustier tomes to find legal ways of relaxing requirements and procedures.

14
Export marketing

Export marketing is a major subject in its own right on which many books and articles have been written and courses held. This chapter will do no more than attempt to set out some of the factors affecting entry into a foreign-language market and to highlight points that experience suggests are likely to cause problems. The preceding chapter considered the special case of an unexpected opportunity for a major contract, and urgency was thus one of its keynotes. Planned entry into a market calls for quite a different approach, characterised by long-term forward planning and thorough research.

Unless there is some special reason for urgency, such as a gap in the target market, it would not be unreasonable for three years to elapse between an initial decision to investigate entering the market and the first batch of products being sold there. Nevertheless a great deal of activity, some of it of rather an expensive kind, has to take place during this period, and once sales have started there will be a further delay before the operation begins to show a profit. Rigorous cost-control is therefore essential and can perhaps best be achieved by a five-year indexated budget with six-monthly review points. On the other hand an organisation that is geared for foreign working and has built up a good library of market and technical intelligence and of its own foreign-language literature (see Chapter 15) will need only a few months to move in and start selling.

14.1   Market intelligence and research

Unless specifically asked to carry out a research project, market research organisations may be able to provide only limited information outside the consumer and consumer durable fields,but there are other agencies which can go a good way towards providing at least background intelligence in the context of specialised products. Among these are: the British Overseas Trade Board, the London Chamber of Commerce, the London Embassy or Chamber of Commerce office of the country concerned and the exporter's Trade Association. A special market research project may be beyond the scope of the budget, but even the commissioning of one will not obviate the need for the exporter's staff to visit the country, consult the British Commercial Counsellor there and build up official and commercial contacts. An ideal occasion for doing this is an exhibition or trade fair, the more so as it is then easy to get to know indigenous manufacturers in the same field. For oddly enough it may very often be that the best way in lies in some form of collaboration with an existing manufacturer who at first glance appears to be a competitor.

14.1.1   Background intelligence

There is a need to build up a picture of the target country's state of economic development, the soundness of its economy, the structure of its industry and the *modus operandi* of its government departments and agencies going well beyond the immediate field of interest. Without such a framework a detailed piece of hot information may be highly misleading.

For instance, to establish the designs and weight classes which he should offer, a manufacturer of vehicles or vehicle components will need to study not only the existing and projected road system but also its relationship to rail, air and water transport and indeed the whole pattern of development of industry and agriculture. Similarly in the case of all but the most basic consumer goods there is a need to study not only the state of and trends in the market concerned, but also the way in which that market is likely to move in relation to consumer spending as a whole.

14.1.2   Economic forecasts

The need for an in-depth study of the history, current state and probable development of the target country's economy needs no stressing, but no less important are factors such as currency shifts which may affect middle- and long-term competitiveness and also the relationship of other actual or potential exporting countries to the target market. It will be of little use spending money on promotions to create a new demand or modify an existing one if this will simply open the way for a larger competitor in another country to move in and swamp the market.

Economic forecasting is an uncertain business at the best of times, but at least it may serve to eliminate some seemingly attractive options and to narrow down the field of subjective entrepreneurial decision.

14.1.3 Target group intelligence

For consumer and trade products alike it is dangerous, tempting as it may be, to extrapolate from one's own or another country to the target market simply by applying some rather obvious adjustments and correcting factors. Even in apparently similar societies the structuring of socio-economic groups differs widely, and within each group there are equally important differences not only, as is well known, in the proportion of disposable income spent on various categories of goods but no less important in taste and custom. For instance, one might suppose that top quality Dundee cake would be a winner in Germany, but in fact this is not so because the convention among those able to afford it dictates that only a new, uncut cake may be offered to guests. Again a combined test instrument designed to suit British practice may be quite unsaleable in, say, France where the nature of the relevant regulations, the structuring of approving authorities and the demarcation line between groups of skill may call for an entirely different breakdown of inspection procedures. It is therefore necessary to build up piece by piece a detailed intelligence picture of the potential market within the given country for the products which lie within the exporter's field of capability. Quite apart from questions of presentation and aesthetic design, an existing range of products may be ill-suited to the target market, while a simple recombination of elements within those products would provide a winner.

14.1.4 Product intelligence

There are two distinct aspects to product intelligence, the first of which has been touched on above. This is the extent to which it meets the *market* requirements. Research may disclose a genuine market gap or a demand partially unsatisfied through lack of indigenous production and imports from other sources. Equally investigation may disclose a gap in demand which experience in other markets suggests could be filled by a well-aimed promotion. Where a suitable gap is found, it is worth focussing all available effort onto it. In other cases there is a need for an exhaustive examination of competing products, both indigenous and imported, and of their price zoning and the way in which they are promoted, distributed and sold. This research may serve to determine, from a wide range of options, not only the characteristics of the product to be offered, but also the presentation, price, promotion and methods of distribution most likely to bear fruit.

The second aspect is the product's compatibility with *statutory* and equivalent requirements. Where sub-systems or components are concerned, the would-be exporter may find himself in a vicious circle, because he can only obtain approval of his product as part of a complete equipment or system and to get it incorporated into such a system means either joining forces with a fellow exporter, which may prove highly inconvenient in the long term, or selling an unapproved component to a native firm. In such cases the only entrée may be through collaboration with an indigenous firm operating in the same field and therefore a potential competitor. But where this problem does not arise it is indispensable to obtain all necessary approvals for the product before attempting to market it even on a pilot basis. If anything that infringes any directly or indirectly relevant regulation is offered for sale, there will be a host of competitors poised to pounce on it and attack it with legal and publicity weapons alike. Description of goods and labelling regulations will often give trouble here, particularly in the foodstuffs and cosmetic fields, both because the exporter will want to use his established label to project his image and because it may be disproportionately expensive to design and produce a new label for a pilot marketing exercise. The use of a supplementary sticker giving the additional information required may offer a solution.

14.1.5 Available methods of distribution

One of the more important facets of the market study will have been the determination of the geographical centre of gravity and distribution of the product market. This, together with evaluation of transport costs, will lead to conclusions on the location of the sales subsidiary or main agency. But to optimise the method of import and distribution it is also necessary to investigate in depth the types of distributive system available, right through to the sales outlets, and their relative importance in the marketing of competing and related products. It may well be necessary to invest a fair amount of money, which will be rather slow in showing a return, on the establishment of a good focal point; but unless the operation envisaged is on an extremely large scale it will be out of the question to set up a special distribution system in the early stages, and the facilities that exist may therefore largely dictate the structuring of the sales operation.

14.2 Laws, regulations and codes

In many countries and for many products the mass of laws and statutory and other regulations faces the exporter with a next-to-impenetrable thicket containing some very sharp thorns, and it is highly advisable to employ a lawyer in the target country to hack a way through this. This step also ensures that there is a responsible person on the spot to deal authoritatively with any complaints of infringement. An agent or other 'fiscal representative' may be unable to produce the correct response or unwilling to do so because he cannot afford any conflict with authority. Further any hint of things going wrong must be treated as an urgent and important matter requiring the immediate intervention of senior management, and scotched before real damage is done. It goes without saying that the acquisition and study of all regulations which might be relevant is a major part of the market intelligence exercise.

14.2.1   Technical regulations and approving authorities

The UK, and in some measure the USA, tend to restrict statutory control to such categories as food, drugs and 'dangerous materials' or surface and air transport, and to leave technical control of other types of merchandise to codes of design and usage developed by their respective standards institutions or by trade associations and professional bodies. It is therefore difficult for the Anglo Saxon exporter to appreciate that in many other parts of the world all kinds of goods are subject to rigorous and penetrating statutory control. A further complication is that in many cases the approving authorities operate on a regional as opposed to a national basis, so that a product which is approved by the headquarters or one regional office will not be accepted in other regions without at least a rubber-stamping process. Sometimes, notably for example in West Germany, responsibility is divided between the ministry concerned and independent but officially approved national or regional organisations. Further certain components or sub-systems within any reasonably complex product, or even for example the contents and label of a can of food, may require approval either by different sections of the same authority or by a number of different authorities. And as if this were not enough a number of factors have over recent years led to, and are likely in the near and middle future to lead to constant changes in the regulations. Among these are technological advance, consumer protection, industrial safety and environmental control. It is thus very possible that an agent in a small way of business will not be up to date on these matters, and the onus lies squarely on the exporter to acquire a knowledge both of the system and of the detailed regulations for himself.

The move towards internationally agreed standards will go a long way towards solving these problems in the long run, but at the moment the existence of these standards tends merely to erect an additional hurdle, as special national requirements are superimposed on them. It is really impossible to provide any kind of generalised guide through this maze, or even on the procedures to be adopted in finding one's own way through it but two things can perhaps be said. The first is that a study of the American, British, French, German and Spanish systems of technical approval will provide foreknowledge of the various combinations and permutations likely to be encountered in most parts of the world. The second is the need to be aware that not only the product itself, but labelling, instructions, sizes and packaging may all require separate approval.

The most useful sources readily accessible are the British Standards Institute, ASLIB and the London Embassies or Chambers of Commerce of the countries concerned, together of course with the secretariat of any international technical organisation that exists in the relevant field. But this does not obviate the need for a detailed check direct with the approving authorities concerned and, of course, for obtaining approval before even pilot marketing or user trials are undertaken. For the point at which an infringement of the regulation arises is normally the taking into use (even for test running) of technical products and the offering for sale of consumer goods.

Having collected all this information, the exporter will if he is fortunate have some of the documents already translated, e.g. from ASLIB or the British Standards Institution, but he is likely to be left with a formidable mass of documentation in the language. For example the German road traffic act fills a sizeable paper-back, and the French weights and measures regulations on the design and calibration of road and rail tankers occupy an A4 loose-leaf folder thicker than this book; and each individual specification is likely to be at least 5000 or 6000 words in length. Formal translation of all this is ruled out by cost and probably by time, and study of it by a non-linguist designer or sales engineer with the aid of a dictionary can be dangerous. It is therefore necessary to employ, either on the payroll or as a consultant, a linguist who also possesses the appropriate technical knowledge to study the literature, extract the key points into oral or written briefs and monitor the design for compliance. A linguist capable of carrying out this task should also be able to make most of the necessary liaison visits on his own, thus saving money and executive time.

Provided that the product does in fact comply with the relevant regulations, there is nothing particularly difficult about obtaining technical approval, provided that the need is foreseen and tackled thoroughly and in time. In fact, as has been remarked elsewhere, officials in even the more hidebound countries will go to very great lengths to help, not only within their immediate scope but also in advising on the procedure as a whole and in providing introductions to other bodies involved. The difficulties and major setbacks that so often arise are almost always due to the manufacturer treating technical approval as a last-minute job or attempting to ride roughshod over some inconvenient stipulation.

14.2.2 *Exchange-control regulations*

The need to check on and keep up to date with the exchange-control regulations of both the exporting and the importing country is so obvious that it sometimes gets overlooked, and the exporter is then either unable to move money out when he wants it, for example to finance a promotion, or to move profits back. The exporter's bank should be able to provide the information, but a direct check on the target country's current rules is worthwhile, as there may be exchange-control clauses tucked away in some other set of regulations such as the public contracts code. Another possible source of difficulty is that not all third-world countries accept the principle that English is the international banking language. If even simple documents such as bills of exchange are being forwarded for clearance by the target country's banking authorities, it is advisable to provide a translation or 'guide' in the language.

14.2.3   Customs regulations

Although the internal workings of customs authorities differ widely from country to country, their procedures and the documentation on which these are based are fairly well standardised, and the main reasons for giving careful attention to customs regulations is the extremely serious consequences of an infringement. The complexity of the labyrinth of red tape is such that once something has gone awry it is almost impossible to set it in order quickly enough to avoid substantial demurrage charges, automatic time-based fines or even legal proceedings. The agent or the customer, i.e. the importer, may be the person technically liable, but unless he can clearly be shown to be at fault it is usually the exporter who has to foot the bill in the end.

So many customs, exchange control and similar problems arise through documentation going astray that it is a good rule to prepare certified copies of key documents before despatching the originals, so that these can be produced instantly if something goes wrong and will at least act as a stop-gap and provide evidence of compliance with regulations.

Five particular problems are perhaps common enough to be worth mentioning. Customs are normally responsible for ensuring that nothing which infringes technical regulations is imported. Where type approval only is called for, evidence of this and any subsidiary approval of components should be included in the customs documentation. For products such as specialised vehicles, pressure vessels or other potentially dangerous matériel which requires final approval of each individual product after importation, customs may require to see the approval documentation before releasing the equipment to the approving authority.

Most customs authorities work by the Brussels Code, but the interpretation of it in terms of assigning items to particular categories is subject to significant local variation and it is as well, on the first occasion a product is imported, to ensure that the agent or customer receiving a new product clears the pro-forma invoice in detail so that no delay occurs on importation.

Where an import licence system is in force, it is of course essential that the licence should be issued and the appropriate copies passed to the exporter before the shipping documents are prepared. The onus for doing this is on the customer, agent or fiscal representative in the importing country, but a combination of inexperience on the part of the exporter and the agent may lead to the licensing requirement being overlooked; and in any event it is essential to allow ample time for the issue of a licence by sending off pro-forma invoices as long as possible in advance of shipment.

With Spain, most Latin American countries and certain other countries with a Spanish tradition there is a need to have certain documents (the details vary slightly according to the country and the method of transport) franked by the importing country's consulate. This is an entirely straightforward procedure, but again is apt to be overlooked when exporting to a new market.

A more important aspect, and one which is going to increase in significance as the EEC and its associated free trade area develop, and more generally as manufacturers tend to broaden their supply base beyond their own national frontiers, is the presence of components originating from countries other than the exporting land. Quite apart from situations where an obvious political implication exists, most importing countries are extremely sensitive on this topic, and the more so where a declaration stating that the entire product and all associated parts are entirely of, say, UK origin, has been signed by the exporter. If a complete section or sub-system of a complex product has been bought in from abroad, this will obviously be included in the declaration and no problem exists. It is where one or two minor components are of foreign origin, for example small standard Japanese electronic components, or the manufacturer has had to switch to a foreign source of supply at the last moment to plug a gap, that this fact may in all good faith be omitted from the declaration. With quantity-produced products, a particular component may come from one place in some and from elsewhere in others, and no-one may in fact know which is which. Experience suggests that it is best in these cases to endorse the certificate of origin with some general rider such as 'other than certain very minor elements' rather than to spell out the situation in detail.

14.2.4 Relevant legislation

Even when all the detailed requirements of technical, fiscal and procedural regulations have been satisfied, there may remain broader legislative provisions to be considered. The aspects most likely to be affected are guarantees for consumer goods and any form of claim made on labels, in instructions or in the course of advertisng or promotion — and it is important here to remember that all forms of sales literature fall under these heads.

The broad trend towards legislation aimed at consumer protection, industrial and home safety and environmental control will gain rapidly in importance over the coming years. The best example at the time of writing this book is probably the West German advertising law, which originally went on the statute book in 1909 but only gained its full set of teeth in 1974. This is a new and somewhat complicated law and the precise import of some of its provisions will probably only come to be understood as the volume of relevant case-law grows, but the broad effect would appear to be that any statement or claim passing by any means whatever into the hands of an actual or potential customer is open to challenge by anyone within West Germany who comes to learn of it; and further that the onus of validating the claim lies entirely on the manufacturer or importer and that all sales and promotional activities may be made subject to an injunction until the case has been heard. The direct consequences of this and the attendant bad publicity are sufficient to push a foreign firm right out of the market, and experience suggests that the competition is likely to gang up in order to achieve just this.

It therefore seems prudent for anyone seeking to export to West Germany, in consumer and specialised fields alike, not only to tone his publicity approach right down to reality and have all his copy checked by an appropriate German lawyer, but also to prepare in advance a detailed formal justification of every claim made and of every statement which cannot be upheld by simple inspection or measurement of the product.

14.3   The use of foreign consultants

Much of what has been said above at first sight suggests that, unless the exporter is in a position to establish at least a sales subsidiary, it is preferable to turn the whole marketing operation over to one or more consultants in the target country. Further arguments for doing so will come up when the method of penetration is discussed. For the legal aspect, including any patent problems, this is indeed the only realistic course. The same is true of television advertising, and unless the exporter knows the target country and its people well and speaks the language, there is a strong case for using indigenous personnel selection consultants in the early stages.

But generally speaking and for most types of product and operation, delegation of this kind leads to disastrous and irrecoverable loss of control. Not only does the tail soon begin to wag the dog, but the cost per wag is apt to escalate uncontrollably. While the logical solution is without doubt the extensive use of native consultants in the early stages, experience suggests that the widespread reluctance of able and experienced managers to adopt it is soundly based. Even if mistakes are made and some of these are expensive in time and money, it generally seems best to field the home team backed up by such outside resources in the exporting country as are needed and can be afforded. It is very difficult to offer any explanation for this. It may be that, if imperfect communication is going to take place somewhere along the line, this is less damaging between the exporter's men in the field and those with whom they deal than it is between line management and those brought in to support it.

The exception is penetration of the Communist bloc. Unless the would-be exporter is fortunate enough to be approached by an East European trade mission — and this more likely to be in the context of a specific contract than of marketing a product into a Comecon country — the establishment of effective contact is at best very slow and often impossible. There are in the UK and Western Europe a number of firms and freelances who specialise in obtaining an entrée, acting either as consultants or as agents or both. The larger concerns are likely to operate in all fields and to all the countries concerned, while the freelances tend to specialise in a particular field and probably a particular country. However most freelances are organised into loose-knit networks, passing introductions and assignments to the most suitable individual.

It may not always be expedient to go direct for the particular national market into which entry is desired, and expert advice on the 'easiest' way in should be accepted. An ideal solution, again best arranged through a consultant, is to exhibit at an appropriate trade fair. As in Western Europe, some of these fairs are specialised within a broad field and others go right across the board. Leipzig is a broad-based one that geographically at least is easily accessible, and both general and specialised trade exhibitions are held in Prague. Showing at one of these fairs will 'legitimise' the would-be exporter and with luck give him access to the full span of the Comecon market.

14.4   Choice of method of penetration

At some point in the marketing process, indeed as early as possible, an irrevocable decision has to be taken on the type of representation and the method of distribution. Major consumer goods and consumer durables manufacturers are normally staffed to plan the whole operation fully and do so with as much care and skill, or even more, as they put into promotions in the home and other established markets. But smaller firms manufacturing specialised trade products often seem to run into serious difficulties through what can only be described as an extremely casual approach. There exists in fact a very wide span of options, ranging from the appointment of an agent through the setting up of a subsidiary to various types of partnership and package deal. (The term 'partnership' is commonly used in this context but does not have the special meaning that it has under British law.) And within each main option there is a further field of choice to be considered.

One quite basic management decision is involved here. For many reasons the most effective method of conducting both export sales and the associated after-sales service and supply of spares is undoubtedly the establishment of the exporter's own outstation within the market. But in the context of a wide-ranging and rapidly expanding export programme this approach becomes extremely expensive in direct overheads and indirectly in the effort required to administer the network, and it may be difficult to recruit permanent payroll employees of sufficient quality who are willing to undertake overseas tours as opposed to protracted visits. A further difficulty is that, for political or politico-economic reasons, the governments of many countries place a rigid limit on the number of nationals of the exporting country that can be introduced on a residential basis. Some years ago for example a consumer goods group of international repute sought to set up a manufacturing subsidiary in an ex-British Far Eastern country and were faced with a limit of four Europeans, none of whom were to be specialists; it was only after much haggling and threats to cancel the project that permission for the additional two specialists needed to make the operation viable was granted. More generally, the greater the 'indigenous' content in both personnel and manufacturing effort, the greater the chances both of obtaining approval from the government concerned and of acceptance in the market. The choice between the establishment of outstations and representation or partnership is thus a difficult and quite fundamental one.

14.4.1   *Agents and their selection*

Many small firms exhibit at a trade fair in the market they wish to enter with the primary intention of using the show to acquire an agent. They may even sign up on the stand the first reasonable looking agent who presents himself, or at most satisfy themselves with a single quick follow-up visit to two or three who have contacted them. Such firms have only themselves to blame when they discover, as they so often do, that the agent is uninterested, incompetent and lacking in live market contacts.

Expensive and difficult as it may be, it is essential to investigate potential foreign agents very thoroughly, insisting not only on commercial and personal references but also on disclosure of other agencies held and proof of appropriate live contacts. Another important factor is geographical location of the agent, and this has to be determined by balancing out transport costs, the geographical centre of gravity of the particular market and location in relation to facilities for distribution. Despite what was said above, it will often be worth employing a suitable consultant in the target country on an assignment strictly limited in cost, time and scope to re-survey the market and short-list two or three agents from whom a final selection can be made. If this is done, however, it is important to check that the consultant himself does not also act as an agent and is thus truly independent.

In any event a straightforward agency arrangement is seldom the best method of penetration. If the forecast or achieved turnover is small and the commission moderate, the more competent agents are likely to have conflicting interests, and an offer of increased commission from another firm whose agency they hold may make their attitude passive or even negative. If the turnover at a reasonable level of commission is sufficient to attract a really good agent, it is unlikely to be far off the point where the money paid out as commission could not be better employed in

operating a two-man (manager and secretary) sales branch or subsidiary.
(The legal definitions of, and distinctions between 'branch' and 'subsidiary' vary from country to country and require investigation.)

In many countries, notably perhaps France, it is often possible to find a man-and-wife team competent and willing to operate an outstation of this kind, in addition perhaps to a small family business, and this can offer a particularly effective and economical solution. Before deciding on a minimal outstation, it is important to cost the proposal out thoroughly on the basis of a manager, a secretary, an office, a telephone and a telex. This exercise must be carried out by direct research in the countries concerned; those who attempt to do it by extrapolating from figures applicable to their own country are apt to end up with a very unbalanced budget. For example (on 1974 going rates) a reasonable estimate for the UK would have been £4000 + £2000 = £6000 in salaries and as much again for overheads and operating costs — say £13,500 including a typical contingency. An on-the-spot investigation in France showed a starting figure of £15,000 for a husband-and-wife team deep in the provinces up to £25,000 or more for a manager and secretary with a minute office in Paris.

If the appointment of an agent is decided on, considerable care is needed in calculating his commission. Commission in other countries tends to be higher than in our own, 15 per cent is probably a starting figure, and it may be necessary to pay up to 17.5 per cent to interest a reputable agent in handling a small turnover. Since transport and associated costs, duty and in some cases a tax element, as well as the commission, have to be sandwiched between an economic ex-works price and a competitive selling price, it may be extremely difficult to show reasonable profitability. Nevertheless where all the factors are right and the agent is adequately supervised, an agency can prove a very valuable outlet. This is particularly the case if the agent also has on his books a range of related products, enabling him to offer a package to major customers, and/or if he covers two or more adjacent national markets.

14.4.2 Local assembly

The first step beyond the simple export of finished products to an agent or sales subsidiary is the export of kits for local assembly. This can produce enormous savings in transport costs, may present a more favourable tax and/or duty situation and, by increasing the indigenous content, will tend to enhance acceptability. The problem is to ensure that assembly, finishing and out-inspection is properly executed, for shortcomings here will not only damage the exporter's repute but may also lead to situations in connection with guarantee or damages claims that are extremely difficult to resolve. Even if the export kit is also marketed for do-it-yourself assembly, it is far from safe to assume that a dealer will carry this out as well as a good amateur might; and where assembly involves relatively complex and tricky processes, as is often the case in the plastics field, extreme care is needed in the choice of an assembly plant.

If the turnover is insufficient to justify the establishment of a subsidiary for this purpose, it is unlikely to attract a local concern with the talent and resources to carry it out properly, and here collaboration with a native manufacturer who would otherwise be a competitor is highly attractive. The exported product may be complementary to the native manufacturer's own range or fill a gap in it; or it may be possible, particularly for two smallish high-quality firms, to arrange a two-way import-export programme, each of them manufacturing one product — say a particular class of sailing dinghy — and each assembling and marketing both in their respective countries. Although the idea of working with a potential competitor, who may also be competing in one's own home market, runs right against the entrepreneurial grain of the kind of firm most likely to profit from it, it is in fact a highly attractive solution on small and large scales alike, offering the partners both high-grade technical resources and a ready-made system of distribution and outlets.

14.4.3   Manufacture under licence

A logical progression from local assembly is manufacture under licence, supported perhaps by the import of 'difficult' components. This term is sometimes used loosely to describe any delegation of manufacturing rights, and a distinction must be drawn between manufacture under licence as such and the various arrangements discussed in the next sub-section.

Strictly speaking a manufacturing licence can only be protected, and therefore should only be established when the product, one or more elements within it or a key production process are protected by patents. The first move towards a true licence arrangement is an investigation into the protection afforded in the target country by the manufacturer's patent, and if necessary the taking out of patents in that country. This is an extremely slow and expensive process, involving the exporter's normal patent agent and an agent in the country concerned recommended by him. Unless adequate patent conventions exist or the taking out of patents in the target country is justifiable in its own right for purposes outside a particular proposal for local manufacture, it may often be preferable to seek some other form of franchise arrangement even where the basic conditions for manufacture under licence proper are met.

14.4.4   Joint ventures and package deals

Where batch or quantity production of standard products is concerned, the advantage of transferring as much of the operation as possible to the target country or to a focus within each broad market area are varied and

substantial. Home capacity remains available for other orders, the costs
of transport are greatly reduced if not eliminated, any problems of
shelf-life that may exist are eased and the consequent broadening of the
supply base, with the possibility of buying in items such as castings at very
favourable prices, may prove extremely valuable to the exporting
company's operations as a whole. And the arguments deployed above for
increasing the 'indigenous content' gain in force as more and more of the
operation is transferred.

While there may often be excellent opportunities for joint ventures in
both high and medium technology countries, it is in the developing
countries that projects of this kind become really attractive. Provided
that the distribution of effort is attuned to the state of development of the
target country's economy and technology and the arrangement is
sufficiently flexible to allow the indigenous content to grow over the
years, a joint venture is ideal from the points of view both of the exporter
and of the government and industry of the importing nation. For the
purposes of this discussion it may be helpful to define a 'joint venture' as a
project in which the bulk of the financial and technological input comes
from the exporter, perhaps with grants and subsidies from the receiving
country's government; and a 'partnership' as an arrangemement in which
know-how, specialised components and possibly capital equipment are
provided mainly by the exporter but financial participation is effectively
shared between him and the local manufacturer or a holding or finance
company to which the latter has access.

The breadth and continuity of scope of such projects can perhaps best
be seen by considering the example of, say, a range of agricultural
machinery and a country whose economy and technology are at a point in
development where the requirement is massive and it will shortly be
possible to move beyond straight importation — roughly the stage at
which many Arab countries find themselves at the time of writing.
Suppose that the exporter is able to establish good relations with a public
or private company in the country, which is contemplating adding a
manufacturing capability to its sales, operating and maintenance
divisions. The first stage is likely to be a straight import contract for
equipment of existing design aimed at meeting the short-term need, at
proving both the market and the suitability of the product for it and at
providing means of training and familiarisation. (It is always prudent to
include this first step even if the capacity for local manufacture exists, to
assess any modifications needed, to build up the distribution and
servicing systems and to arrive at performance and reliability standards
under local conditions of operation and maintenance.) The next move
would be the supply of the simpler machines in kit form for local
assembly, and from there one might proceed to the local manufacture of
simple components such as trailer bodies either to the exporter's standard
designs or in forms designed locally under the exporter's supervision.
These activities provide a framework round which design, manufacturing
and inspection facilities can progressively be built up and personnel
organised and trained. At this stage it would be logical to start

introducing locally manufactured standard components, if needs be modifying the design in detail to accept them, and to put in hand local manufacture of some special items such as castings.

At these early stages of development of the project it is important to maintain breadth, balance and flexibility and to avoid thrusting too rapidly ahead in a particular sector only then to find that the requisite supporting services are inadequate. As a prelude to extending local manufacture, the exporter may well have to offer, within the framework of the broad collaborative agreement, to advise on factory layout, to recommend suitable machine tools, test equipment etc. and very probably to supply these. Once a proper mechanical engineering production unit with its associated design, stores, tooling, maintenance and inspection facilities has been established, progress to complete local manufacture involves changes only in degree.

In any event the exporter will wish to retain under his own hand the manufacture and supply of certain specialised items as an insurance against infringements of his rights under the agreement.

Before entering into an agreement of this kind at all, the exporter must thoroughly investigate not only his potential partner but also the possible effect of internal or external political pressures and the contract law and regulations of the country concerned. Having reduced the broad entrepreneurial risk to an acceptable level, the exporter must proceed on the assumption that his partner is commercially and technically reliable, whilst making sure that his rights are very clearly established and protected in contractual form. Even where a licence agreement as such cannot be made to stick, there are many ways in which the exporter can protect his interests. He will for example initially limit the sales territory of his partner to the country concerned and possibly certain specified neighbours, while leaving open the possibility of extending outlets at a later stage; these clauses can be reinforced by some kind of reciprocal arrangement under which the local manufacturer passes to the exporter any enquiries originating outside the former's territory.

Again the exporter can limit by size or nature the equipment to be included in the local assembly and manufacture programme with an understanding that the local manufacturer will place with him any orders he may obtain for other equipment within the full product range. Generally the aim here should be to arrive at rigorous contractual safeguards continuing up to the point where mutual involvement becomes irreversible in practical terms, while leaving the longer term options open to take best advantage of the shape in which the project actually develops.

No less important and considerably more difficult than commercial protection is the assurance of quality of locally manufactured items. It must be a condition of the agreement that the local manufacturer accepts the exporter's own standards of quality and methods of quality control. To this end the exporter must have a contractual right of free access both to the manufacturer's plant and delivery park and to the plants of local sub-contractors and suppliers; in fact the exporter should retain for himself the right to approve or veto these. Provisions of this kind are easy enough to write in but often very difficult to enforce without impairing the good relations on which the whole project depends.

On the financial side, except of course in advanced Western markets, the exporter may be very much at the mercy of the law and statutory regulations of the target country. On the one hand, in dealings with a Communist bloc or other highly socialised countries, the relationship may have to remain a purely contractual one even in the long term. On the other, in most South American countries for example, projects of this kind are required to be 'partnerships' with at least 50 per cent indigenous financial participation. Probably the arrangements most favourable to the exporter, unless his long-term aim is the establishment of a subsidiary in the country concerned, are an ongoing contract containing provisions for review and revision and an appropriate mix of cash payments, credit arrangements and royalties.

Major companies in all fields are highly expert in launching joint ventures and other major collaborative projects and generally have great success with them despite numerous and occasionally expensive teething troubles and the risk of major political upheavals. On the other hand some large concerns seem determined, sometimes for good economic reasons but sometimes probably through chauvinism, to keep manufacturing potential very firmly under their own hand. But the opportunities in this direction are equal, perhaps proportionately greater, for medium and small-medium companies with a good range of products, some patents or at least exclusive design features and ample know-how.

14.4.5 The establishment of subsidiaries

The solutions discussed above share two related drawbacks. They sacrifice direct control of operations in the new market; and more particularly they make no provision for on-the-spot management in the critical early phases. There will often be a strong case for the exporting company to have direct representation at policy level in the country right from the start, and this is certainly necessary for consumer goods where a demand has to be modified or created by promotion.

The best legal formula for establishing this cell will depend on company law in the exporting and target countries and on the relationship between these codes, and of course on any restrictions that may be in force on the movement of money and the employment of foreign nationals. And apart from any direct restrictions, international currency control measures such as the need to move capital through Eurodollars or Investment Dollars and pay a high premium rate for the privilege will influence decisions of principal and detail.

The choice of method must in fact depend on expert advice taken at the time—yet another argument for the early appointment of a legal representative in the target country — but generally it will be possible to start with no more than a 'branch office', treated legally and otherwise as a division of the company. This involves no irrevocable commitment, only minimal setting-up costs and no capital investment in fixed assets. But, as mentioned earlier, it does need to be carefully and realistically costed out. Once the pilot stage is past and a firm decision to go ahead in the market has been taken, there are advantages in converting the branch into a sales and holdings subsidiary. This need not lead to any increase in running costs or the immediate acquisition of fixed assets, but there will be the formation expenses — probably of the same order as they would be in the home country — and of course the need to move capital. On the other hand the existence of a company greatly increases operating scope and flexibility and offers the opportunity to attract indigenous capital. Unless the short- and middle-term scale and nature of the operation can be firmly defined in advance, it is probably better to start with a minimal holding company with at most a sales function — in effect no more than a management cell — and to use this as a launch-pad for the formation of one or more operating companies.

One reason for this course is that, even where no absolute insistence on indigenous majority participation exists, a company without this may be at a disadvantage in both fiscal and practical terms. A two-level structure may enable the exporter to retain control of the central or holding company and use this as a base from which to take a majority holding in operating companies, thus exercising control of the latter at one remove.

An alternative is to take a substantial stake in the company with which collaboration is proposed, but here again it will usually be impossible for an exporting company to take a majority holding direct. One can do no more here than expose the broad range of possibilities and to stress the need for expert advice; the course chosen must depend on the particularities of time and place and on the nature of the operation envisaged.

14.5   Costing

All too often an exporter successfully penetrates a market only to find that his operation shows minimal profitability or even incurs losses which he cannot sustain. As is inevitable with any new project and as has been stressed early in this chapter, there may be a preparatory phase of two years or more followed by a pilot operation before a return can be expected. This in itself may be a serious enough matter for the smaller firm, but it is very different from spending good money on launching an operation under conditions which make it incapable of showing a healthy profit. Planning must therefore include a series of comprehensive and rigorous forward costing exercises at frequent intervals. These will enable the exporter not only to spot a basically unprofitable situation in time but also, by comparing the results of successive exercises, to forecast the profitability trend resulting from movements of prices in the two markets concerned and of the respective currencies.

It is quite logical to launch a marketing operation with predictably limited profitability as a platform for further and more profitable enterprises in the same market. But managements with inadequate costing procedures may well go in blind, and one sometimes feels that the psychological pressures to export mentioned in an earlier chapter override financial judgement and cause boards to bury their heads in the sand.

On the other hand forward costing procedures should not be so detailed and rigorous as to create an illusion of accuracy that masks a host of fairly wild assumptions. At a time when all economies and the relationships between them are in a state of flux, forecasting is not going to give an accuracy better that ± 5 per cent or more probably 10 per cent. This margin of error can be catered for to some extent by including adequate contingencies, but there will always remain an element of entrepreneurial judgement. Thus rather than attempt to produce a year-by-year costing using estimated indexation rates for a large number of factors some of which may not be directly connected with one another, it may often be better, unless there are strong indications to the contrary, to make a broad assumption that the movement of all the cost elements concerned will be roughly in harmony and to cost on a year close enough for assumptions about revenue and expenditure to be reasonably firm. This year should preferably be the one in which the bulk of the initial capital expenditure is planned to lie.

14.5.1 Forward ex-works cost

In times when it is difficult enough to arrive at a realistic quotation price for a specific long-lead order, the forecasting of production costs, or the basic cost of supplying a service, in broader terms and further ahead may be seen as no more than an academic exercise. Nevertheless it is essential to arrive at a figure which contains reasonable contingencies but not such a large safety factor as to make the project stillborn, for without this the rest of the costing is meaningless.

14.5.2 Transport cost

Again an attempt must be made to estimate transport costs. This is even more difficult because these are outside the exporter's control and their inflation is compounded by subsidiary elements such as insurance. Although transport costs probably form a small proportion of the whole and the impact of variations in them is thus of second-order importance, their unpredictability may well call for a specific effort at the planning stage to minimise them, for example by exporting the product in knock-down rather than fully finished form.

The need to make sufficient allowance for operating costs in the target market, whatever form they may take, has already been stressed. The key point is that they must be estimated on the basis of current costs in the target country and not extrapolated from home market experience.

A particular problem for the smaller firm which may lack financial reserves is the need to carry the cost of a minimal on-the-spot team (manager and secretary) on the return from the earnings on the initial small-scale operation. These costs can in fact have quite a decisive effect on the scope and build-up rate of the first phase. One might venture two yardsticks here: once the pilot project is completed, build-up to the point at which local management costs can be contained at 20 per cent of earnings should be as rapid as possible; and the reduction of this element to 10 per cent may be a helpful basis from which to determine the final scale of the initial operating phase. (This last figure, of course, assumes a more economic mode of operation than the conventional agency.)

The exporter who is for some good reason developing his own operation rather than using an agent is thus likely to be faced at first with an embarrassing management cost gap, and this in the critical year or two astride launch when intensive high-grade management effort is required to get the operation off the ground. Boards will always, and very rightly, prefer to find this effort from within their payroll staff, but the combination of the executive time required and the language problem may make this impossible. In this event it may be worth buying in management in the shape of a consultant until the project can sustain its own management team on the ground. Whether this consultant should be based in the home or the target country must be decided by weighing off control against constant on-the-spot availability and relative fee levels against travel costs.

14.5.4 Language costs

The operations under discussion in this chapter are so varied in nature that it is impossible to give any yardstick figure for language costs; one can say only that they will lie somewhere between the 1 per cent or so mentioned in the preceding chapter and the 20 per cent or more quoted in Chapter 16 in the context of producing foreign-language literature. Certainly their level, combined with the tight cost margins involved, justifies a well-planned effort both to forecast and to contain them while avoiding the dangers of failure of communication in the contexts of negotiations and more particularly of publicity and promotion.

Since the cost of written translation and foreign-language copy will vary rather closely with its quality, savings here must be looked for in minimising the extramural translation effort by good planning and the setting-up of sufficient in-house resources to deal with routine work. The ways and means of doing this are discussed under the appropriate headings elsewhere in this book.

Interpreting is another matter. On the one hand, conference interpreters apart, fees are considerably higher in most other countries than in our own; and in any event an interpreter casually recruited on the spot and unfamiliar with the project may not give satisfactory results. On the other the cost of taking an interpreter out on every visit is equivalent to carrying a spare senior executive around. It is therefore important to confine the use of interpreters to the few major meetings where their services are indispensable. Either the firm must field a linguist executive to lead the project, or the additional person brought in and expensively moved around must be able to contribute a good deal more than just interpreting. Since it may be impossible for an executive of the required level of talent to be made available for work that in the early stages represents only a minute proportion of turnover, there is a further argument for the retention of a consultant who speaks both the languages concerned and who can carry out all but the most important visits on his own. His fees will be higher than those of an *ad hoc* interpreter, but since expenses are likely to be roughly double the interpreter's fee, there is a direct saving both in money and in the project leader's time.

14.5.5   Cost to end user

The sum of all the cost elements discussed above plus any indirect costs arising out of the particular situation provides a first estimate of the minimum selling price. But unless the market is a 'money no object' one or the product neatly fills an evident market gap (in which case success will depend mainly on factors other than price), the cost to the end user must also be quite separately assessed from the market end. This study will not only set upper and lower limits but, more important, will determine at what level in the market the product can best be inserted. It will be of little use pricing the product so that it competes directly with an indigenous product or an established import, and an effort must be made to find 'vertical' gaps in the price structure as well as 'horizontal' ones in the range of products already available. There may be a need to change the specification or quality of the product, recycling this into the forecast production cost, and a decision on market position is certain to affect the types of outlet chosen and hence the method of distribution and the transport costs.

Only when the costing has been recycled in this way and the coincidence or otherwise of the economic selling price and the price acceptable to the market has been found will it be possible to judge whether the project is a viable one in its own right or whether the risk and forecast amount of losses justify going ahead with it as a launch-pad for other operations.

Promotion is a major subject on its own, calling for a high degree of expertise, and this section will do no more than ventilate a few points that are peculiar to promotion in foreign-language markets.

14.6.1   Product familiarisation

Where extensive promotion is required to create a new demand or modify an existing one, establishment of a brand image will clearly be a major element in the promotion plan. What is perhaps less obvious is the need for product familiarisation both for consumer products competing for an existing demand and for trade products.

Anyone who is reasonably well-travelled and familiar with the field in question can spot the country of origin of a product with fair certainty at a glance, before he even reads the manufacturer's name on the inscriptions on any labels. It is very difficult to state in objective terms just how one does this; it is probably a combination of characteristic traits of external design and presentation; but it certainly applies right across the board from boxes of chocolates to machine tools and computers. There is for example a very clear-cut distinction between the clean lines of a Scandinavian or modern German design and the relative fussiness of a similar product from the Anglo-Saxon or Romance countries.

Conversely if one walks into, say, an electrical shop in a foreign country, it is not always easy to tell the toasters from the hair-dryers by their appearance.

It is usually pointless and often harmful to redesign in imitation of the competing indigenous products, for unusual or exotic appearance may be a strong selling point. Since verbal communication lacks the speed and power required here, a means must be found of making the product identify itself visually. Special point-of-sale material depicting the product in use will be required, and advance advertising must use a particularly judicious balance of visuals and copy to implant the (literal) product image in the customer's mind.

In the case of trade goods and capital equipment however, as well as of some consumer durables, adaptation of the design to the market may well be required. Control and instrumentation layouts and any interlocks or other safety devices must conform not only to local industrial safety regulations but also to the usages in the country of destination. Failure to do so will add to the time required for familiarisation and training and may even lead to errors and accidents when men are tired or working under stress.

14.6.2   Promotion and launch

The promotion and launch of a consumer product in a new market are more heavily dependent on language and national characteristics than any other aspect of export marketing. A single word misused or misplaced, dated slang or ignorance of a new slang meaning can destroy all impact and turn a promotion costing many thousands of pounds into one great giggle. Not long ago for example a Continental perfume manufacturer included in an English-language advertisement the caption 'A gay smelling session'. The visual showed a group of men with their heads bowed together over the perfume bottles—the message conveyed was not quite the one intended!

But language is only the beginning of the problem. As was highlighted in Chapter 5, themes, angles and brands of humour that are surefire in one market may be poison in another. Thus the slant and style of the copy, the subject and composition of visuals and the design as a whole have to be thought through afresh. And the same goes for material aimed at an aural impact. For promotion and advertising campaigns in the consumer and consumer durable fields, as opposed to the production of sales literature for specialised products, the sponsor has really no alternative but to go to a consultant in the target country or, for the third world, in that country's former imperial or economic master. The problems of control under these circumstances are discussed in Section 16.1, and this factor, together with the need for putting across personalities and for instant decisions, make it essential for the exporter to set up at least a branch office run by his own management and very probably a subsidiary before embarking on a major promotion and launch.

14.6.3   The marketing of consumer products

Whatever the scale and manner of launch intended, a pilot marketing programme is desirable even with a proven product and a brand name well-known in adjacent and apparently similar markets. Quite apart from the evaluation aspect, there is a need to prove the suitability of the sales literature and other publicity material and the efficacy of the supply and distribution system. Assuming that all necessary approvals have been obtained and a check of conformity with all laws and regulations has been made in advance, the product aspects most likely to require close study are size distribution, packaging and presentation. The exporter of an established brand product may well decide to retain, as far as regulations on labelling permit, his standard presentation in the hope of attracting customers who have seen and possibly bought the product in his own home market or elsewhere. But if a new presentation has been specially designed for the market, it may well be necessary to see the product on the shelves alongside its competitors and to study customer reaction before reaching an irrevocable decision.

The pilot marketing phase will require some support in the shape of promotion and publicity, but it seems preferable to keep this in a rather lower key than one might choose for a similar exercise in the home market. It is essential to avoid gimmicks that may impair credibility or even give offence, and in particular any flash-in-the-pan impression which may result if lavish publicity is followed by a gap in time before the main launch. There is also the matter of cost.

At the two extremes there are appropriate clear-cut solutions. For a large volume mass-appeal product which, if the pilot scheme is successful, will almost certainly be produced in the target country or at least moved in bulk and packaged there at an early stage, the scale of the operation is sufficient to justify and support a major promotion and to carry the associated management costs. With a luxury speciality product introduced through an agent to selected specialised outlets, it may be best at first to confine publicity to the point of sale and let the product stand on its merits and the resulting recommendations; the operation can then be expanded with the support of a carefully planned advertising campaign after there has been time to obtain retailer and customer feedback. But between these extremes there lies a dangerous grey zone of insupportable and uncontrollable costs. Home-based language and PR expertise is unlikely to give the campaign the right shape and the necessary impetus, while even if the budget will run to the fees and recharges of a PR consultant in the target country, it is unlikely also to cover the management effort needed to keep him and the agent under control. In this situation, as in others discussed elsewhere, the possibility of some form of complementary collaboration with a potential competitor in the target country becomes extremely interesting. Each partner then runs the marketing of the other's product in his own home market, reciprocity providing the motivation to make a good job of it. Even if one product succeeds and the other fails, the party whose own product has failed will get some return from handling the successful one; in any event both firms will have established a genuine mutual interest, broadened the base of their operations and established access to the other's market for future products.

The best way of obtaining information on possible partners is to join the national Chamber of Commerce concerned through their London office; most of them publish regular bulletins which include lists of facilities offered and business opportunities sought. For some countries, notably France and Italy, the commercial section of their London Embassy may be a better channel.

14.6.4 *Marketing trade products*

As has been remarked elsewhere, there is a widely held and probably valid school of thought that the advertising of trade products does little more than to inform and remind the reader of their existence. The main method of acquiring new customers is to establish a reputation in the target trade for technical quality and commercial reliability. This in turn will lead to personal recommendation. The problem is therefore getting the first entrée, and effective and relatively cheap ways of doing this are

the maintenance of a good network of contacts by visits to the country
and attendance at conferences or seminars held there, and exhibiting at trade fairs.

However, there is a need to put in a considerable amount of spade-work on the target market's technical press, with the aim of getting editorial cover. Since many trade publications are sponsored by or associated with the national trade association concerned, an exporter may meet heavy resistance. This can best be overcome by going in at a fairly high level through the London office of the national Chamber of Commerce concerned, the commercial counsellor at the British Embassy or best of all of course a potential customer with whom good personal relations have been established.

14.7   Stocking, spares and after-sales service

Many British exporters have in the past damaged both their own prospects and their country's commercial reputation by failing to ensure that adequate initial stocks and follow-up supplies of products and, where applicable, a sufficient inventory of spares is in position before the product is placed on the market. This is expensive because it may delay the launching, it will tie up a good deal of money in stock before any substantial return comes in and it may also attract significant storage charges. On the other hand delay in the execution of guarantee repairs does not create the best of images, and a supply failure just as the volume of sales is building up will be disastrous. Disappointed customers are unlikely to lend a very sympathetic ear to hard-luck stories about factory or transport strikes, the less so in view of Britain's current reputation. It is therefore necessary not only to stock up in the country against all foreseeable requirements but to position a cushion stock as a safeguard against interruptions of follow-up supplies.

Whether the exporter proposes to put his own service engineers on the ground, or whether engineers are to be recruited locally, all concerned must be completely fluent in both the languages concerned, and time and money may thus have to be provided for language training. Experience is so important in the work of a service engineer that it will generally be necessary to field at least one man from the exporter's existing staff at least for the first year or two. On the other hand there are strong arguments for using existing staff of the agent (if he has a technical department) and/or the distributors. In this event there will be a need to run a training programme either at the factory or at a suitable location in the target country; both to ease the training problem and to ensure ease of communication later, it is highly desirable that those selected should speak both languages. This requirement does not apply in a large-scale operation where the exporter tends at a fairly early stage to set up a subsidiary with its own training facilities in the target country.

This problem apart, the language aspects of after-sales service are twofold. The technical documentation such as spares lists, catalogues and procedural and technical instructions must be translated and in position before the operation starts and preferably before any training programme. A procedure must also be established that will ensure that new instructions on revised procedures or modifications to the product are translated and distributed as soon as they have been prepared; even where the initial documentation effort is well planned and executed, the need for up-dating is often overlooked.

The second need is to ensure that there is no language hiatus in the channels of communication used for ordering new supplies or spares. Because they will need to be handled quickly by a large number of fairly low-level employees, it is preferable to arrange for these instructions to be transmitted in English. Where this is impossible or likely to lead to errors or misunderstandings, the exporter must have the necessary rather elementary in-house language resources and all communications must be addressed for the attention of the person who can translate them.

14.8   Communications aspects

This chapter has already thrown up many communications problems in both the broader and narrower senses of that term, and the intention here is to discuss only internal communications within the entire exporting set-up from factory to end-user or retailer. While failures of communication are both most probable and most serious in the planning, negotiating and launching phases of the operation, it is surprising how often hitches occur in routine operations, and how crises are aggravated by misunderstandings even after things have run smoothly for some time.

14.8.1   Channels of communication

The first requirement is to ensure that the physical means of communication are adequate. This means telex. Post is too slow, even straight across the Channel; cables are expensive and fairly subject to garbling at one end or the other, depending on which language they are sent in; and the telephone often offers inadequate quality of transmission for the passing or reception of detailed information by someone working in a language other than his own, is subject to delays and can quickly run up surprisingly large bills. For any telex terminal which will have to send in a foreign language the extra cost of a punched tape facility is worth while.

Having set up the necessary physical means, one must then set out in writing in all the languages concerned a standard operating procedure covering all likely contingencies, and this must list a named contact and a stand-in at each functional or geographical point in the system. If a communication in a foreign language on an operation with which he is not directly concerned lands on an executive's desk, it usually goes straight to the bottom of his pending tray or even into the waste-paper basket. For obvious reasons it is preferable that all the named contacts and their stand-ins should be able to speak both languages.

Experience suggests that particular care must be taken with channels and procedures where a shipping agent, an insurance company or other organisations outside the system directly under the exporter's control are involved. While shipping agencies and similar organisations handle routine standard messages fast and accurately across the language barrier, experience suggests that their procedures are not always adequate to deal quickly with non-routine matters and emergencies. It should therefore be a matter of drill to copy any communication sent to a forwarding agent to the agent or other principal in the country of destination, or if the latter originates it, to the factory.

It is impossible to say in general terms what precise measures are needed or what problems are likely to arise; one can only stress that a great deal of thought and effort, with perhaps an element of over-insurance, should be put into establishing the means and procedures for internal communication.

14.8.2   Local recruitment

If and when a responsible manager on the exporter's payroll is established in the target market, responsibility for local recruitment should be delegated to him, or for the senior appointments on his staff carried out by him under supervision from the exporter's personnel or appropriate functional department. Even if one speaks the language, it is extremely difficult to interview and assess candidates unless one is actually living in their country; even if one has known the country very well in the past, fashions change and there are nuances of language, dress and manner which are all too easy to overlook or misinterpret unless one's finger is right on the pulse of the society from which the candidate is drawn. Further it is extremely expensive in executive time to interview in the foreign country and in travel and subsistence costs to bring long-list candidates over.

The difficulty thus arises in making the first one or two key appointments for the branch or subsidiary to be established, since even if its senior executive is to be found from the exporter's existing payroll, he will not be in position at the time these appointments have to be made. The only reasonably cheap and really satisfactory way of making these first few key appointments is by personal knowledge or from personal recommendation by a reliable contact. Thus from the moment his senior staff first start visiting and reconnoitring the market, they should be on the lookout for likely candidates.

Unless one is successful in imposing the traditional Anglo-Saxon requirement that everyone concerned should speak English, reasonable in-house language resources are a prerequisite for economical and speedy operation. In the smaller firms these are however likely to be insufficient in quality and capacity to cope with all the work involved, particularly in the critical formative stages of the project. Until the 'foreign end' is not only established but is considered fully trustworthy, there will thus be a need to back-up these in-house resources by call either on a language consultant as such or on a consultant who specialises in the appropriate field and speaks the languages concerned. If this consultant is to earn his fee and more particularly to justify his expenses, he must inspire sufficient confidence to be sent on his own to carry out the less important exploratory and liaison visits.

A lawyer (who should of course be an English-speaker) based in the target country is indispensable from the earliest stages onwards, but otherwise, certain special cases apart, it is preferable to avoid the use of consultants based there unless and until the exporter has sufficient management on the ground to monitor and control them. Major international consultancies are ideally equipped to advise on and perhaps to carry out an operation of this kind on an exporter's behalf, but the cost of employing them will often lie outside the smaller exporter's budget.

15
Technical documentation

The product of foreign-language technical documentation is both costly and time-consuming; if not fully planned in advance it can make an unpleasant dent in profit margins, particularly as in many countries, especially Eastern Europe, delay penalties are apt to be levied on missing documentation as if it were a part of the equipment itself. Perhaps one reason why things often go wrong is that in many organisations this advanced planning involves departments which do not otherwise need to be brought in until just before the delivery stage. A second is that of costing; to be safe the full cost of documentation has to be carried on the initial contract in a new language market or by the first batch of exported goods. Yet the production of technical documentation in a given language for a given product is a one-time operation which if all goes well can be spread over follow-up contracts or batches as well. This is yet another area which in single-language working need scarcely attract the attention of negotiators and top management, but which becomes very well worth negotiating on, planning and costing in when a particular language barrier has to be crossed for the first time. To highlight this point with just one example among those discussed in detail below, persuading the customer to accept only a list of recommended spares in the language and the full illustrated parts list in English may represent a

220 saving of several thousand pounds in the case of a complex product.

The question of conversions between Anglo-American units and the metric system and of aligning specifications originated in different countries was aired in Chapter 4 and is further discussed below; but since it involves engineering philosophy and is likely to be with us, even in the United Kingdom, for some years, it merits a rather broader look before the reader gets too deeply entangled in the trees of detail. A product that has been designed to Anglo-American formulae or codes and made of materials specified in Anglo-American units on machines also designed for them cannot be precisely specified in the SI system without running into strings of decimals at which even the trained engineer's mind boggles and which go well beyond the practical limits of everyday metrology. Rounding errors both in constants and in dimensioning may not only lead to significant differences between the specification and the actual product, but also make it impossible for the customer and his approving authorities to check the specification details by recalculating them either forwards or backwards. Yet a specification presented in its original Anglo-American units is just as difficult for an engineer trained in the metric system to both visualise and comprehend quickly as metric specifications still are for many of us. In the absence of advance agreement on the handling of this problem between all concerned, the exporter may be forced either to 'go up one' in his design and accept the consequence of increased cost and possibly of impairment of some performance or weight/size characteristics which directly influence the cost-effectiveness of the product, or to risk rejection of his design by the foreign approving authority at the delivery stage when the cost penalties of a change would be disastrous. In practice the order of magnitude of such deviations is low and they are more than taken care of by safety factors, apart from the problem of fits which are mainly already covered by international standards straddling in some way or other the two systems of units. Thus they can probably be dealt with when specifying by putting some kind of numerical or other qualification on the safety factor sufficient to cover any risk of this being challenged while still leaving its minimum value acceptably high. Once again difficulties can be avoided by awareness of the problem and timely decisions to overcome it.

15.1 General factors

15.1.1 Requirements

Ridiculous as it may sound, it is often far from easy to establish the full range of requirements for technical documentation in advance, and this is yet another aspect on which exhaustive research is necessary. It is relatively easy to agree with the end customer or agent the nature and scale of documentation he will need and to write this into the contract. But this is only the beginning of the story. The customer himself may not be too familiar with the details of statutory requirements, and even the approving authority for the complete product may, either through an oversight or initial lack of detailed knowledge of the product, fail to draw attention to some special approval required for a component or sub-system. In the case for instance of a specialised vehicle carrying equipment which is to be connected to the mains electrical supply, the vehicle or even the sub-system approving authority may fail to give warning of the need to get the switches separately approved.

In the more bureaucratic countries researching and preparation of the approval documentation may be a significant time and cost factor if the embarrassment and probable expense of goods sitting on the quayside while the mills grind yet again is to be avoided. Much preliminary help can of course be obtained from the official agencies of Great Britain and the importing country such as the British Overseas Trade Board, the commercial counsellor in the British embassy of the country concerned and the London embassies — or if they exist, Chambers of Commerce — of the target country. The British Standards Institution with its Help To Exporters Service, some of the more sophisitcated British Trade Associations and in some cases the appropriate engineering or scientific professional institutes can also be of great help. But whereas general information from such sources will usually suffice to establish the requirement for commercial documentation, direct discussion of the technical approval requirements with the approving authorities concerned is highly advisable if not essential. This also gives opportunity to discuss with them any relaxations or specification problems and ways and means of approval inspections, thus enabling a coordinated delivery and handover plan of the kind envisaged in Section 13.5.4 to be established.

15.1.2 Planned layout

Careful planning of the layout of foreign-language documentation and the establishment of a good library and filing system for it can yield significant savings in time and money both in the short term and in the long. Most firms have a section operating a well organised system for their English-language technical documents, but perhaps because of the lack of suitable in-house language resources this rather seldom extends to foreign languages. On the level of detailed layout, it will pay to keep legends and notes of drawings, diagram sheets, etc., replacing them by a suitable number or letter code. It then becomes possible to use the same drawings and to pair each of them with a similarly coded glossary sheet for each language. This sheet can then be inserted facing the diagram or, in the case of large fold-outs and separate drawings, the appropriate language legend can easily be overprinted onto a standard panel left blank on the master.

The next principle is to break down major documents such as handbooks and workshop manuals into sections and sub-sections relating to each 'brick' in the build-up of the product. It then becomes easy to assemble the documentation for any one of a range of complete products from these sections, and the only need for fresh editing and translation lies in the index. In the same sense the amount of matter on the pages of the English should occupy only some 60 per cent of the space available, so that pagination can be held in the longer languages; and each section should be separately page-numbered with the addition of a key letter for the section to the page number itself, so that supplementary pages covering special ancillary equipment or modifications can easily be added and no problem arises in indexing the assembled document. It may also be advisable to include on each page a key heading in English as well as in the language so that no confusion can occur if documents are being assembled by someone who speaks only English.

With documentation based on this glossary sheet and brick system it is relatively easy to establish a multilingual library of bricks which can be added to as required and from which the required documentation can quickly be drawn. This should of course extend to manufacturers' leaflets, etc., of regular sub-contractors or sub-system suppliers. This library like any other will require an index, but in devising the index it is particularly important to include some means of discovering quickly and certainly whether the document in question has already been translated and if so where copies of the translation, if not held, can be obtained. Once established, this facility can readily be extended to cover not only the major technical documents but also instructions and standard forms for approval documentation.

A system of this kind will not only prevent panics and reduce direct language costs but can also be used to minimise printing costs. Diagram sheets will be standard across all languages and can therefore be printed in economic quantities. But it may be quite uneconomic to have the foreign-language texts actually printed unless it is certain that these are or will be required in substantial quantities. A wide choice of options is available here, but for the major documents of complex specialised equipments, where the quantities in any one language market may be small, it is usually acceptable to type the text using carbon ribbon or a special litho ribbon onto short-life litho plates and run the sheet as required. Since it may often be necessary to show at least a heading on diagram sheets, it is worth choosing a method for the reproduction of these which will allow the required language text to be similarly typed onto blank secondary masters or plates. The process chosen should also be one, such as the Brunning process, which produces second-order prints of acceptable quality, as it may not always be possible to obtain masters of sub-contractors' and suppliers' drawings and diagrams, and these firms may be unwilling or unable to conform to the system adopted.

The operation of a system of this kind is one of the relatively few places where a linguist who does not also have secretarial qualifications can be accommodated within the smaller firm. The real annual cost of employing someone for this purpose will be directly recouped in reduced translation effort and in the avoidance both of panic trips to sort out approval problems and of contract penalties for delayed documentation.

While most of the content of technical documentation, being related to the equipment itself, will of its nature be standard across all markets, it is important to ensure that operator and workshop manuals and other maintenance instructions are related to the intended conditions of use and to the general circumstances prevailing in the customer's country.

Perhaps the most important aspect under this head is lubrication instructions and charts. These are usually prepared, and often for good reason, to cover the full climatic range of possible markets, but it is very easy to read an incorrect lubricant grade or frequency figure off such multi-purpose charts, particularly as those who use them are often working in a maintenance bay under difficult conditions. A further factor here is that the carefully condensed text, extensive abbreviations and rather dense layout often used to accommodate the chart within the format of the manual or a multiple of it are likely to make the clarity of layout less than ideal after translation into the longer languages. Unless the market in question covers a wide range of climatic zones or other conditions, it will usually be worth preparing single-purpose charts, at least to cover those systems where an error in lubrication would be critical. It is also common practice to state the range of lubricants required by referring it to a particular brand of lubricant common in the manufacturing country, often admittedly with a note saying that equivalents may be used. This is fine in theory, because all suppliers of lubricants are supposed to hold international tables of equivalent grades. But here again an error can easily occur in reading the small print, and in any event experience shows that many third-world countries cannot in fact cope with this situation and customers in them are apt to choose a locally available lubricant by hit or miss methods. It is the work of a moment to obtain from the customer or his lubricant supplier in the course of preliminary technical discussions lists of the types and grades of lubricant available to him and with the facilities available in the UK it is equally easy to match these to the lubricants normally specified and provide a chart which the customer can use without difficulties or risk of error.

A second area requiring special consideration is that of expense stores which the customer may need or wish to stock up with or replace by local procurement. In the case for example of standard electrical components it is only necessary to find out what is available in his country and specify this by make and part number as an alternative to the component normally recommended. By and large, apart perhaps from items with specialised threads, metallic spares present little problem; it is with non-metallic components such as friction linings, and more particularly with specialised plastics used for thermal or electrical insulation or for self-lubricating bearings, that problems arise over specification, quality and even over practical performance where these appear to be met.

Another simple but important point concerning spares is the need to indicate clearly in manuals and spares lists where and under what arrangements spares can be ordered. This applies particularly in the cases of large organisations moving into a new market, where the extension of an existing spares organisation may not have been planned when documentation is prepared, and of complex engineering products containing a number of specialised sub-systems made by sub-contractors. Unless and until an after-sales service and spares organisation is established in the market, it will probably be best for the exporter to instruct his customer to order all spares through his own head office and accept the additional administrative load involved.

Both the design itself and the technical documentation must take full account of the proposed conditions of use. These may call for quite extensive revision of, for example, maintenance schedules. This need is obvious in the case of vehicles, vehicle-borne equipment and machinery and plant for outdoor use, but static equipment too may be affected by higher than usual ambient temperatures or relative humidities. The customer's shift length, operating hours and maintenance system may also have to be taken into account. Good maintenance being in the interests of supplier and customer alike, it may be worth studying the customer's maintenance schedules for his existing equipment and attempting to accommodate to these. For instance British vehicle maintenance tables are normally based on intervals of, say, 500, 1000. 5000, etc., miles. Even when generously rounded these come out to 750, 1500 and 7500 km, while an operator already using equipment originating from a metric country is likely to have based his planning on around 1000 or 5000 km intervals. Adaptation to these, where possible, will clearly not only be a strong selling point but will help to ensure that maintenance is properly carried out.

15.1.4 Characteristics of users

Those concerned with preparing operating, maintenance and repair instructions work on the tacit assumption that the grouping of skills and standards of skills and education in the target market are broadly similar to those of their own organisation. Apart from the need, discussed in Chapter 4 and below, to take particular care in ensuring that texts intended for translation are clear of ambiguities and local terminology, this assumption by and large holds good for technologically advanced countries. The situation in the third world is very different and, because it is related to the education problems of the developing countries, is unlikely to change more than gradually over two generations or so. Training of maintenance and repair supervisors and technicians, while necessary and valuable, does not always supply a complete solution. Middle-level and junior executives and supervisors are apt to be working at or often beyond the ceiling of their capabilities, and technicians, while often at least the equal of their counterparts in advanced countries in purely practical skills and particularly expert in improvisation, are likely to lack the broad education necessary to absorb even elementary theory or carry out instructions calling for calculations. Just as it used to be said in the Services that 'soldiers cannot measure', so one might say of many third-world technicians that they can measure but cannot calculate or deduce.

Consider for example the setting up of a control circuit. For the home market it may be enough to say simply: 'Enter the circuit diagram at the first potentiometer P1, follow through adjusting potentiometers in succession, and repeat this cycle until satisfactory running speeds and accelerations are obtained'. Similarly one might ask the technician to determine a particular setting by substituting in a simple formula. For third-world markets it will probably be worth setting out the process step by agonising step and replacing the formula by a table of pre-calculated values for each setting. Similar considerations apply to the use of substitutes. For example, if a welder in an advanced country runs out of a particular type of electrode, he or at least his supervisor will probably be able to look up the material specifications in question and use these and other technical data to enter tables of electrodes and find an acceptable substitute, if necessary slightly modifying the welding procedure. His fellow in the developing countries not only lacks the ability to do this but may also be temperamentally inclined to place the matter firmly in the hands of Allah and either do nothing or, with the best of intentions, pick an electrode at random out of a nearby bin.

This leads one to the question of attitudes. Despite the tendency of Anglo-Saxons to deprecate the competence of those of other races who are not born with a clock in their heads, the exporter to a third-world market probably has more going for him there than in many European countries today, if only he knows how to turn this situation to his advantage. One only has to talk to individuals at all levels in the developing countries to realise that most of them are genuinely and deeply motivated by patriotism, belief in their country's political and economic system and confidence that despite teething troubles the country will achieve its economic and technological aims in the end. Even if combined with a tendency to lethargy, this strong motivation can be put to good use in helping the customer to obtain high standards of operation and maintenance by appropriately framing both courses and instructional manuals. A few words of introduction explaining the equipment in simple terms and stressing the ways in which it represents advanced technology and has been adapted to the particular needs of his country or concern will encourage the operator to take a pride in his equipment. Instructions carefully matched to his ability to comprehend without in any way writing down to him will make him feel that he is doing a good job and at the same time improving his knowledge.

15.2 Scope

The technical documentation required will vary widely with the nature of the product and the marketing operation, but the requirement as a whole will usually fall under some or all of the heads set out below; even where not all of them apply, they will at least serve as a planning guide.

15.2.1   Technical sales literature

Even where the export project derives from preliminary personal contact and takes the shape of a firm contract to a particular customer, there will be a need for some kind of explanatory literature of a sales nature. Sales literature in general is discussed in the next chapter, and only the points that particularly affect technical literature will be covered below.

The first problem is at what technical and linguistic level to pitch such leaflets, and here one must first discover where the final decision to purchase is made and what kind of person makes it. Many third-world countries present particular difficulties in this respect. First they tend to be socialised often to the point where the approval of the sponsor ministry is required and almost always to the extent that the treasury or its equivalent will have to give financial approval of transactions requiring foreign exchange. Political considerations such as the desire of many non-aligned countries to maintain a balance in their purchases from the Eastern and Western blocs will often involve broader consultation at ministerial level. Obviously some of the politicians involved will lack technological awareness, as indeed they may in advanced countries too. The difference lies in the quality of advice they get from their senior civil servants. At least for another generation key posts in developing countries may frequently be filled by individuals lacking both the general ability and specialised competence to give solid advice. This may be for the very understandable reason that they have been given posts as a political reward for services in the attainment of independence, or simply because the kind of talent needed does not yet exist. Gaining the interest and favourable opinion of these decision-makers calls for a rather high standard of language and a very elementary level of technical content. On the other hand the engineers who examine the proposal in detail and advise on it at lower levels are likely to be highly competent and experienced in their own fields but of limited general education, so that they will on the one hand resent being written down to technically and on the other may be unable to appreciate, or perhaps even to understand, high-flown language.

This conflict is too extreme to be solved by compromise, and the production of two separate leaflets does nothing to ensure that they will filter through the bureaucratic channels to arrive at the places for which they were respectively intended. It is therefore probably best to prepare leaflets of this kind in two parts, carrying to an extreme the practice often followed in technical sales literature for the home market, which contains an introductory section aimed at top management and a second more detailed section for the specialist. It is however important that the first section should contain sufficient technical and operational background to serve also as a tactful brief for the non-specialist decision-maker. The

In the minister: 'Ah, these people really respect us and understand our problems'.

And in the engineer: 'Ah, these are really down-to-earth people who know their job and appreciate exactly what we need.'

To produce this double slant without making it glaringly obvious makes particularly exacting demands on the translator. In fact it is fairly unlikely that any one translator will be able to handle both parts of the leaflet satisfactorily, and to send them out separately will inevitably lead to clashes in terminology. Thus translation needs to be a team effort, and the need for meticulous briefing makes it preferable that the team should be directly accessible to the exporting firm. Even when these conditions are satisfied, the style and content of this kind of leaflet is so critical that it is best to get the draft vetted by someone who has his fingers right on the pulse of the target market and indeed of the prospective customer within it.

This first stage in technical documentation is also of particular importance because it will establish much of the terminology that will run through all subsequent parts. Thus apart from briefing on the document itself, time and effort must be allowed for the thorough briefing of and consultation with the translation team at this very early stage. One detailed point in technical sales literature is that the translator must be told whether any specifications included are or are not actual or potential contract specifications. In French for example and in a number of other languages this will affect the word chosen to render the heading 'Specification', and the use of the word *Spécification* to cover what is in fact no more than a list of general technical data may cause complications even if it is supported by the usual reservation of the right to change specifications. The choice of units within the metric system in a technical sales literature as opposed to documentation of a purely engineering nature is also a difficult one. This is discussed more fully below, but designation of the length of a bale of hay in millimetres, for example will not ring any very notable bells with a farmer.

15.2.2 *Contract specifications*

No matter whether we are considering a standard product being marketed generally into an area or specialised equipment being sold to a specific customer under a special contract, the formal or contract specification is a key document. In the interests of supplier and purchaser alike, it must be precise and unambiguous and in every sense of the word acceptable in both or all the languages concerned, and it must be sufficiently detailed to provide a basis of costing on the one hand and of acceptance of the goods supplied on the other. In the case of a broad-based sales operation, the product will have been—or at least should have been—certificated in advance by the national approving authorities concerned and/or appropriate commercial laboratories. It is good practice to submit the draft specification in the language for approval along with the product. Most approving authorities, however rigorous they may be, realise that it is not easy for an importer either to understand or to meet every detail of their requirements, and they are generally more than prepared both to advise in detail on any modifications necessary and to comment on the related documentation. Obtaining advance approval of the specification in this way can avoid a host of difficulties vis-à-vis both the customers or agent and the authorities directly concerned with importation.

Where a single-customer contract for specialised or complex equipment is concerned, the problem is less simple. Unless the collection and handling of market intelligence has been exceptionally good and preliminary technical level discussions unusually thorough, it is rather unlikely that the specification which accompanies the initial proposal will stand through the contract stage to execution of the project. On the other hand any change after signature of the contract inevitably leads to revised costings and to a generally contentious situation. The approach needed is therefore a combination of extreme flexibility in the early stage, when lack of mutual understanding and confidence may broaden the scope of usual give and take, with a determination to get all technical problems finally resolved and the solutions incorporated into the specification before a firm contract is signed. Here one must refer again to the establishment of mutual confidence and of a broad spirit of collaboration; for no specification can be completely comprehensive and express every detail of the working compromises struck between what the manufacturer can supply and what the customer needs and is prepared to pay for.

Presentation of the specification and any associated drawings is far more important than many firms seem to consider it. In the advanced and developing countries alike the tendency is more and more to go out if not for worldwide tender at least to a very broad field. And the same trend towards internationalisation means that more and more contenders are likely to respond. Since the commercial aspects of the proposal are likely to be covered in a few sheets, of which only the quotation proper will require analysis in detail, and the technical side may run into at least tens of pages accompanied by drawings which are not particularly easy to handle off a drawing board, the bulk of the work of examining the tenders falls on the technical staff and in the last resort on a single individual or a small team. While engineers in most countries are accustomed to rather moderate presentation in much of the documentation they use, in circumstances like these they will inevitably tend to study more carefully and to favour specifications which are well and clearly presented and make minimal demands on their ability to decode and read between the lines.

A particular point here is the quality of prints of drawings and the legibility of their legends, but problems here as in all other aspects of presentation and accuracy are apt to arise from rush. For even if the tenderer's internal procedures are faultless, the time available to get out a complete complex proposal, perhaps covering a whole range of related equipment, to have it translated into and decently presented in a foreign language and to get it into the prospect's hands by the closure date will never be enough—particularly when the technical documentation has also to be phased into and coordinated with commercial documentation and costing.

The only satisfactory solution is thus to get the bulk of this work done in advance, justifying the direct and indirect costs on the grounds either of a general intention to enter a particular language market or of a promising specific opportunity indicated by intelligence. For standard products this situation results automatically from submitting specifications for approval along with the equipment itself; once again it is in the context of a single or multiple contract for specialised major equipment that longer-term and more detailed advanced planning is necessary.

If genuine innovation is needed to meet the requirement, then there will inevitably be a development and proving phase, perhaps under a separate development contract, which will allow ample time for the preparation of costings and documentation before the stage of a firm offer is reached; but for many and evident reasons manufacturers prefer to export into new markets and importers to procure from new sources matériel that is proven in general design if not in detail.

If the kind of foreign language technical library discussed in Section 15.1.2 has been established, this facility can easily be extended to cover specifications for standard 'bricks', each representing either a particular type of basic unit to which ancillaries or extensions can be added as required, or an ancillary unit which may be common to a number of basic units. For example an automatic lathe will require a control unit, a swarf-removal system, an infeed system to bring blanks to it and a delivery system to remove the machined components. Each of these ancillaries with only minor modifications will also be necessary and suitable for, say, a milling or slotting machine. Such elements of a specification as material specifications, testing, inspection and calibration requirements, or standard sub-systems, e.g. vehicle lighting, can also form 'bricks' in the system. Given a library of this kind, it is relatively quick and easy to pick out the relevant standard sheets, revise or complete them, for instance with dimensions, sub-assembly quantities or performance characteristics, and then to prepare and have translated a general covering specification showing how they relate physically and functionally in the complete equipment under offer. Exactly the same principle will often apply of course to drawings, and even when for some reason a special drawing has to be made, a standard legend can be used on it. With an approach of this kind, the only time-critical problem likely to arise is the typing of the contract technical documentation, since most countries' contract law requires contract documents to be submitted in original; nevertheless it may be possible to get away with high quality photo or litho copies at the initial proposal stage.

The not inconsiderable problems of detail which arise in writing or translating specifications apply also to other elements in the technical documentation and are therefore discussed in the next section. There are however certain points of presentational and costing tactics which are peculiar to specifications and become important when the tender is being made in response to a 'worldwide' request for tenders. Here one must put oneself in the position of the customer's engineering staff, who will be faced with the task of comparing and selecting from a large number of competing specifications that are in fact rather similar but differ widely in terminology, format, presentation and the amount of detail included. Being human, these people will inevitably favour the tenderers who have made a real effort to make their task easy. Particularly where public contracts are involved, the enquiry documentation may contain quite detailed instructions on the form in which the tender specification is to be submitted, and it goes without saying that a very great effort to comply with these is worthwhile.

Perhaps the first tactical decision, the results of which finally appear in the quotation proper but which will inevitably be reflected in the structuring of the specification, is whether to quote a genuine all-in price or to give a basic specification and price with a string of 'optional extras', most of which are in fact essential if the product is to fulfil its intended purpose. An all-in price supported by a lavish specification will look absurdly high against a competitor's basic price and may give the customer the impression of being taken for a ride. On the other hand an important third-world customer was heard to remark that they had accepted a certain quotation because it gave them a clear-cut figure of what the equipment was actually going to cost them, and that they lacked the statistical talents to make the combinations and permutations needed to reach such a figure from a leading competitor's quotation. One practice that is rather frequent and certainly disastrous, because it implies lack of respect for the customer, is to quote a price for the product made to UK standards and a supplement for 'additions and modifications to comply with... regulations.' Unless there are indications to the contrary, the best course is probably to quote an all-in price for something that will just genuinely meet the customer's stated requirements and to superimpose genuinely optional extras which will give added performance or versatility. The specification must, of course, be structured along the same lines.

A more fundamental and delicate situation arises when an enquirer, generally through lack of experience or confidence, over-specifies by calling for an unfavourable or even unfeasible solution to his requirement when a perfectly satisfactory one exists. The obvious move of going and talking to him about it may be the wrong one, as many countries, at least where public contracts are concerned, refuse to hold direct discussions with tenderers before the closure date for quotations in case this is seen as showing undue favour. If time is short the only way out is to submit a

standard specification with an explanation of why it meets his
requirement; but since it will not be easy to shift him from his *idée
fixe* and he may regard any attempt to do as a slight, it is preferable
when time and capacity allows to submit alternative costed proposals,
one following the enquirer's approach and the other the solution
recommended by the manufacturer.

15.2.3 Approval documentation

A good deal has already been said on the difficulty and necessity of
obtaining advance information on approval procedures for special-to-
order products, so let us assume here that we have a list of the approvals
required, instructions on the procedures and a set of the relevant forms in
our hands in good time. These forms may be rather massive. In the case
of a specialised vehicle going to France or a country with 'French-based'
regulations, the documentation for a moderately complex specialised
vehicle may amount to a dossier of twenty to thirty pages. Quite apart
from problems of language or detail, the prospect of coping with a young
book like this as opposed to the usual brief and simple inspection
certificate may be something quite new to a manufacturer's
out-inspection organisation and even to particular individuals within an
inspection authority such as Lloyds. If the contract involves delivery of a
large number of units of several different types at a high production rate,
it is scarcely an exaggeration to say that a mini-production line for the
associated paper work has also to be planned. Certainly it will be
necessary to devise, set out and prove a detailed standard operating
procedure before deliveries begin.

A particular and very real practical problem here is that the inspectors
and clerical staff who will be handling the actual sets of documents to be
completed for and go out with each unit are fairly unlikely to have any
knowledge at all of the language. The preparation of bilingual forms
would make the bulk of the documentation absurd, and these might in
any case be unacceptable to the authorities at the other end. In fact it is
probably unnecessary to expend money and time in having the various
instructions and forms translated into English in full. If the exporter has
an experienced linguist on his payroll or working closely with him, he
should be allowed to play a full part in, if not to lead, the discussions on
the out-inspection and documentation procedure and prepare an
instruction in English to go with each form that has to be completed in
the inspection bay. As an added precaution it may be advisable to make
the final out-inspection certificate and any inspection label which has to
be attached to the product itself bilingual, as these will usually be quite
short and simple. For more complex documents, which may be standard
for each particular product or can be filled in from an instruction, the
identifying headings such as 'Model number' and 'Serial number' should
be shown in both languages to help the clerical staff who finally make up
the dossiers.

Since the cost and effort involved in the preparation and completion of documentation of this kind is far from negligible and the consequences of omissions or errors may also be expensive, it is probably worth taking out the draft in the language, after it and the associated procedure have been agreed internally, and getting the approval or comments both of the customer and of his inspecting authorities.

Inevitably some sets of documents will get lost en route or equally probably in the files of the importing country's bureaucrats, and it will then be necessary to produce authenticated duplicates extremely quickly if expenses such as demurrage and the payment of customs fines on the customer's behalf are to be avoided. On the other hand it is quite uneconomic to complete and file a full duplicate dossier for each unit. The best compromise here is probably to have a document check-list for each unit which can be ticked off as the documents are put into the dossier and can also cover in a separate section any customer documentation such as user handbooks; and to retain duplicates of the shorter key documents such as test and final out-inspection certificates for each unit together with a limited number of spares of the other documents. It will then be possible to make up a duplicate dossier containing authentic copies of the key documents very quickly and easily should the need arise.

Since many equipments being imported into the more bureaucratic countries will have to go through three or four separate stages of inspection and approval before becoming available to the end user, queries and snags are virtually inevitable. It is worth going to a good deal of trouble to provide oneself and the customer with a watertight case to argue from and the ability to produce fresh sets of documents quickly when required.

15.2.4 User handbooks

Many aspects of the production of effective foreign-language user handbooks have been covered in Section 15.1 above, and similar considerations apply when instructions to operators are issued in the form of boards to be placed by the machine or labels fixed to it. Once a mutlilingual library of 'bricks' has been set up and thoroughly indexed, the compilation of instructions for issue with each unit delivered should present few problems. Discussion under this head can thus be confined to the problems of getting a new section or complete handbook prepared and translated and the practical difficulties that so often seem to arise in connection with instructions emanating from suppliers and sub-contractors.

The 'Japanese camera leaflet syndrome' has become a byword among exporters, translators and communicators in general, but it would be unfair to suppose that all exporting countries are not equally at fault in this respect. With the exception of scientific papers in new fields and those literary works which depend heavily on communication at the

aesthetic level, instruction books and workshop manuals are probably the
most difficult task with which a translator is faced.

The sponsor must face the fact that errors are going to arise and to pass right through the chain unnoticed until the customer's supervisory staff have had time to become thoroughly familiar with the equipment, since up to that point there may be no one person with a really full grasp both of the product and of the foreign-language text. One might perhaps quote here the translation of an instruction to heavy-vehicle drivers 'not to ride the kerb' as 'avoid pavements for horses', but where engineering, pharmaceutical and other products are concerned errors can lead to injury and loss of life.

To look on this dark side first, sponsors of such translations should always ensure that any translation agency or free-lance they use is covered by 'professional negligence' indemnity. But even if the blame can be firmly pinned on the translator, as it rather seldom can, this insurance may not begin to cover claims arising from a fatal accident, and exporters of potentially dangerous products would do well to examine the position with their own insurers. A more serious example than the above of how dangerous errors can arise even between English and French lies in that fact that English-speaking electrical engineers usually speak of a switch which is 'on' and of a circuit through which current is flowing as 'closed', and of a switch which is 'off' or a circuit which is broken as 'open' (though even in English the inverse terminology is conventional in certain fields). The French also speak of a live circuit as *fermé* ('closed') but to them a switch is 'closed' when it is off and 'open' when it is on, on the analogy of a tap or cock. However expert and conscientious the translator and any reviser or editor may be, there is quite clearly a serious risk here of a dangerous error if a procedure on an apparatus involving a number of switches and circuits is being described.

This said, it may not seem unreasonable to advise allowing as much as one year for the start-to-finish production of a user and/or workshop manual for complex equipment. If the English text is written within the manufacturing firm, and a translator or language consultant capable of going through this on the machine itself and picking up any ambiguities and errors is not available, it is prudent to have this text checked by an outside consultant engineer or technical author before it is passed across to a remote translator. Remote or otherwise, the translator must be briefed and indeed encouraged to come back with queries on any point at all that is not absolutely clear to him. With luck the non-standard terminology should by this stage have been established either with the purchaser or with existing customers in the same language market, so that provided one translator or translation team has been used throughout the project terminology should present little problem. The sponsor should ensure that the foreign-language text is read by at least one reviser—ideally a fluent speaker of the language who has not seen the machine or the English text before should go over the foreign-language text on the machine. Experience suggests that, tempting as it may be, it is not advisable to send drafts of user and maintenance instructions to an agent in the importing country or to the customer himself, as they will not at this stage be familiar enough with the equipment. On the other hand training courses for the customer held at the manufacturer's plant offer a splendid opportunity of proving both the terminology and the full text of any tricky parts of the written instructions.

Forward planning and close collaboration with the linguist or translation team concerned should overcome most of the hazards inherent in producing instructions on the manufacturer's own equipment, particularly if one of the team has had an opportunity of interpreting in or being present at discussions with the customer. But for some reason that is never very apparent problems often seem to arise over instructions on specialised sub-units or devices which are bought in. Frequently the texts and diagrams provided by suppliers and sub-contractors arrive in such a botched-up state that they require rewriting in the language rather than translating, and even major multinational firms producing standard equipment in a number of countries and marketing it worldwide often seem unable or unwilling to produce instructions in any language but that of the main equipment manufacturer. These instructions are often longer and more difficult than those on the main equipment, so that duplication of translation can cause a really substantial waste of time and money, quite apart from producing a less than ideal translation because of lack of contact with the sub-contractor or supplier. It would seem that while a request to supply one set of instructions per unit in a language other than English may produce the answer that the translation does not exist, an offer to buy the edition in the required language at a negotiated price per copy may suddenly lead to its existence being discovered.

ASLIB keeps an extensive library and index of translations and will make a search free for members and at a small fee for non-members. Alternatively if the item in question is also produced in, say, France or Germany it may be worth writing direct to the subsidiary in that country, again offering to pay an appropriate price per copy as they will not be supplying the item itself. In cases where the item is one that is in virtually worldwide use, it is also worth checking with the customer himself whether he already has copies of instructions of it in his language and arranging with him to get a sufficient number of these reproduced. This slightly tedious and seemingly avoidable problem has been discussed in some detail as it is one that no-one would expect unless he had met it.

Finally it is worth restressing the need to brief the translation team very thoroughly not only on the equipment itself but also on the broader factors such as conditions of use and characteristics of the intended users. This will hardly be necessary if the target country is their own, but a Frenchman is no more likely to know an ex-French colony than an Englishman is to have been to, say, Singapore.

Maintenance and workshop manuals take all the problems of user handbooks one stage further, with the compensation that those using them are likely to be more expert than the operators and to have more opportunity to study the documentation under reasonable conditions and to consult their superiors. One must comment here that the English of workshop manuals on specialised equipments quite often contains significant editorial errors or misprints, such as misprints of the reference codes of valves or switches in explanations of sequenced procedures. In the English these are often obvious to an informed and careful reader, and will certainly become apparent to an experienced maintenance engineer when he attempts to carry out the procedure. But unless the translator is equally alert and familiar with the equipment and the principles that underlie it, he may not only carry the error over but also, in an attempt to avoid ambiguity, render the passage in such a way that no-one reading the foreign-language text would spot the mistake. It is therefore essential that key passages are physically checked back onto the machine before being cleared for translation.

For reasons given earlier maintenance and repair instructions may have to be substantially revised or specially written to suit conditions in the target country. Because of climatic or workshop conditions or perhaps of the limited capabilities of the customer's maintenance personnel, it may often be prudent to recommend unit replacement of an assembly that would normally be repaired on the workshop bench. Ideally the writer of the manual, the translator and a representative of the customer should get together to discuss both the changes in actual procedures and the revision of instructions which call for an unusually high level or a particular grouping of skills. Another point of detail which can usefully be cleared in this way is the conventions to be used on drawings and schematics. As was mentioned above training courses held at the manufacturers' plant offer excellent opportunity for such discussions without the slightly humiliating need to consult the customer formally.

It will also be worth attempting to structure the technical manuals in a way that will suit the customer's maintenance and repair organisation and in particular the extent of repairs normally carried out at various levels of workshop or passed out to specialists. If the manual has been prepared and compiled in small sections as has been suggested for other reasons above, this should present no great problem.

15.2.6   Spares lists

Occasional problems over detailed terminology apart, spares lists are perhaps the most problem-free element in foreign-language technical documentation. Since however they are expensive and time-consuming to reproduce, it is important to establish at the contract stage exactly what the customer's needs are, both in the nature of the lists to be provided and in the number of copies of each. He may well be prepared to accept a list of spares recommended for x years of operation in the language and the full illustrated parts list in English, provided of course that the latter is well illustrated with exploded diagrams in which the part numbers are given. Or again he may accept a full parts list with illustrations only, omitting the supporting lists of part numbers and full designations. In this case the only additional work needed will be the preparation of an index in the language so that the user can quickly turn up the illustration required. The extent of spares documentation which the customer may insist on and/or the supplier may consider advisable will depend to a considerable extent on whether the supplier intends to have a technical representative in the importing country either for a considerable period after delivery or permanently. The point to bear in mind is the time taken to translate full parts lists and more particularly the expense of reproducing them in quantity.

15.3 Language aspects

The decision on how to handle the language work involved in technical documentation must depend both on the part played by technical documentation in the operation as a whole, on the nature of the product and of course on time. Fortunately for once most of the arguments within these factors march together, leaving the sponsor with a clear-cut option between on the one hand getting the work done in the country of the language, either through a reliable agency or direct to a freelance recommended perhaps by a customer in that country, and on the other working closely in with a language team in his own location. For consumer durables, where the technology is widely known and fairly well standardised, the terminology well established and topicality of language all important, the first course will usually be preferable. In some minor fields which are oriented towards the consumer or the distributive trade and yet specialised, such as furniture components or domestic fittings in general, it is indeed the only satisfactory one. The texts themselves should be accompanied by ample and well thought-out briefing material in the shape of illustrations and drawings. It is also worth providing a full written description of any novel or unusual features to ensure that the translator does not misinterpret any summarised or passing references to them in the text. It is also essential to include actual copies of any illustrations to be captioned or diagrams and drawings with a legend which requires translation. As has been stressed elsewhere, it is not enough just to provide the wording. It is advisable to allow one month even for very short texts and three months for longer texts such as manuals, with a cushion for postal delays over and above any agreed timings.

In the case of capital equipment and specialised trade products it is greatly preferable to work in close liaison with a linguist on the spot, and in fact to arrange for him to work at the exporter's plant during the early stages when constant discussion is necessary. He will then become closely involved not only in the technical documentation but in the project as a whole and can advise on the best way of handling any particular language problems.

15.3.1 Establishment of terminology

In scientific work and in the newer and more sophisticated engineering fields such as ADPS, terminology presents little problem. Most notably perhaps in organic chemistry, but to a large extent in the other hard sciences too, terminology is fully standardised and the names in fact represent a descriptive code, so that it is only necessary to know the code in the two languages to translate with precision. Further, such a high proportion of innovations of the past twenty to thirty years have originated in English-speaking countries, notably in the United States, that in fields such as computing and telecommunications even the other major technological languages have either borrowed the English term as it stands or transliterated it into a form convenient for the language in question. Nevertheless in texts intended for translation or even for international use in English, it is advisable to back up verbal terminology with symbolic or mathematic expressions rather more lavishly than would be necessary for single-language working in one's own country.

It is in the more traditional areas of civil, mechanical and electrical engineering that, as the discussion in Chapter 4 shows, more difficult problems arise, and these are compounded by the need to get the terminology right first time at a stage when little is known about the project or the customer. This is a situation in which the best may be the enemy of the good. It calls for a conscious decision, preferably taken in consultation with a linguist, on the amount of money and more particularly time that can or should be spent on getting the terminology absolutely right, i.e. in complete conformity with the customer's own usages, as opposed to just linguistically correct and clear. In addition to the general considerations discussed earlier in this chapter there are two major factors here. The first is the part which documentation as opposed to hardware plays in the project as a whole; for instance perfection of terminology is of relatively little importance in a contract mainly concerned with the supply of finished products, while it is in the full sense of the word vital where manufacture under licence, local assembly or some package deal of this kind is involved. Even with a new language market and a new language team, it will rather seldom be necessary to treat the establishment of terminology as a separate phase in terms of time and cost planning; but since this process is always implicit in the preparation of technical documentation it is worth discussing in some detail.

The first aspect is the study of the shape and function of standard minor components such as 'pins', 'studs', and 'bearings', and a decision on which of the various foreign words lying within the equivalent zone of meaning best matches the particular component. Unless the translator is given full access to drawings and even to the product itself, he is unlikely to choose the best word and his translation may thus become difficult for a foreign engineer to follow. For instance a 'pin' may require a quite different translation depending on whether or not it protrudes from the part into which it is inserted and whether its function is location or the transmission of load; and to give an accurate word-picture of a bearing one must know not only the type of bearing but also the principal plane of loading and the way in which it is mounted. Obviously it is neither necessary or desirable to state such detail repeatedly in either the English or the foreign-language text — the clue lies in choice of the right word by the translator.

The next stage, which applies mainly but not always to specialised machinery such as packaging machines or the transfer units within an automatic line, is the research or where necessary coining of terms for specialised components or modes of operation; this calls for a certain boldness of mind on the part of the translator, but unless he has acquired a complete understanding of the functioning of the machine, this boldness becomes mere rashness. Here particularly it is essential to get away from the English term, which may well have been coined by the manufacturer and be unintelligible as it stands even to his English-speaking competitors or customers, and to consider the object or process purely in terms of the language of translation.

The third step in the establishment of terminology is to assign a term to each one of a series of similar sub-units or assemblies which may be present. For example the transfer and feed system supplying an automatic with small workpieces or products is likely to consist of a series of conveyors, hoppers, vibrator plates, fixed and moving guides and feed-control monitors and actuators, i.e. of a number of assemblies similar but distinct in form and function. In a description of the feed as a whole it will usually be clear from the context and sequence which of these similar items is being referred to, but when mention is made of them in other parts of the descriptive text or in maintenance procedures involving the machine as a whole, they can be identified only by their designation. In an ideal world the translator's task would be confined to finding sufficient alternatives in the language to match the various English terms used, but often the writers of the original are themselves so familiar with the hardware that they are less careful than they might be about assigning distinctive terms and using them consistently.

Unfortunately it is not always enough to accept the customer's terminology even when one is able to discover it in time. Engineers in every country are given to using 'private' terms, and the translator may thus find himself poised between a manufacturer and a customer neither of whom uses terminology that would be generally regarded as correct. The only really valid sources are the relevant approving authorities either in the target country or in the mother country of the language or, where international standardisation exists, the authority that controls it. This means gaining access to the foreign standards or specifications concerned. Experienced technical translators do build up their own reference libraries for the fields and languages in which they work, but this is rather unlikely to be comprehensive since the number of standards involved in a broad field is extremely high. Likewise, unless the linguist has been brought in really early in the planning stage, there is unlikely to be time for him to get his hands on these source documents in time for the quotation stage at which much of the terminology will be established. It is on the other hand relatively easy for a manufacturer to build up a library of, say, the French and German standards and specifications relating to his particular product, and this is yet another important function for the multilingual technical library envisaged early in this chapter. There is usually no difficulty in obtaining these documents either from the London office of the Chamber of Commerce of the country concerned or from their London Commercial Counsellor, or again direct from the national or international agency concerned; but it does take time. The British Overseas Trade Board or the British Standards Institution can often supply English translations of at least the more important standards and regulations, but these are of little help to the linguist looking for the terminology of the original, and to obtain this it is usually easier to go straight to the source.

It may sometimes be a worthwhile safeguard to get a clause written into the contract to the effect that the customer agrees and accepts the terminology used in the proposal and, if the original specifications are subsequently revised, in the contract specifications. This at least places the onus of any subsequent misunderstandings on him.

15.3.2   *Conversion of units, choice of standards*

It is difficult for those of us who are attempting to accommodate to the metric system in general to realise that the international SI system does not entirely coincide with the systems of units in common use in various 'metric' countries. For example the centimetre, which is as widely used on the Continent as the inch is with us, does not appear in the SI system; and traditional terms such as *Zentner* or *livre* are often used in everyday parlance to designate their nearest metric equivalents. Generally speaking engineers everywhere accept and understand the SI system even if they sometimes revert to long-inculcated habits; but users of machinery, most of all perhaps of agricultural machinery, may find almost as much difficulty as we do in visualising, say, a length expressed in millimetres when they are used to thinking in terms of centimetres and metres. Also it is slightly absurd if not unsound to convert an approximate length expressed to the nearest inch or foot into unrounded millimetres. Thus in semi-technical sales literature aimed at a readership which includes consumers or non-technical users as well as engineers, it will often be preferable to use the appropriate 'national' metric system rather than the SI system.

In use of or conversion to the SI system itself, the three points at which problems most commonly arise are pressures, specific gravities and horsepower. The first difficulty arises over a widespread tendency to regard kg/cm², bars and atmospheres as identical units, while in fact 1.0 atm = 1.0 kgf/cm² = 0.980665 bar. Incorrect conversion can lead to significant differences where pressure vessels or high-pressure hydraulic systems are being discussed. A more important area of confusion is a failure to distinguish between absolute and gauge pressures. This is not helped by the fairly common English practice of writing 'psi' when 'psig' is intended. Since apart from the obsolete German abbreviation *Atü* all metric pressure units are absolute unless specifically stated to be gauge, it is much safer to work in absolute units throughout except where specific reference must be made to a gauge pressure reading. Generally speaking other language conventions do not quote specific gravities as pure figures in the way that we do; they are usually quoted in g/cm³ or the equivalent referred to a litre or cubic metre. The problem over converting horsepower is twofold: first the very small difference (conversion factor 1.01387) between Anglo-American and metric horsepower leads to absurdities in converting the output of low horsepower motors, and it is usually better to stick to the original figure indicating which it is; and second the French among others still use in many contexts the concept of *puissance fiscale,* a nominal figure derived from a formula not unlike the old RAC formula, instead of BHP.

More generally the problem of rounding is the strongest of several reasons why the manufacturer should carry out metric conversions for himself rather than leaving it to the translator. It needs very intimate knowledge of the equipment to judge correctly the extent to which small linear and other measurements may be rounded and in many cases the direction in which they should be rounded. Outside the laboratory, the instrument shop and the toolmaking shop, in circumstances, that is, where we would specify in thousandths of an inch, 0.01mm is probably the finest difference that can be measured. The more fundamental problems associated with rounding were discussed at the beginning of the chapter. For the sake of clarity it is probably best to choose between one of two practices: one is to show metric dimensions only, in which case any roundings must be agreed by the designer; the other is to use the English dimensions in their original form and accompany them with boldly rounded 'nominal' metric equivalents, prefacing the document with a note explaining this and also indicating the normal British abbreviations for any British units used.

Wheel and tyre dimensions and, of course, the designations of British and American threads are always written in their English form.

The best handy reference book on units known to us is the *Dictionary of Quantities and Units* by J. V. Drazil (Leonard Hill, Intertext Series, 1971); this covers English, French and German. For wider language coverage including Russian and Japanese, and for the tracking down of national units, including some splendidly obscure traditional ones, the Elsevier *Lexicon of International and National Units* is also very useful.

The standard abbreviations for international units are of course universally accepted and understood, but outside these the interpretation, or rather decoding, and coining of abbreviations presents one of the trickiest problems in technical translation. Oddly enough the logical French and the methodical Germans allow themselves far more latitude than we do over the coining and use of abbreviations and tend to abbreviate inconsistently to suit the space available or even the state of their liver, so that three or four different abbreviations of the same term may appear within one text or legend. The ideal would probably be to follow the practice of the Services and 'avoid all use of abbreviations in communications with allies'. However in many technical texts the result of doing so would be so unwieldy as to negate the clarity aimed at. Where abbreviations are used in the actual English designations of assemblies or components or more particularly in drawings, schematics and wiring diagrams, it is probably best to stick to the original English abbreviation and give its foreign definition in full, although the orthographic significance of the abbreviation will then be lost. Frequently as it occurs, it is quite wrong to introduce an abbreviation in English or any other language without explaining it, and the best practice is to write the term in full the first time it is used with the abbreviation in brackets after it. If the text and its supporting graphics contain a large number of abbreviations which the reader may come upon out of context, it is advisable, just as it is in English, to include a table of abbreviations and their definitions.

Incomprehension frequently arises through reference to standards, notably material specifications, with which the reader is unfamiliar or to which he does not have access. SAE standards and codes are known of in most countries, and a reference to them is thus likely to be accepted even if a particular document is not available to the reader; German standards (DIN) are also very widely known and accepted; but unfortunately British Standards themselves and the specifications and codes of British professional institutions and trade associations are apt to ring no bell whatever outside the Commonwealth. Since many SAE and ASI standards are fully or virtually identical with British ones and a number of British manufacturers who have gone metric are working to DIN, it may often be possible to substitute the American or German equivalent without further ado. But where such a fallback does not exist or technical considerations preclude its use, the exporter must either annex a translated copy of the standard to the documentation or at least include an explanatory note in the product specification and offer to produce the standard itself if so requested. The gist of materials specifications is quick and easy to translate and reproduce, and the inclusion of these, together with notes on other standards or codes referred to, will often impart sufficient confidence in the customer to obviate the need for the translation and inclusion of long and complex documents. It is however always worth finding out whether the British Standards Institution or other sponsor has copies available in the language required. It is the approving authority rather than the customer himself who is likely to prove the main hurdle here, and provided that a major effort has clearly been made to study and comply with that authority's regulations, it may well be possible to clear any doubts over British standards and codes in discussion with the authority's inspectors.

The converse problem of obtaining foreign standards is perhaps most likely to arise in relation to enquiries from Eastern Europe or the USSR. This is on the one hand because the state import-export agencies tend to include in the general specifications supporting their enquiry a requirement that certain mechanical or electrical components should comply with their national or with Soviet bloc international standards, and on the other because these standards are often neither immediately available nor easily obtainable. By contrast most other country's requirements are based on if not identical with those of the major European industrial nation that sponsored, imperially or otherwise, their economic and technological development. It is therefore wise, at a very early stage in negotiations with the state import-export agency or with any specialist intermediary being used, to request copies of all relevant standards. There will then be time to get these analysed, effectively translated and compared with the corresponding British standards before the actual enquiry arrives or at least before the closure date for quotation is imminent.

Finally under this head mention must be made of engineering drawing conventions. Great care must be taken here to make drawings intelligible and unambiguous to the customer without imposing too great a strain from the use of unfamiliar methods, with a consequent risk of errors, on the designers and draughtsmen. However the national differences are not too great, much information on agreed or at least internationally acceptable conventions and abbreviations is available in government and other, e.g. the British Steel Corporation's, publications dealing with metrication, and both documentation and direct advice can be obtained from the Help to Exporters Service of the British Standards Institution and in some instances from the appropriate engineering institute or trade association. Where time is short, an experienced technical translator, working at the manufacturer's establishment as was suggested above in another context, will be able to give the drawing office direct guidance on the spot and to monitor their work. Often one or two of the brighter young draughtsmen may welcome this opportunity to broaden their knowledge and, if allowed to specialise in foreign-language work with a certain amount of encouragement and supervision initially, will quickly become quite expert. Conversely, allowing draughtsmen with no knowledge of the language to transpose legends either from a glossary or from drawing to drawing without supervision usually leads to results that, to misquote Wellington, are likely to astonish the enemy rather than surprise him.

There is a chestnut about the motorist who stopped in a village and asked a yokel the way. With all the deep wisdom of the countryman the latter replied: 'If you want to get there, don't start from here.' Sad to say the same advice might be applied to many technical texts offered for translation. Whether or not these are fully intelligible to the expert English-speaking reader for whom they are intended is a question outside the scope of this book, but they certainly make the task of translation far from straightfoward for the translator, particularly if he does not have frequent and easy access to the originator. Naturally these strictures only apply in certain instances; no problem is likely to arise where the manufacturer has a professional technical author and/or illustrator on his payroll or contracts out to a specialist firm. But in some smaller engineering firms making highly specialised products for a limited market, the English-language technical documentation simply does not provide an adequate basis for translation in terms of presentation, language, freedom from ambiguity or sometimes even accuracy. However, even if the existing technical documentation is good, it is likely to need some up-dating, editing and slanting before it is ready for translation, and a review of all relevant documentation, which will also indicate what new texts have to be written, is a step that should be taken very early in any foreign-language export programme. If a suitably qualified and well-trusted linguist is available to the manufacturer on the spot, he should be invited to participate in this task or even to carry it out and produce the results for approval, as this will ensure not only that he is completely briefed but also that any obscurities or language-technical problems are sorted out in the English before the translation proper gets under way. Where time allows this review could for instance well be combined with the exercise to establish terminology discussed at the beginning of this section.

When the documentation is to be sent away for translation, thorough preparation of the base texts and graphics is even more important, as the translator will have no choice but to translate what he has in front of him. Particular points that must be checked are: that the system of headings and sub-headings, together with any numbering or lettering of sections, paragraphs and sub-paragraphs is clear and consistent; that all cross-references and references to components by code letters or numbers are correct; that any abbreviations used are explained; that all metric conversions have been made and entered; and that the text and drawings are free of all ambiguities and inaccuracies. If as is often the case the translation is required to follow the pagination of the original, the English should not take up more than two thirds of the space available on each page. Finally some method of page or paragraph numbering and leads to the next page must be devised, so that the translation can be assembled without risk of error by someone with no knowledge of the language.

The prime requirement in a technical translation is that the terminology should be clear and above all consistent, but it is also important that the style should be suitably pitched, subject to all the conflicting factors discussed above, for those who are actually going to read the documents. More generally it is important from the point of view of establishing good relations that the language used should be generally pleasing to the customer. The quality of the translation will play a large part in putting across the manufacturer's image, particularly in the critical early stages, and the authors can say from experience that, perhaps strangely, third-world customers are more sensitive to style than their European counterparts, perhaps because they regard good style as a mark of respect to them. It is worth tactfully obtaining feedback on this aspect from the customer when opportunity arises, as this will encourage the linguist to keep up the good work or to mend his ways in certain particular directions. Although it may appear an extravagance, early contact between the linguist and the customer, for instance by taking him out as an interpreter in the preliminary negotiations, will do more than any other one thing to achieve the terminology and style that is most acceptable to the customer. And psychologically the fact that both parties know the linguist personally will do much to improve relations between the principals by improving mutual confidence and reducing the feeling that they are forced to work at one remove from each other.

15.3.5   *Technical correspondence*

The accepted convention of each party originating correspondence in its own language works very well in Europe but ex-colonies using that of their occupying power may have very limited ability indeed to work in any other European language. In Algeria for example, despite vigorous efforts to create a pool of English speakers by bringing English into the educational system and by running intensive courses for the executives and specialists of national companies, it will be some years yet before there is an adequate supply of those who can translate or interpret at a reasonably high level between French and English, let alone of English-speaking managers and engineers. The language in which correspondence associated with the project is to be conducted must therefore become something to be discussed and agreed between the parties. On the technical side in particular, both because of the probable lack of technical translators in the customer's country and because of the overriding need for consistency of terminology, it may well be preferable if not essential to conduct all correspondence in the customer's language, even if this is not called for — as it sometimes is — in the general conditions accompanying the enquiry. Admittedly this represents an additional expense for the exporter, but it is one that he can cost in if he knows about it in time.

Technical translation is expensive, and because the demand increasingly exceeds the supply it is likely to become more so. Once again it is meaningless to quote prices, but supposing 100 arbitrary cost units per thousand words be the going rate for 'information only' non-specialised translation between English and French, the rates are likely to be 250 (plus) for French, 300 for German and up to as much as 400 for minor European languages; and work for publication in the true sense, e.g. for technical sales literature, could be another 30 per cent up on these. Where tabular work, captions or legends are involved, as they inevitably will be, the overall cost per word may, as has been pointed out elsewhere, be even higher.

It is however perhaps in technical documentation more than in any other field of language work that close-knit collaboration with a language consultant pays off, and for the major European languages at least it may be more realistic to look at costs in these terms. Referring back to the yardstick of 0.5 to 1 per cent of the total contract value quoted in connection with a substantial engineering export contract, between two-thirds and three-quarters of this would probably be taken up on technical documentation. An in-house typing facility of the requisite standard will produce some savings, although the linguist may prefer to work within his own secretariat on complex documentation; and the existence of a multilingual technical library of the kind described above will yield not only substantial savings in time and direct costs but also a much more satisfactory result.

Again more perhaps with technical documentation than with other types of work, and even if the linguist is experienced in the particular sub-field, the direct language costs are likely to be rather high for the first penetration into a new language market with a particular specialised product and to fall off very markedly as experience is gained, and here one is thinking of reductions as high as 50-75 per cent in the time required for a particular task after several years of working with a client.

A checklist for arranging technical documentation for an export product is given in Appendix 8 and an optimisation procedure in Appendix 9.

16

Foreign language promotional literature

The production of foreign language promotional literature is undoubtedly the most intractable and in management terms the most difficult of the problems that arise in foreign working. Most of the others will yield to a combination of good forward planning and know-how; the difficult decisions are only indirectly connected with the language barrier and are entrepreneurial rather than managerial in kind. But here the difficulties arising from the highly subjective nature of judgements on promotional literature are compounded on the one hand by a similar but a distinct area of subjectivity in target response and on the other by the cost and sheer technical difficulty of arriving at a satisfactory solution. We have to admit that we have not so far accomplished a project of this type without major perturbations of some kind, either when working into English for foreign clients or vice-versa; and the reader may like to enter this chapter with the background thought that, whenever possible, it is advisable to take two bites at this cherry—the first one being as modest as image will allow.

16.1 Where to do it

The first decision to be taken is whether to execute the project in one's own country or in the target language area(s), and here the marketing manager is in fact in a no-win situation straight away. On the one hand, when design and printing as well as copywriting are taken into account, it is next to impossible to produce in one's own country a set of literature that will appear to have originated in the target market. On the other working direct to a foreign agency can easily lead to a loss of control extending to every aspect of the project — not only of cost and timings but also of presentation and indeed content. Where the originator of the literature has an established agent in the target area, it is very tempting to use him as the co-ordinator. But experience suggests that, even if they are prepared to take this on, agents often lack the necessary drive and expertise and the loss of control is even more serious than in working direct to foreign experts. Thus the only organisations not faced with this dilemma are those large enough either to have a full-scale subsidiary with its own marketing organisation in the target market or to face the very substantial cost and not always satisfactory outcome of turning the whole project over to one of the leading international advertising or PR firms.

Our experience rather surprisingly suggests that on balance loss of control is the most serious hazard and it is therefore better for the originator to keep the project under his own hand. Since the lion's share of the cost will probably lie in printing, the additional expense of seeking out and using to the full really first-rate language facilities will be proportionately small and will yield a considerable dividend. Even if some of the actual foreign copywriting is done in the target country, the use of a linguist under the originator's own hand will enable him to retain a sufficient measure of control.

The exception lies in major consumer promotions, particularly those involving television advertising. These must be done in the target country or countries, and should therefore only be undertaken after a fully adequate coordinating organisation has been established there.

16.2   Selecting and setting up a team

The production of foreign language promotional literature on any scale involves a rather large team of which some members are likely by the nature of their callings to be highly individualistic in approach if not actively temperamental. The first step in the project must therefore be the assembly of a team and the proving during the planning stage of their ability to work together.

16.2.1   Composition of a team

The hard core of the team needs to consist of three individuals — the sponsor's representative (say the marketing manager), a PR or advertising consultant and a language consultant. The two elements to be built round this are on the one hand the production group of copywriter/researcher, designer, photographer and printer and on the other the language group of copywriters/translators in the languages concerned. As will be seen below, every member of the team is likely at some stage to be required to act in an advisory capacity as well as carrying out his basic task.

16.2.2   Selection factors

It is essential that the sponsor organisation should appoint one man to run the project, and that he should be at once senior enough to carry full delegated responsibility and far enough down the line to have time to devote to the many ramifications that will arise. The need to refer back to director or full board level over every problem that comes up will cripple smooth working of the team. Intervention at this level should be confined to two stages — approval of the team, the budget and the timings; and approval of the outline design, the visuals and the English base text.

It will seldom be possible to build up a team all of whose members are colocated, especially if minor languages are involved. But to achieve the requisite ease of liaison the hard core should be within very easy reach of one another, and the next in priority for colocation are the printer and then the designer.

Since genuine conflicts of opinion and interest are going to arise, personalities and mutual confidence are even more important than usual. Relationships within the hard core must be good enough for uninhibited questioning and mutual criticism. Since the PR consultant and the production group are likely to be used to be working together, the next most critical relationship is between the language consultant and printer, for it is between them that battles will have to be fought in the later stages when reserves of money, time and tolerance are running low.

Conversely, while the language consultant will presumably select translators in whom he has confidence and with whom he is used to working, the PR consultant and for that matter the sponsor must also have confidence in the translators, since the process of slanting to the target market will involve a critique of the concept as a whole and of the English base text. In fact it is the translators or foreign copywriters as much as anyone who determine the success or failure of the project. They must be native-speakers of great talent and experience who are on the one hand completely in touch with life and current slang in their own country and on the other either possess or have the opportunity to acquire direct knowledge of the subject of the project. In fact it is unsafe to use translators who do not have either copywriting experience or published works to their name.

16.2.3   Nomination of a team leader

However much this team operates as a horizontal hierarchy, it must contain somebody other than the sponsor who is authorised to take decisions and present them to the sponsor. The team leader will normally be the person with whom the sponsor places the main contract, and will thus be either the PR/Advertising consultant or the language consultant. Logic argues for the PR consultant, since the bulk of the cost will lie on the production side and he will probably be better geared to deal with the technical intricacies of production. On the other hand it is the language consultant, backed by his translators, who can offer the more valid advice on content, slant and presentation, and it is important that his advice should not be unreasonably overriden by technical considerations of design and printing which may be based on nothing more valid than habit. In fact the PR and language consultants need to work with the sponsor as a pair, so as to give him the best possibility of reaching a correct decision when conflicts arise.

16.2.4 *Method of working*

Experience suggests that the most common snag in operations of this kind lies in the fact that virtually every action taken or change introduced by one member of the team repercusses on the work of all the others, but unless the person who takes the action has exceptionally wide experience, he may not realise that it does so. For instance a last-minute change in a visual will obviously call for a new caption; the new visual may have to go to a translator at a distance or even abroad for captioning, and this will delay the completion of setting. Then the new caption may not fit into the space available, or may call for a slight change in one or more of the foreign-language texts, so that the designer and the language consultant will again have to come in. Then there will be the need to identify the changes in the foreign-language copy to the printer; and so on. . . The first clue to smooth working thus lies in excellent coordination and communication; the team leader or one of his staff must ensure that everyone in the team knows of every development and decision, whether or not it appears to affect them, and is given time to react. Further it is not realistic to plan a project of this kind on a simple straight-chain programme. The programme required is one which the mathematician would call successive approximation but it might be clearer to term optimisation by recycling — and time and money has to be allowed for this process. Both for this reason and simply to foster sound team-working it is also important to budget for at least one and preferably two meetings of the entire team, even if this means bringing some members from a distance or from abroad. An attempt is made to represent the recycling process in Appendix 10.

16.3 Basic decisions

In developing single-language publicity material, it is both logical and customary to start by deciding on exactly what documents are required and what broad format they should take, and to proceed from here to the planning phase proper. In multilingual projects, however, the scope is very apt to be the first victim of the recycling process, and it is therefore better to start from a broad directive on aim, subject matter and targets and to come to decisions on timings, budget and scope via a series of basic technical decisions.

16.3.1   Choice of languages and number of editions

The sponsor's desire to have foreign-language promotional literature will stem from some marketing plan he has made, and he is therefore likely to come up with a request for languages directly related to these markets. The first need will be to examine this choice in depth in the light of the considerations discussed in Chapter 1 and arrive at a priority list of languages which represents true cost-effectiveness in the short and middle terms. It is often surprising to the language consultant as well as to the sponsor what a drastic revision of the plan this examination produces; and a priority list rather than a firm one is needed to put sufficient flex into the recycling process as a whole and into the timings, budget and contingency allowances in particular. Thus even if the target immediately in the sponsor's eye is a minor-language market, it may well pay to go into one or even two major languages first and then decide whether to give that particular target full or 'minor-language' treatment. A further factor here is that it is as a rule very much easier to plan and debug the project in the major languages, where expertise is both at a higher level and more readily available. Also the cost and duration of production of full-scale literature is such that an opportunity target needing a quick response is often best dealt with by low-cost improvisation.

Once a provisional decision on the languages is reached, the next step is to make a firm decision between polyglot literature or separate single-language editions. For serious promotional literature it is fair to say that single-language editions are strongly to be preferred. First, something written entirely in his own language makes the reader feel that the sponsor is interested specifically in him and does not just regard him as one more or less important member of a bunch of foreign prospects. Second, few of us with any knowledge of more than one language ever take in the contents of a polyglot leaflet properly; we are far too busy comparing the various texts and looking eagerly for the 'Japanese camera leaflet syndrome'. Physically, if the copy is of any substance at all, polyglot presentation will lead to overcrowding and thus force the designer into almost every known point of bad design. And given careful coordination throughout the team — in particular between designer and printer — and careful choice of printing techniques and the use of colour, separate single-language editions need not cost much if any more than a polyglot brochure. There are perhaps two exceptions to this rule. One is where the presentation is almost entirely (85-90 per cent) visual and the copy consists of nothing more than page or section headings and long captions. Here, with careful wording, a polyglot document can give an impression of internationalism, the personal impact on the reader being made by the visuals. The second exception lies in data sheets or price lists made up almost entirely of figures and used in support of other documents—here the personal impact has already been made if the reader gets to study them at all, and the appearance of other languages will serve as a gentle reminder that he is not the only fly in the ointment. Further, documents of this kind usually date quickly and therefore need to be produced as cheaply as possible in a form which simplifies the production of new editions when needed.

Since it will be used to cover English-speaking and certain minor-language export markets, the English edition too requires some thought. It is now almost certainly preferable to write this in American English, giving dimensions, etc., in both Anglo-American and SI units. Slanting presents a problem, but since many of the minor-language markets have either heavily absorbed American culture or at least become used to dealing with North American organisations, a carefully chosen and rather generalised slant towards the United States market is likely to prove an acceptable compromise. Whether it is necessary to produce a separate UK edition in British English is a managerial decision which should depend on the need to adapt slant and content rather than on presentation.

16.3.2 *Format and number of pages*

Small formats should be avoided; they are usually too big for the pocket and tend to get lost in a file, and in particular they allow very little scope for compensating for the various language lengths. The best best basic size is undoubtedly A4, with A3 fold-outs where necessary. For brief introductory leaflets, such as might be given out at conferences or shows, A4 folded twice crossways and presented either horizontally or vertically is ideal, as it is easy to handle and accommodates both to pocket and file. It is important to bear in mind that many countries now follow the United States practice of 'top filing', and this is one of the many factors that argues for the slight initial cost of loose-leaf binding with one of the various plastic binding systems now available. These are elegant, allow the full width of the page to be used and are easy to strip and remake when the need arises to insert supplementary sheets or amendments. They also give much more scope for length adjustment (since one is no longer tied to multiples of 4 pages for economy of printing) and allow documentation to be made up *ad hoc* to cover selected products within the sponsor's range or to include an introductory page or supplement aimed at a particular market. It is in the choice of format, layout and number of pages that the next to insuperable problem of accommodating different language lengths must be faced; this is discussed in more detail in Section 16.7 below.

There will, of course, be occasions in both promotional and technical documentation when marketing plans impose a high priority on one or more minor languages, but the sponsor should examine the need very carefully with the support of his team before venturing into these. Language and printing problems, combined with the smaller number of copies required for a minor language edition will escalate cost disproportionately, perhaps by 30 per cent or more in terms of cost per copy as compared with the major language editions. Timings too are likely to go haywire, because the translator will almost certainly be in the country of the language and he may have to do the proof-reading; there may also be delays on the printing side in obtaining the required characters, accents etc., and in fact the availability of these will often limit the choice of typeface or size. More important perhaps, it is in practice extremely difficult to produce copy in some of the minor languages that is up to the standard which a good firm will require in its promotional literature, and particularly so, for every kind of reason, in the fields of science and technology.

It is, therefore, usually best to make use of the most appropriate major language as the main vehicle for communicating with the minor-language market and to cover the appropriate major-language editions with some kind of introduction in the minor language. This can vary from a kind of glorified compliment slip or introductory letter to three or four pages of copy, perhaps illustrated, slanted to the market and summarising the main features and selling points. One of the purposes of this introduction is to offset any impression of discourtesy that might otherwise be implied in not using the minor-language throughout. It should therefore be aimed specifically at buttering up the reader, and could well include a personal signed message from the chairman or managing director.

An alternative approach, where the timings of the marketing plan allow it and the cost justifies it, is to produce the relevant major-language edition first and then arrange for the minor-language copy to be prepared from this and set and proof-read in the country of the language, the plates then being returned to the original printer to be dropped in. Since there will be a firm design to work from and the space available for copy will be precisely defined in visual terms, most of the communications problems mentioned above will solve themselves; and if a market is of sufficient importance to justify a minor language edition, it is probable that the sponsor will have effective representation and contacts there by the time the major language editions are produced.

Many of the difficulties and indeed failures associated with the production of foreign-language promotional literature stem simply from the fact that the sponsor has allowed totally inadequate time. It is not unusual for a public relations consultant to be asked to produce literature for, say, a show or trade fair in a month or less. This inevitably leads to disaster, and when a situation of this kind arises it is probably better to go for a typed and litho'd supplement to be handed out with the English documentation. Something that is good in itself but patently provisional is far more effective than a botched-up glossy.

From experience we are convinced that 9 months from conception to delivery is an absolute minimum for the production of a good set of promotional literature in 3 or 4 languages; a year is more realistic, and 15 months would be the safest figure for planning purposes. This may look ridiculous to the layman, but the complexities dealt with in this chapter may serve to point the need for it, and it is not out of tune with the lead times of good marketing planning. This long lead time adduces yet another argument both for flexibility in make-up and for staying with the major languages; the commitment of money so far in advance on a specific minor-language market may quite likely be followed by a decision not to enter that market after all, but the major-language editions will always find application within the export programme as a whole. A more detailed indication of timings is given in Appendix 10.

Once the documentation has been established in the major languages, and more particularly the production team is thoroughly run in, revision and addition becomes a relatively quick, cheap and simple process. Here it would not be unrealistic to talk in terms of weeks rather than months, although time must be allowed for research if new technical terminology is involved.

16.3.5 Budget

The practice of going out for fixed-price tender for the production of a major set of multilingual promotional literature may be pleasing to the accountants but is unlikely to produce satisfactory results. Even if the sponsor finishes up with adequate literature, he will also be faced with a chorus of 'never again' from the production team. While the sponsor must start the ball rolling with an indication of the sum he has in mind, both the long lead-times and the nature of the task call for a realistic and flexible approach to budgeting. Any experienced organisation asked for a fixed-price quotation for such a project will be bound to put in and maintain as long as possible such heavy contingencies that the sponsor may not get full value for his money, and even an indexated price established in advance is unlikely to be wholly satisfactory. The final budget is best established at the end of the planning stage after recycling of the basic decisions dealt with in this section and of the scope; and even then some elements in it may have to be indexated. The sponsor can then see exactly what he will get and decide what it is worth to him and, in consultation with the team, on the best distribution of funds between the various aspects of the project. We are convinced that a major undertaking of this kind should be treated as a phased operation, with a fee determined in advance for the first planning phase which would culminate in a report giving costed and timed recommendations for the execution phase.

Nevertheless, given this approach and reasonable timings, a great deal can be done to contain the ultimate cost and optimise cost-effectiveness. To quote just two examples, paper can be bought in at the end of the planning phase, and the photography plan can be attuned both to seasonal conditions, if these apply, and to the convenience of the sponsor if special events or hardware are to be photographed.

16.4 Scope

Despite what has just been said about budgeting, it would be unrealistic to embark on a project without a guideline ceiling cost, and for this reason if for no other the complexity of the various factors themselves and of their interplay dictates that final decisions on the scope of the documentation can only be taken at the end of the planning phase. To contain long-term costs it is probably best to determine scope and format in terms of the extent to which various sections of the documentation are likely to date, thus:

Long term   The main long term item is the body of the company profile. This can probably be made to hold for as much as 10 years, provided that the sections on current personalities and on plant or facilities are laid out in such a way that they can be replaced separately.

Middle term   The sub-section of the company profile on *plant and facilities* can be 'written ahead' so that it may with luck hold for four or five years. Any exciting new machinery can always be displayed on a separate sheet as a frontispiece, leaving the body of this sub-section untouched.

Again with luck, *selling copy* slanted to a particular market will hold for a number of years given reasonable foresight in drafting it.

A section that can be rather more safely regarded as middle or even long term is the *conditions of sale;* it is important to establish these firmly as the translations should ideally be checked by an official agency or lawyer in the country mainly concerned, to ensure that they are free of legal ambiguities and they conform to the law of that country.

Short term   However stable his company's situation may appear, a
sponsor would be well advised to treat any matter on personalities and
any mention of other companies such as key sub-contractors or
suppliers as short term, keeping it physically separate from the long-
and middle-term items although it can be made to appear to follow on
naturally from these.

The main short-term section is that on product information, and
this must be so laid out that there are no cost or time inhibitions on
including or omitting specific products, on up-dating technical
information or of course on adding new products.

Now and probably in the future *price lists* are so short term that it is
probably not worth printing them at all. The need here is to have a
simple polyglot skeleton into which revised prices or new products can
quickly be slotted at minimum cost.

The reader will have perceived that he is being steered towards
producing his foreign-language promotional literature in the form of
a single loose-leaf set of documents which can be made up, revised and
added to as required. A pocket in the inner back cover will allow price
lists and any stop-press items to be presented without spoiling the
appearance of the folder as a whole.

Returning once again to the question of trade-offs, this approach
will allow the production of foreign-language promotional literature
to be treated as a long-term continuing project rather than as a
once-for-all operation. It becomes possible to stagger the cost by
starting with, say, essential product information covered by a short
provisional profile and to develop the full profile later; similarly the
establishment of a flexible system will yield great savings in cost and
time if a decision is taken to produce an edition in an additional
language.

16.5   Market intelligence

Much of the intelligence needed to produce effective foreign-language
promotional literature will either be generally available or will have been
acquired in the shaping of the marketing plan. There are however two
aspects that will require rather more specific and penetrating analysis
than might be necessary to arrive at marketing decisions.

16.5.1   Product intelligence

One can assume that research into the technical suitability of the product
for the market and of the existence of a demand or the feasibility of
creating one will have been covered in the broad marketing plan. But for
purposes of promotional literature it is necessary to study not only the
characteristics of competing products or the nature of a gap which it is

hoped to fill, but also the selling points employed by competition and the detailed way in which the product is likely to be used. This is a truism in home market promotion and advertising and rather more than lip-service is often paid to it when other English-speaking markets are being considered. But the need often appears to be overlooked or written off as too difficult where foreign-language markets are concerned. The collection of a comprehensive set of competitors' literature to order against a deadline is in fact a remarkably laborious and time-consuming operation and hence an expensive one, but foresight on the part of the sponsor can save a great deal of time and money. For example an executive visiting a trade fair or show can be briefed to collect sets of the competiton's documentation with only minimal disruption of his other activities, and this is meat and drink to the PR consultant, the designer and the linguist alike. A relatively quick study of it will pay off in four areas — pitch and slant, the selection and presentation of selling points, do's and don'ts in design and not least important the specialised terminology actually in use. There is no need to waste time and money having this agglomeration of paper translated; once the language consultant gets his hands on it, he can quickly go through it and give the PR consultant and the sponsor an oral briefing.

It is also necessary to find out what approvals are required for the product and which of these must be mentioned in the literature. A search of relevant patents in the target countries together with a review of the sponsor's own patent cover in those countries is also worthwhile if time allows.

16.5.2 Target readership

Conventional market research parameters which classify target groups in terms of sex, age, income or occupation are doubtless adequate for the consumer products and consumer durables for which they are mainly intended. However, more specific information and careful thought rather than statistical analysis are required where specialised products or invitations to invest are concerned. This need can perhaps best be illustrated by two examples.

Suppose first that one is trying to persuade West German firms to set up in a particular region of the UK. The first problem here is that German managements come very much in three kinds: first there are those who adhere closely to German management traditions; then there are firms which are completely dominated by American management concepts; and finally, quite apart from the multinationals, managements which are concerned with developing new 'European' ways of working.

Clearly there is no one approach that will appeal greatly to all three, and so it is necessary to determine in which category most of the more likely starters fall and to plan the attack accordingly. Again, whom does one primarily seek to persuade? The top decision-makers who actually control investment are very likely to be impressed by a hard headed approach couched in economic terms, but they will have to persuade some of their senior managers and their families to move to the UK and settle there. Even the hardest-headed tycoon of soap opera is in fact likely to be extremely sensitive to the importance of building up and holding a first rate management team. One should therefore perhaps keep the economic aspect down to bare essentials and concentrate on selling the region as a good place to live and raise a family in. The decision reached on these two factors will dominate the content and presentation of the entire documentation.

Second, consider selling a specialised product to a third-world socialist country. Here, as was mentioned in the preceding chapter in the context of technical sales literature, the documentation must be designed to appeal at once to the politician who takes the final decision, to the senior civil servants who advise him and to the middle-piece engineers within a nationalised company who are the actual end users. In these terms the selection of material and slanting become highly complex and specific problems, and the most one can hope to do in general terms is to make the reader fully aware of them.

16.5.3 Good and bad angles

Many of the factors affecting the choice of angles were discussed in Chapter 5, and what has been said there and under various heads above will suffice to underline the need for deep research and careful deliberation in the choice of an angle. There are perhaps two facets that determine when this decision actually has to be made. The first is the need to offset Britain's declining image by a very determined effort to demonstrate technical and commercial credibility, bearing in mind that one has got to take the reader along with one at least far enough to incite him to deeper investigation. Thus in the case of a medium or small firm it would be logical to slant the company profile more heavily in the direction of both past and recent history than would be the case in literature destined for the home market, and to highlight products or events that illustrate advanced design and high quality on the one hand and the ability to meet deadlines in face of difficulties on the other. And the choice of examples should be designed to show that a solid tradition of quality and performance is being maintained and even improved upon. In the same sense personality profiles are important, and these should stretch veracity to the limit to make the most of any foreign qualifications and international experience that those concerned possess. For obvious reasons success in industrial relations and good labour availability are particularly telling points; and since no-one ever really likes to think of a foreigner making money, any initiatives that may have been taken in the fields of social or charitable activity or pollution control are also worth stressing.

It is very tempting to call in a consultant from the target country to advise on the choice of angle and presentation, but experience suggests that this is both very costly and rather unprofitable. He will not feel highly committed to the project, in fact he will probably be convinced that he could do it better himself; and in this very subjective area foreign experts are just as likely as our own to offer completely contradictory opinions. Good homework and free-ranging discussions by a well-picked team including the linguists are likely to produce a better result at no added expense; for they will be fully informed on and identified with the project. It is, however, worth making the rounds of the appropriate Commercial Counsellors, London branches of Chambers of Commerce and similar organisations to get their views. If time and money permit, the most useful advice of all is likely to come from the Commercial Attachés and other staff of our own embassies in the target countries.

16.6 'Translation' aspect

The inverted commas in the heading are used to make the point that the word translation is used here simply as a convenient label for getting the message expressed in the languages required; for psychological, linguistic and technical reasons alike, direct translation is not the way to produce foreign-language copy. Unless the sponsor has sufficient confidence in the linguists in his team to give them a free hand, he would do well to confine his foreign-language documentation to the bare essentials of product information. Otherwise the result, even if not laughable and thus detrimental to his aim, will certainly represent the spending of money to no good effect. In fact it is preferable to write the final English copy in parallel with the foreign-language copy from a contents and format draft annotated with the special points and slants for the various language markets rather to release finalised English copy as a basis for the foreign copywriting; otherwise if the English copy is effective it will grip the linguists concerned too tightly and they will fall somewhere into the rather wide gap between the stools of translation and of writing copy from a brief. If the sponsor is not content with the assurance of his language consultant that the foreign-language copy is correct, it is probably worth the time and cost penalty of having this freely written and then back-translated literally so as to avoid tying the foreign copywriters down in advance. It is far from easy to find suitable people to write the foreign-language copy, but this ball is firmly in the language consultant's court and he will have to reach a decision after weighing the conflicting factors of specialised writing talents, field knowledge, background knowledge of the sponsor and ease of communication.

16.6.1 *Choice of style, angle and slant*

Although a number of other sources will have been consulted in reaching decisions on pitch and slant, the individual who is to write the foreign-language copy must be prominent among those consulted, and points in which his opinion is overriden must be fully cleared with him in discussion. Copywriting is one of the most difficult forms of writing under the best conditions, and no-one can hope to achieve success in it unless he has complete faith in what he is doing. The reader will appreciate from all that has been said above that very drastic compromises will have to be struck, and unless the writer is fully in the picture and convinced of what he is doing he will be unable to weigh these off correctly and to develop the required message between the lines.

Quite apart from the need to strike a compromise across individual sectors of a language market or groups or specific organisations within a market, it is probably best to avoid the kind of liberties and excesses that are often smash hits in one's own language and market. For example one hears the attractive and successful Avis 'number two' angle quite severely criticised in British business circles simply because, one suspects, it is known to be American in origin. While the home ad-mass and even specialist customers will usually fall for a good gimmick because they really prefer to buy home-produced goods anyway, the foreign consumer or export customer will need to be convinced by solid argument well backed up with fact and is apt to suspect 'clever' angles as being some kind of cover-up. One must avoid the trap of trying to be more Roman than the Romans.

16.6.2 *Expertise*

Tempting as it may be to use professional copywriters of the mother-tongue concerned, the need to compromise across the various sectors of a large language market and to avoid extremes, together with the extreme difficulty of briefing them to the required extent, militate against this solution. The ideal, if he can be found within reasonably easy reach, is an experienced top-grade freelance who combines both literary and commercial translations with writing or journalism. Such people do exist. It is best of all if he lives in the sponsor's country, preferably of course near at hand, frequently visits his own country both professionally and on holiday and is familiar with as many other sectors as possible of the target language market. With luck such a person will combine the prerequisite qualities: command of the language, the ability to adapt his style to the need and the discipline of writing to length. Provided opportunity exists to brief him fully, a person of this calibre will have little difficulty in acquiring subject and product knowledge to the necessary level. In fact copywriting is one of the few activities covered by this book where expert knowledge of the subject may prove to be a disadvantage, as it may lead the writer to use technical terms that are not fully comprehensible to some key members of the readership—a pitfall well enough known to all those who have ever been concerned with semi-specialised writing.

It follows from what has been said above that the briefing of the foreign copywriters is a major and highly important exercise in itself. Once selected, they should be brought in as much as possible in the planning phase, and where distance makes this difficult the arrangement of one occasion at which the whole team assembles for an on-site briefing by the sponsor is next to essential. The next stage at which they come into play is when they are consulted as suggested above on content, pitch and slant on the basis of an early ideas or contents draft. But however extensive this preliminary familiarisation may be, it will not obviate the need for them to be given a clear and comprehensive brief for their main task. The preparation of this brief can best be done by the language consultant, because he will have a better idea of any linguistic problems than the sponsor or the PR man.

Whoever prepares this brief, it must contain five main elements:

1 A base text in the form of an agreed contents and layout draft (or less desirably, but sometimes unavoidably, the finalised English copy).

2 A stat of the dummy, clearly marked up with the space available for copy on each page and preferably within each panel of the grid, with an indication of the maximum number of characters and of the placement of pictures and graphics together with their captions or legends. An important point here is that all artwork requiring translation should be included in the base text and an indication of its position and maximum acceptable length given in the dummy. Many a well planned production has been delayed or finished up with blemishes because a few phrases in the artwork were not passed for translation at the proper time.

3 A set of proofs, stats or mock-ups of all visuals to be used. These must be of the best quality available at the time; the sketched-in indications in the dummy are not good enough, and if half tones are provided in low-quality copies they may have to be annotated. Unless the dog sees the rabbit in time, there may be a need to revise captions at the page-proof stage, which is a most undesirable and uneconomic process. If the final choice of visuals has not yet been made, it is better to include all possible starters and get them captioned at this stage rather than have to go back at the last minute for a new caption.

4 The fullest possible terminological briefing material, preferably in the form of competitors' literature (see also below).

5 A full, clear, purpose-written brief on the aim, the target readership, the selling points to be emphasised and any special slants on them, and of course very clear instructions on exactly what he is required to do, e.g. to write certain sections free within a fairly generous length limit, to write others strictly to the length indicated in the dummy and to

translate others (such as technical descriptions) directly even at the
expense of going over length.

The deliberate use of a writer/translator as opposed to a specialist technical translator is likely to create a terminological gap. In most of the major fields a person capable of doing the task properly should also be able to fill this gap by research and informal consultation with colleagues and contacts; and of course ample briefing material is normally available. But in some minor specialised fields, such as furniture fittings sold to the trade, it may be impossible to find anyone who is capable of carrying out the task and has or can gain access to the jargon.

In this event it may be necessary as a preliminary step to assemble the minimum of technical material needed to cover the terminology and send this for translation through a conventional specialised bureau. The result will then serve as an authoritative brief for the copywriter.

16.7 Technical aspects

16.7.1 *Language length*

In the days of metal setting, when the lines of type were grouped and secured in a frame and the visuals dropped into this frame in the form of blocks, it was relatively easy to accommodate variations in language length by putting some superfluous visuals into the English and simply omitting these blocks to fit in the longer languages. But with offset litho printing in four colours, which is now almost universal practice, this cannot be done without making up a separate set of four colour plates for each language edition, or at least for the pages where space is critical; and this is quite simply prohibitively expensive. The variation in type size which will make the document appear either like an elementary reader or similar to the back of an insurance policy is only four or at most six points, and even with type faces which also offer the option of condensed and standard type there is not enough play to accommodate variations in character count which may amount to plus 40 per cent on the English — and in terms of space, for reasons mentioned below, even up to 50 per cent. Similarly a well-balanced gridded design will not take variations of this order in white space. Thus it is probably true to say that an advance in printing technology has put direct translation of good taut English copy into the longer languages out of court. This leaves three options. One is to hold the design until the longest language copy is available and design round this, and then to pad out the other languages to the required length. This will however tend to produce a copy-heavy design and flabby copy in the shorter languages. The second, equally unsatisfactory, is to write 40 or 50 per cent of padding into the English copy and then instruct the foreign copywriters to write to length omitting the padding; a further drawback here is that to get the amount and nature of padding right the base copy will have to be written by a fairly expert linguist who is unlikely to regard it as a particularly sensible or acceptable activity. Thus, technically as well as from other points of view, the only satisfactory solution becomes free writing of the foreign-language copy from a base text backed up by a comprehensive brief.

16.7.2 Column widths and language structure

As was mentioned above, most modern designers like to use a six-panel (vertical) or eight-panel (horizontal) grid on A4 format. This gives a column width of only 60-70 mm and, with 12 or 14 point, a line length of only 35-40 characters. This presents few problems with English and the Romance languages, but it plays havoc with the Germanic and some of the Slav languages, which combine a rather generous orthography with a liking for compound words, particularly in the scientific and technological fields where even before compounding a syllable or two may be added, e.g. march, marschieren.

In passing, this example also illustrates the need to work on character count as opposed to word count. There are rather strict rules about where these long words can be split, and incorrect or excessive hyphenation makes them virtually unintelligible at first reading. Moreover no one printer is likely to have setters who know the rules in all the languages concerned, and although there are specialised printing manuals which give these rules, they seldom seem to be available when they are needed. Equally it is impossible for a linguist to stand breathing down the setter's neck and correcting him as he goes along. On the other hand the need to correct large numbers of improper word splits on the galleys reduces the corrected galleys to chaos, is apt to make the proof-reader overlook other errors and will bring in its wake consequential printer's errors which have to be taken out by running second galleys or at the page-proof stage.

The first need which a combination of narrow columns and, say, technical German imposes is the abandonment of justification. This is because the space variations used to justify sometimes open up to the point where they are indistinguishable from the word spaces in the fuller lines, with the result that the text becomes difficult to comprehend at first reading. The abandonment of justification, though it raises gasps of horror in some of the more conventional British circles, is probably no great loss, as most other countries appear to regard justification as old-fashioned and a ragged edge as good modern practice.

The problem is greatly eased if not eliminated if the designer can be persuaded to work on a four-panel (vertical) or six-panel (horizontal) grid and balance off his visuals and captions in sub-panels within this. But this is a matter in which designer and printer are apt to gang up against the linguist with a whole array of aesthetic and technical arguments, and only to confess their error when it is too late; and there are of course often perfectly good technical reasons for sticking to a narrow-column grid.

Finally it will be clear from the discussion above that the use of narrow columns optimised for English will, whether or not justification is adopted, still further increase the effective additional space required by the longer languages. Typically the overlength of French with respect to English will go up from around 25 to around 35 per cent, and German (usually considered to be the worst case) from 33 to 45 per cent or more so that if German—or for that matter Dutch or Russian—is involved, the lowest safe planning figure is 50 per cent.

16.7.3 Graphics

The first point is that any lettering on graphics which varies must be in the same colour as the copy, and this straightaway imposes a restriction on colour planning in design and on certain forms of colour coding. The 'key number and glossary' system suggested in the preceding chapter for engineering drawings is quite simply not acceptable in high-grade promotional literature. On the other hand if too much language-variable legend is included in the graphic design itself, the problems of length restriction and positioning become almost overwhelming.

One difficulty here is that, thanks partly to the widespread and uninterrupted influence of the Staff Colleges of their respective Armed Forces, the British and Americans tend to standardise abbreviations and to explain at some convenient point any special abbreviations which they use. In other languages the system of abbreviating is far less organised and it therefore becomes very difficult to use abbreviations other than the internationally known scientific and engineering ones in promotional literature, where it may be inelegant to explain them even if space allows. The solution appears to lie in the maximum use of carefully designed symbols which can be both indicative of their meaning and aesthetically attractive — and of course multicoloured — and can be explained either in a panel at the edge of the graphic or, if they apply throughout the documentation, on a special 'symbols legend' page, which for obvious reasons should ideally be a fold-out. If a separate page is used, there will probably be a fair amount of space to play with, and it is both economical and aesthetically quite pleasing to make such a page polyglot, using different colours for the various languages.

While the layout and conventions of most scientific and technological diagrams and schematics, like the abbreviations and symbols used in them, are by and large internationally standardised, the same is not true outside these fields. For instance in the simple matter of organisation charts there are considerable differences between American, British, French and German practice. This is a problem for the designer, who will need to examine specimens of the kinds of graphics needed from all the markets concerned and produce a design that is at once visually acceptable and readily intelligible to all potential readers. It is probably a good general rule to make graphics even simpler and bolder than one would seek to have them for documentation intended for one's home market.

Printing costs will always form a substantial proportion of the budget, and can easily escalate beyond control if a deliberate effort is not made to contain them in both planning and execution phases. The ground rule is perhaps to ensure that all language-variable content, including artwork, is in one colour. This admittedly imposes some constraint on design but offers a double economy; only one special-to-language plate is needed for each page or spread; and the other three colours can be printed in one single run each covering all editions.

A second rule is that right from the start the space allotted for any passages which cannot be written to length must be that of the longest language, using the 50 per cent yardstick mentioned above, and planning in advance to accommodate differences in length by an optimised combination of variations in type size and white space, both of course within acceptable limits. This applies on the one hand to short passages such as legends of graphics, symbol definitions and captions, and on the other to legal documents such as conditions of sale which require matching texts, and sometimes to technical descriptions.

Once all relevant points have been firmly and sensibly tied up at the planning stage, the containment both of printing costs themselves and of secondary costs arising from printing factors is largely a matter of really careful coordination and briefing.

16.7.5   Proof-reading problems

It is absolutely essential that galleys, stats of final artwork and page-proofs including all the visuals are read at least by the language consultant and preferably by the foreign copywriters. It is the artwork that usually goes wrong, and errors here are apt to be conspicuous. For example in the German edition of an expensive tourist brochure the word *Wasserwege* was omitted from a main heading, so that it read *Befahren Sie die reizenden britischen*; as the picture to its right was of a delightful girl with rather little on, this error may in fact have scored a plus in promotional terms — but one will not always be as lucky as that. The lettering destined for artwork is usually set in to the galleys, but checking these is not enough (particularly as the design department often seems to work from an uncorrected set of galleys!). Errors can occur right up to the stage where the final artwork is pasted up, and it is difficult if not impossible to correct omissions of the kind mentioned above at the page-proof stage.

Experience suggests that in, say, a four-language project one set of galleys will be disastrous; one does not of course know in advance which this will be. It is therefore in everyone's interest to insist that the galleys are run on paper with wide margins for correction and not on narrow strips. Quite apart from the physical impossibility of inserting more than a certain number of corrections in narrow margins, it is highly desirable that the proof reader should write the corrected word out in full as well as using the conventional sign; otherwise there is a high risk of secondary error. It is important that all proof readers concerned (and the printer!) should have copies of BS1219 or of the appropriate equivalent standard if printing is being carried out abroad; but since it is extremely difficult to correct proofs using a strange convention, the printer should also provide himself with copies of the conventions used in the countries of the languages concerned.

Another good practice is to make sure that all sets of foreign-language galleys are clearly marked as 'corrected' or 'uncorrected'. With the rather complicated passage of proofs that takes place, it is fairly easy for an uncorrected copy to get back into the printer's hands and, since he will have no means of knowing whether there are or are not errors, he may take a disaster one stage further under the impression that he has done a superb job.

Finally there appears to be a kind of statistic based on human error of the number of corrections a checker or proof-reader will make per unit length of text at one reading or even on a second reading of the same draft or galleys. It is absolutely essential to get errors out before the page-proof stage, when correction of them is very expensive and apt to break deadlines. The printer must therefore be warned in advance of the possible need to produce second and even third galleys if requested to do so.

This nest of problems makes it tempting to recommend the use of a major international printing establishment. But quite apart from cost, a small or medium sponsor firm which has only occasional requirements would then have all the disadvantages of being a small fish in a large pool, and distance may make communication difficult. The difficulties sometimes met with smaller printing firms unaccustomed to working in foreign languages almost always arise from lack of the planning and teamwork which has been the theme of this chapter.

16.8 Clearance of drafts

For obvious reasons some sponsors feel themselves very much in the hands of their language team, and they may feel tempted either overtly or covertly to get the foreign-language copy checked by some other individual or organisation. This invariably ends in tears; one only needs to imagine what would happen to a piece of draft copy prepared in one advertising agency or PR consultancy and then passed to another for comment. We must confess from our own experience that the temptation to tear someone else's translation to pieces is equally irresistible, and while the sponsor is of course perfectly entitled to carry out any checks he wishes, these should be discussed and agreed in advance with the language consultant.

On the other hand it is essential that the users of promotional material should have confidence in it, and the language consultant should therefore insist that time is allowed for clearance of the draft with any senior linguist executive in the sponsor company, with the management of any subsidiaries in the markets concerned, and with any reliable and established agent. We know of one case some years ago in which a complete print of a Spanish brochure, costing some £4000 even in those days, had to be scrapped because the firm's South American agent would not accept it. We are talking here of course not of major errors in language or terminology but of matters of style in which judgements are purely subjective. One problem is that, in the case for instance of a German draft, German, Austrian and Swiss agents may produce different and often directly conflicting comments. These will have to be resolved by the language consultant and the copywriter concerned with advice from the sponsor on his market priorities.

The need to clear any legal texts with an official agency or lawyer of the country concerned was mentioned above and for many countries it is now advisable to have the whole of the draft similarly cleared. West German advertising law, for example, is now so stringent that it is virtually necessary to have a complete proof of any claim made prepared in advance if the risk of bad publicity and even a stay on distribution as the result of legal action, perhaps by a competitor, is to be avoided.

16.9 Costing

The need to recycle the budget along with the other basic decisions has already been stressed, but the sponsor and other members of the team will need to arrive at a first approximation to feed into their examination of the problem. The sponsor will almost certainly have data on the printing costs of his English language promotional material and these, updated if necessary, will serve as a point of entry. From there the following yardsticks may be used, provided it is understood that they are extremely rough and the result obtained will have an error zone of, say, ± 15 per cent:

Coordination, research, English copywriting and design	25%
Language costs including consultancy	20%
Production of visuals	25%
Printing	30%

Again in the most approximate of terms the addition of a major language is likely to involve a cost increase of 15 to 20 per cent overall and that of a minor language perhaps some 25 per cent. If the sponsor has his own advertising/PR cell and works direct to a language consultant, the proportion of costs listed above under the head of coordination, etc., will remain about the same in real terms but will be distributed between the sponsor organisation, where it will appear as both direct and indirect costs, and the language consultant.

One decision needed for the finalisation of costings and probably best taken by consultation within the hard core of the team is the choice between writing in rather massive contingencies for the longer lead items and indexating these. The choice here rests of course with the sponsor and will depend on his budgeting system, but as a general rule it is more cost-effective to cover the long lead items by indexation and to restrict contingency allowances to those items in which genuine contingent expenses may arise.

Finally delay always costs money and the more so in times of inflation. The containment of costs and the realism of the budget will depend not only on good planning and communications but also on agreement by all concerned to a realistic time schedule. If the sponsor through lack of forward planning or more probably from failure to appreciate the complex problems involved in the production of foreign-language promotional literature imposes an unreasonable deadline on the team, quality will inevitably suffer and cost can easily run out of control.

Conclusion

This book really consists of numerous variations on three simple themes. For managements that understand its nature and the techniques and resources needed to cross it, the language barrier presents no more formidable problems than do many other facets of management. Like most potentially hazardous physical environments, the language barrier can be turned to their own advantage by those who have proper awareness of it. Working in a foreign language means more time and significantly, but not overwhelmingly, more money. But these factors need prove no drawback if they are appreciated in advance and planned and costed in. The language barrier is a ruthless exposer of bad management; it will bring down those who ignore it or try to ride roughshod over it.

There can be little doubt that the trend towards working in a limited number of 'major' languages will continue at an accelerating pace, but the slow response time of educational progress and the cultural and hence political associations of language make it unlikely that English or any other language will become a universal *lingua franca* in the foreseeable future.

This book has shown how organisations faced with the need for multilingual working can establish, at relatively low increases in cost and

over a period of one to three years at the most, in-house resources which
will cope quickly, cheaply and adequately with the bulk of their language
needs. Once multilingual working has become customary, linguist
executives and specialists will tend increasingly to gravitate into the
places they are needed; the motivation of an aspiring or up-and-coming
executive to learn a language to a useful standard will become
progressively stronger — and what is more important he will become
increasingly likely to make enough use of his languages to keep them in
shape.

Thus we can expect, and we should certainly hope, that the demand
made by commercial and professional organisations on extramural
language resources for run-of-the-mill work will diminish to the point
where they represent on the one hand the requirements of concerns too
small to have a staff structure and on the other languages too little used
to justify standing resources. On the other hand there will always be a
proportion of language work which because of its specialised nature,
urgency or importance, or simply because of the complexity of the
circumstances surrounding it, will call for recourse to extramural
language resources certainly by medium and small organisations, and not
infrequently by large ones. Linguist executives' time may also be a factor
here. Successful fielding of these fast balls will require professional
linguists who combine experience and quality of mind with a number of
specialised skills outside their languages, and with whom top
management is happy to operate some kind of rather easygoing, retained
arrangement so that they are always in the picture when called on to act.
Equally there will be a continuing need for conference interpreters as
such and for consultant interpreters or intermediaries prepared to act in
the client's presence or independently in whatever way he may wish and
they may jointly see fit.

The problem that is likely to be with us longest because it arises from a
genuine language-technical difficulty and not from mutual ignorance of
management and the language profession or from the latter's
organisation, is technical translation. Increasing concentration on the
major languages, coupled with the accelerating progress that may be
expected in the establishment of international standards with
concomitant agreed terminologies will tend to improve matters as time
goes by. But the brutal fact is that the effective translation of highly
specialised scientific and technological texts calls not only for an excellent
and up-to-date knowledge of the language as it is used in the field in
question, but also of a knowledge of that field sufficiently expert to be
able to get into the writer's mind even when he has expressed himself
badly. Now that the age of the polymath is past, there are after all
relatively few experts in specialised fields who can express themselves
lucidly and objectively even in their own language. Anyone who can
combine this ability with a knowledge of one or more foreign languages
should be able to find — in the country of one or other of his
languages — more satisfying and rewarding work than translation. Good
technical translators are perhaps most likely to be found among those

who have withdrawn through choice or necessity from a conventional full-time career.

This problem strikes us as such a serious one as to call in the long term for eradication rather than solution. It was not very long ago that most scientists could read and understand a paper on their subject in English, French or German and many could understand these spoken languages. Russian admittedly presents a problem because of the Cyrillic alphabet, but this should in fact give little worry to those used to working with the Greek alphabet in mathematical expressions. The fact that fewer and fewer specialists have any understanding of foreign languages results simply from an unfortunate dichotomy in the educational system acting in concert with the 'two cultures' cold war. If languages — as they logically should be — were allotted the same place in the educational system as they can be shown to occupy in employability and career patterns, namely that of an increasingly important second string, the language barrier would be cut right down to size. In the past 30 years nations as different as the USSR and West Germany have shown us that this is an attainable educational aim.

APPENDICES

1
Language coverage by population and gross product

1 Languages are given in alphabetical order.
2 Population is given in thousands, GNP at market prices in millions of US dollars.
3 Figures are abstracted from the World Bank Statistics for 1972.
4 The aim of this table is to show the comparative coverage of some of the major world languages and perticularly of European languages, and at the same time to indicate those languages that might be used for commercial correspondence in a particular country. The heading 'Primary Language' covers the country of origin of a language and those countries now peopled by an overwhelming majority of inhabitants originating from or speaking the language of the country of origin, e.g. Australia and New Zealand in the case of English, Brazil for Portuguese. Secondary cover indicates that a language is widely spoken in a particular country as a result of previous economic or political domination, educational tradition or other factors. If primary cover is shared between two languages, e.g. French and English in Canada, the population and the GNP have been broken down to reflect the actual number of persons speaking those languages as their mother tongue; these countries have been indicated with and asterisk in the table. In the case of secondary cover where more than one language is widely understood, e.g. German and Russian in Poland, the total population and GNP figures have been kept, since the use of one of these languages gives access to a maximum potential market.
5 In several countries which represent significant markets, the language used for correspondence may be one of a number – English, French, German and possibly Spanish or another. These countries are listed separately at the end of the table.
6 In certain cases, notably some South American countries, the division into primary and secondary cover present problems which have been resolved for these purposes largely in terms of the size of the market. We recognise that such a division must in the last analysis be arbitrary.
7 *Dutch secondary coverage* Afikaans has been treated as a separate language. There may well be some residual use of Dutch in former colonies such as Indonesia and Surinam, but we have been unable to confirm this.
8 *Arabic secondary coverage* There appears to be a trend towards the use of Arabic in certain non-Arabic countries that are wholly or primarily Muslim.

Language and primary country(ies)	Population	GNP	Secondary country(ies)	Population	GNP	TOTAL Population	GNP
ARABIC Algeria, Egypt, Bahrein, Iraq, Jordan, Kuwait, Lebanon, Libya, Mauritania, Morocco, Oman, Qatar, Saudi Arabia, Sudan, Syria, Tunisia, United Arab Emirates, Yemen	129,568	46,330	See Note 8			129,568	46,330
CHINESE China, Taiwan, Hong-Kong	805,647	145,100				805,647	145,100
DUTCH Netherlands, Belgium*	18,185	53,510	See Note 7			18,185	53,510
ENGLISH UK, Channel Islands, IOM, Ireland, Australia, Canada*, New Zealand, USA	298,260	1,428,270	Bahamas, Bahrein, Bangla-desh, Barbados, Botswana, Brunei, Burma, Cameroon, Ethiopia, Fiji, The Gambia, Ghana, Grenada, Guyana, Hong-Kong, India, Iraq, Jamaica, Jordan, Kenya, Kuwait, Lesotho, Liberia, Malawi, Malaysia, Maldives, Malta, Mauritius, Nigeria, Oman, Pakistan, Panama, Phili-pines, Qatar, Rhodesia, Saudi Arabia, Sierra Leone, Singapore, Soth Africa, Swaziland, Tanzania, Thailand, Tonga, Trinidad & Tobago, Uganda, United Arab Emirates, Zambia	1,048,909	127,360	1,347,169	1,600,630
FRENCH France, Belgium*, Canada*, Luxembourg*, Switzerland*	66,093	244,120	Algeria, Burundi, Cameroon, Central African Republic, Chad, Congo, Dahomey, French Guiana, Gabon, Guadaloupe, Guinea, Haiti, Ivory Coast, Khmer Republic, Laos, Lebanon, Malagasy Republic, Mali, Mart-inique, Mauritania, Morocco, Niger, Rwanda, Senegal, Syria,				

Main language-group table (column values: the two "Total" columns equal the sum of the primary-country and other-country figures):

Language / Primary countries	Population	GNP	Other countries likely to use the language	Population	GNP	Total Population	Total GNP
Austria, East and West Germany, Luxembourg*, Switzerland*	88,438	271,600	Bulgaria, Czechoslovakia, Hugary, Poland, Rumania, Yugoslavia	107,998	142,830	196,436	414,430
ITALIAN — Italy, Switzerland*	56,410	114,900	None			56,410	114,900
JAPANESE — Japan	106,960	247,890	None			106,960	247,890
POLISH — Poland	33,068	49,640	None			33,068	49,640
PORTUGUESE — Portugal, Brazil	108,006	59,620	Angola, Ginea-Bissau, Macao, Mozambique	14,444	4,780	122,450	64,400
RUMANIAN — Rumania	20,700	16,770	None			20,700	16,770
RUSSIAN — USSR	247,460	377,700	Bulgaria, Czechoslovakia, Hungary, Poland, Rumania, Yugoslavia	107,998	142,830	355,458	520,530
SPANISH — Spain, Argentina, Columbia, Mexico	135,506	122,050	Bolivia, Chile, Costa Rica, Cuba, Dominican Republic, Ecuador, El Salvador, Equatorial Guinea, Guatemala, Honduras, Nicaragua, Panama, Paraguay, Peru, Puerto Rico, Uruguay, Venezuela	85,910	55,450	221,416	177,500
SWEDISH — Sweden	8,120	36,350	Finland (population figure includes a proportion of native Swedish speakers)	4,630	13,000	12,750	49,350

SPECIAL CASES

Country	Population	GNP	Primary language (italic) and other languages likely to be in use
Arab Republic of Egypt	34,840	8,340	*Arabic*, English, French
Iran (Persia)	31,169	15,220	*Farsi*, English, French, German, (Russian)
Israel	3,080	8,050	*Hebrew*, English, French, German
Turkey	37,010	13,650	*Turkish*, English, French, German

2

Requirements for in-house language resources

A Languages (see Chapter 1)

1 What major languages?
2 In what priority?
3 Is a minor language required?
4 If so, which?
5 In what priority with respect to major languages?

B Workload

6 What is breakdown of past workload by languages and nature of work? Viz.

Language	Correspondence To: From:	Visitors	Documentation To: From:
	(number of items)	(number)	(number and length of items)

7 Is documentation specialised? If so:
- technical?
- legal?
- promotional?

8   What proportion of total workload does (7) represent?
9   Have you the resources, e.g. foreign executives, to take
    on this specialised load (7 and 8) in-house? If not,
    assume extramural support needed.
10 Subtract (8) from (6) to obtain base figures for in-house
    load.
11 Use market trends and marketing plans to extrapolate
    forward (say two years) from base figures at (10).
12 Reshape present figures (11) to obtain:
    - volume of in-house work from each language as a
       percentage man load
    - volume of in-house load into each language as a
       percentage man load
    - level and nature by languages of qualifications for
       English staff
    - level and nature by languages of qualifications for
       foreign staff

Answers from A and B

13 The figures at (12) will give you a list of linguist staff
    required. Normally the *first* unit in each language/mother-
    tongue combination *and any fractional loads* should be
    annotated as *multilingual secretaries*.
14 Then apply the results from A to convert this list into a
    LINGUIST RECRUITMENT PRIORITY LIST.

C Deployment

15 Reshape the figures obtained at (11) to give breakdown by:
    - departments
    - senior executives within departments
16 Using the list (14) and the figures (15) and ignoring
    other factors, allocate linguist staff to departments/
    specific posts, thus drawing up a first draft deployment
    list.
17 Are any specific posts in list (16) blocked? (That is,
    filled by good employees of long standing.)
18 If so, what is the next best deployment for linguist in
    question?
19 Does this involve a further reshuffle of list (16)?

Answers from C

20 Recycle to optimise and produce LINGUIST DEPLOYMENT LIST.

Final short-term answer (A + B + C)

21 Recycle list (14) with list (20) to optimise and produce
    LINGUIST RECRUITMENT AND DEPLOYMENT PRIORITY LIST.

D Long term

22 Take the figures (10), (11) and (12) and make a rough
    five-year forecast in the same way.
23 Make a similar rough long-term forecast of specialised
    work (7 and 8).
24 Marry these forecasts to give value of work by language,
    direction, level and field.
25 If any one item at (24) represents substantially more
    than one man load there is a case for:
    -   recruitment of a staff linguist, *or*
    -   further training of a multilingual secretary recruited
        under the short-term plan.
26 If three or more items at (24) represent more than one
    man load each, there is a case for forming a language
    section in the longer term.

3

Planning of extramural support

A Languages

1-5 As Appendix 2.

B Workload

6   Analyse as at (6) of Appendix 2.
7   Proceed as at (10-12) of Appendix 2.
8   Subtract from list (7) any workload currently or
    potentially covered by in-house resources.

Answers from A and B

9   Use the answers from A to arrange list (8) in order of
    priority.

C Type of support required (see Section 10.6)

10 Does list (9) contain more than three field/language
    combinations?
11 Is/are (two) minor language(s) involved in list (9)?
12 Is *total* of man loads in list (9) greater than three?
    (NB this is not the same as (10).)

13 If (10-12) are all 'Yes', go to a major agency.
14 If any two of (10-12) are 'Yes', bring in a freelance linguist as consultant.
15 If one or none of (10-12) is 'Yes', seek out one or more good freelances.

D Coordination

16 Do you have, in order of preference:
 - a language section with a head?
 - an in-house language panel with a coordinator?
 - a senior multilingual secretary?
 - a linguist librarian, research assistant, etc?
 - a linguist executive on the administrative side.
17 The first 'Yes' in (16) should be your coordinator for extramural language resources.

4

Advance planning for conferences

```
Lead times: major conferences one year
             small conference/seminar three months

1   Appoint conference executive and in-house supporting team.
2   Lay down provisional budget.
3   Bring in language consultant (interpreter?).
4   Make first key plan.
5   Cost and time first key plan.
6   Recycle first key plan with budget and proposed date.
7   Select method of interpretation.
8   Go out for equipment quotes.
9   Decide venue.
10  Provisionally book interpreters, equipment and venue.
11  Recycle plan.
12  Confirm bookings (10).
13  Issue provisional invitations/advance publicity.
14  Book guest speakers.
15  Recheck facilities at venue.
16  Book audiovisual, etc., equipment (if not under (10) and
    (12)).
17  Decide on nature and format of audiovisual aids.
18  Make detailed plan for secretariat and appoint key
    members.
```

19 Set up translation facility.
20 Initiate preparation of audiovisual aids.
21 Initiate preparation of documentation.
22 Prepare and issue instructions to *all* speakers (including advance submission of scripts).
23 Initiate detailed administrative planning:
    - transport
    - catering
    - entertainment
24 Recost plan and recycle against budget.
25 Establish a planning board or diagram that will ensure that progress of all aspects is checked weekly until they are finalised.
26 Issue firm invitations, etc./middle-term publicity.
27 Finalise attendance list and numbers.
28 Update whole plan and recycle to ensure facilities adequate for numbers and costs within budget.
29 Lay down firm deadline for completion of each aspect of preparation (aids, documentation, etc.).
30 Recheck all bookings and earmarkings of personnel and equipment.
31 Make up and send out interpreters' briefs.
32 Check all audiovisual aids for compatibility with equipment and correctness.
33 Finalise:
    - executive arrangements
    - availability of speakers
    - conference documentation
    - aids
    - secretariat
    - equipment
    - transport programme
    - catering
    - entertainment
    - delegates' folders
    - host brooches/briefs, etc.
34 Take over conference accommodation.
35 Set up and test equipment (make sure there is no optical or electrical interference between subsystems).
36 Assemble and brief all hosts, staff (including interpreters) and main speakers.
37 Rehearse main speakers as necessary.
38 Recheck all equipment, documentation, etc., in position.
39 Update guest list, seating plan, etc., for last-minute changes.
40 Get all staff into position and recheck all equipment *just before* first delegate arrives.

5

Conferences: one-time procedures

This checklist covers, in effect, the setting up of a conference/presentation management team and the establishment of the basic facilities and documentation.

1   Nominate conference/presentation, etc., executive.
2   Nominate conference production and/or language consultants.
3   Prepare standard operating procedures to cover all types of conference, presentation, etc., required. (This must include checklists.)
4   Develop audiovisual aids and documentation of general application, i.e. 'long term, in all languages required.
5   Establish costing methods and yardsticks (indexated).
6   Work out initial and operating budgets.
7   Decide on what equipment is to be bought; select and procure.
8   Build up card index/dossiers on venues, interpreters, equipment, secretarial support, transport, etc.
9   Check loading of mobile equipment into car boots, boxing for air transport, etc.
10 Revise standard operating procedures as necessary.

6
Conferences: routine procedures

The following procedures should be used for each presentation:

1   Lay down aim and audience.
2   Fix approximate date(s).
3   Reconnoitre venue.
4   Finalise audience list.
5   Check availability of presentation team.
6   Check availability of outside support - interpreters, secretariat, etc.
7   Check availability of audiovisual aids, documentation, hired equipment, etc.
8   Put drafting/translation in hand as necessary.
9   Check serviceability of own equipment.
10 Go firm on date.
11 Book venue.
12 Book interpreters.
13 Book equipment to be hired.
14 Make catering and transport arrangements.
15 Send out invitations, administrative instructions and reply cards/forms.
16 Assemble and check all scripts and aids.
17 Prepare and reproduce programme, attendance list, reception checklist and visitors' folders.
18 Prepare and send out interpreters' briefs.
19 Rehearse.
20 Update numbers and administrative arrangements.

7

Conferences: final and daily checks

```
1    Are rooms clean?
2    Is all equipment in position and working?
3    Are all audiovisual aids in position?
4    Are all emergency exits/fire doors accessible/in order?
5    Are all conference personnel in position?
     -  nominated hosts
     -  chairmen
     -  speakers
     -  interpreters
     -  engineer(s)/projectionist(s)
     -  receptionists
     -  guides
6    Are transport arrangements working?
7    Are catering arrangements working? Confirm numbers.
8    Have seating, table, etc., plans been updated?
9    Are visitors' folders in position?
10   Is Chairman briefed on any last-minute changes he needs
     to know about?
```

8

Technical documentation for an export product

A Languages (see Chapter 1)

1 What major languages are required?
2 In what priority?
3 Is any minor language involved?
4 If so, can its use be confined:
   - to technical sales literature only?
   - to some introductory or covering document only?
5 If (3) is 'Yes' and (4) 'No', can the customer/the agent arrange to have it done and the cost offset against the main invoice?

B Resources

6 What methods of reproduction will you use? (Maybe different ones for different parts of the documentation.)
7 Are the reproduction resources sufficient to handle the volume of work in time?
8 Do the resources cover all types of reproduction required?
9 Is there an unbroken chain of facilities to carry foreign language matter of all types involved through from MS or tape to finished product?

10 Is effort available for collating documentation within the required time?

11 Is enough suitable effort available in-house to prepare new English texts in good time?

12 If (11) is 'No', can this work be delegated either to a specialised firm of technical authors/illustrators or to the language organisation used?

13 Have you ready access to available extramural language resources for the language required?

14 If 'Yes' to (13), is sufficient specialised translation effort available at the time(s) required?

15 Who will be responsible for coordinating presentation details?

16 Who will be responsible for coordinating programme:
   - in exporting firm?
   - in language organisation?

C Scope

17 What documentation is required?
   - sales/descriptive
   - specifications
   - inspection/approval documents
   - user handbooks
   - workshop manuals
   - recommended spares lists
   - complete spares lists
   - labels
   - safety warning notices, etc.

18 How much of (17) already exists in English?

19 Is it up-to-date?

20 How much of (18) already exists in the language(s)?

21 Is it up-to-date?

22 Is it acceptable in terminology and style?

23 What is the deadline for delivery of documentation?

24 What documentation is required in advance of this, and when?

25 Do penalties attach to delays in supplying documentation?

Answers from A, B and C

26 Obtaining answers to (6-25) and recycling them progressively should enable you to draw up a plan for the production of technical documentation with timings.

D Inspection/approval documentation

27 Establish the official inspections/approvals required in the target country.

28 Establish the customer's requirements for qualitative and quantitative acceptance.

29 Obtain all the documentation connected with (27) and (28) above.

30 Compile a flowchart of inspection/approval acceptance starting at the *manufacturer's out-inspection* and running through to *retail sale/commissioning*.

31 Prepare instructions for English-speakers to fill in formal documents (29).

32 Design bilingual or foreign-language documents for own out-inspection and to complement formal documents.

33 Agree a completed specimen set of *all* documents (29) and (32) with customer and all approving authorities concerned.

34 Obtain details of and procure all plates, labels, stamps, markings, etc., required.

35 Arrange any factory inspection, calibration, etc., to be carried out by approving and/or insurance authorities.

36 Incorporate checking of plates, etc. (34) into manufacturer's out-inspection procedures.

37 Revise out-inspection documentation if necessary.

38 Prove complete procedure up to despatch.

39 Revise documentation and/or instructions as necessary.

40 Organise clerical effort for collation and despatch of documents.

41 Organise filing system to include:
- spare copies of key documents
- data from which a full set of documents can quickly be reconstructed.

9
Promotional literature: optimisation procedure

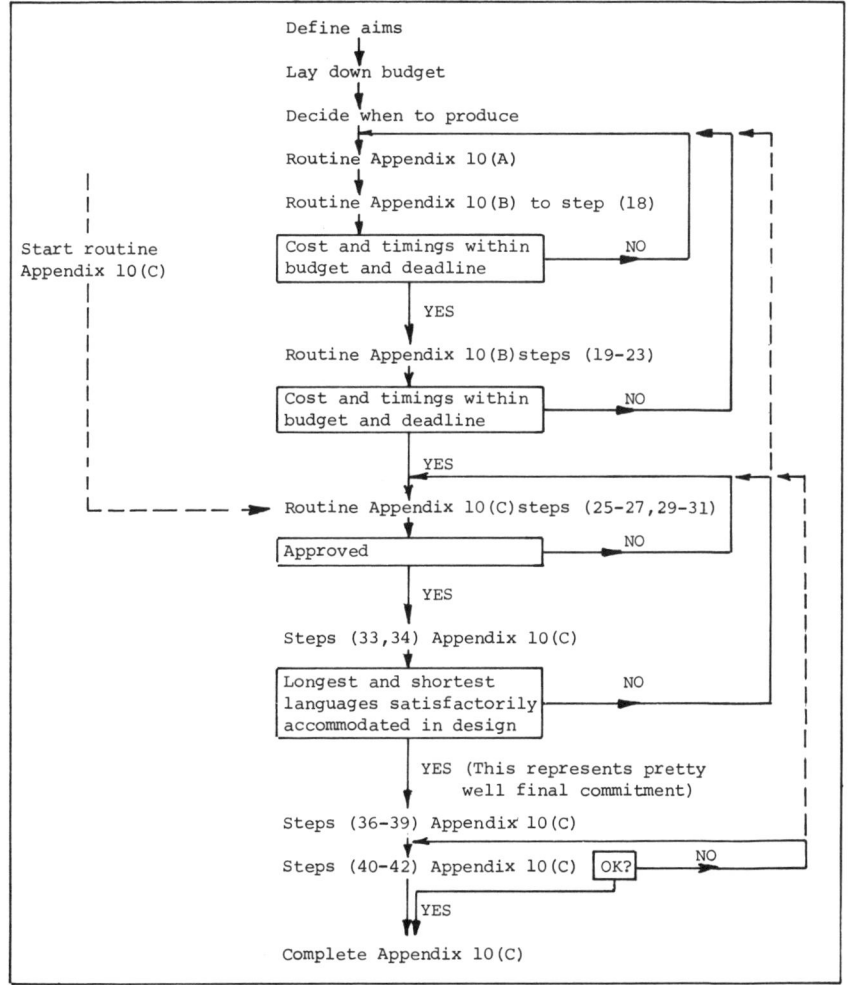

```
                        Define aims

                        Lay down budget

                        Decide when to produce

                        Routine Appendix 10(A)

                        Routine Appendix 10(B) to step (18)

                        ┌─────────────────────────┐
                        │ Cost and timings within │  NO
                        │ budget and deadline     │──────→
                        └─────────────────────────┘
 Start routine
 Appendix 10(C)
                                │ YES

                        Routine Appendix 10(B) steps (19-23)

                        ┌─────────────────────────┐
                        │ Cost and timings within │  NO
                        │ budget and deadline     │──────→
                        └─────────────────────────┘

                                │ YES

                     →  Routine Appendix 10(C) steps (25-27,29-31)

                        ┌─────────────────────────┐
                        │ Approved                │  NO
                        └─────────────────────────┘──────→

                                │ YES

                        Steps (33,34) Appendix 10(C)

                        ┌─────────────────────────┐
                        │ Longest and shortest    │  NO
                        │ languages satisfactorily│──────→
                        │ accommodated in design  │
                        └─────────────────────────┘

                                │ YES (This represents pretty
                                        well final commitment)

                        Steps (36-39) Appendix 10(C)

                        Steps (40-42) Appendix 10(C)  ┌────┐  NO
                                                      │OK? │──────→
                                                      └────┘
                                │ YES

                        Complete Appendix 10(C)
```

10
Promotional literature: outline planning and promotion procedure

A Setting up team

1   Define provisional aim.
2   Make first approximation of budget.
3   Decide where to produce literature - own country, target country?
4   Appoint sponsor representative.
5   Appoint PR/advertising and language consultants.
6   Complete make-up of team.
7   Appoint coordinator.
8   Assemble team for briefing.
9   Arrange channels and methods for passing information within team.
10 Arrange team meetings well in advance (2-3 for whole programme).

B Basic decisions

11 Choose languages and assign priorities (Chapter 1).
12 Decide between polyglot and single-language editions.

13 If more than one polyglot edition, decide language grouping.
14 Decide between British and American English.
15 Decide format. Size? Top or side filing?
16 Decide number of pages.
17 Make plan for dealing with any minor languages involved.
18 Work out planning times.
19 Recycle budget and plan.
20 Decide scope of literature.
21 Decide production method for each section.
22 Acquire/update/review market intelligence.
23 Choose angles.
24 Recycle budget and plan.

C Production

25 Produce first dummy.
26 List visuals and plan production.
27 Submit dummy and list of visuals and artist's impression for client approval.
28 Revise/resubmit till approved.
29 Start production of visuals.
30 Draft English copy or base text.
31 Submit copy for approval.
32 Revise/resubmit till .approved.
33 Check copy length against space (for longest language).
34 Decide on policy for coping with length variations. (Good stage for full team meeting.)
35 Recheck and recycle project.
36 Issue approved copy and briefing material for translation.
37 Start plate-making and prepare to run three of four colours, i.e. all non-verbal matter.
38 Call-in and collate foreign-language copy.
39 *Character*-count to check for length (averaging acceptable but simple *word*-count inadequate).
40 Marry copy to dummy.
41 Recheck visuals and captions. (Good stage for full team meeting.)
42 Adjust as necessary.
43 Clear non-verbal matter for running.
44 Set verbal matter.
45 Make any last-minute revisions.
46 Proof-read (must be done by linguists).
47 Drop in copy for each language edition.
48 Page-proof each language edition.
49 Check all aspects of page-proofs (must be done by linguists).
50 Clear fourth colour (verbal matter) for running.

Business
and
language